Traditional Jewish Wisdom
for Healthy Eating

FOOD
FOR THE
SOUL

Chana Rubin, RD

gefen גפן
publishing house בית הוצאה לאור
JERUSALEM ◆ NEW YORK

Copyright © Chana Rubin & Gefen Publishing House, Ltd.
Jerusalem 2008 / 5768

Typesetting: Koren Publishing Services
Cover Design: S. Kim Glassman
Cover photograph: Tim Hill
Author photograph: David Shemesh

ISBN 978-965-229-406-7

3   5   7   9   8   6   4   2

Gefen Publishing House, Ltd.
6 Hatzvi Street, Jerusalem 94386, Israel
972-2-538-0247
orders@gefenpublishing.com

Gefen Books
600 Broadway, Lynbrook, NY 11563, USA
516-593-1234
orders@gefenpublishing.com

www.israelbooks.com

Printed in Israel   *Send for our free catalogue*

For David

*You gave me the confidence to cook "beyond the recipe" and
the inspiration and opportunity to write this book.
Thank you for listening, learning, editing,
cooking, and so much more.*

— CONTENTS ⸻

"When one eats just to satisfy physical desire, it brings a certain sadness. But eating in a sanctified manner increases joy and pleasure." (Rav Avraham Yitzhak HaCohen Kook)[1]

Each month, the women of our community gather to learn, socialize and participate in *tzedakah* projects on *Rosh Chodesh* (the new month). At these meetings, I cannot help myself. During the presentation, I silently take a headcount, which ranges from 20 to 60 English-speaking women of all ages from the Beer Sheva area. What a delight to see such a diverse group of Jewish women gathered together. Then I take a second count – how many of us are overweight or obese? Unfortunately, the answer ranges from 25 to 40 percent, matching figures of the general population, both in Israel and the United States.

The health issues related to obesity – heart disease, Type 2 diabetes, hypertension and others – are as high in our community as in any other. Being Jewish, educated and worldly does not give us extra protection when it comes to diet and health.

While there is still much research to be done, we now have access to a remarkable amount of information on nutrition and health. We know that the risk for many serious diseases can be reduced by following a healthy diet and a lifestyle that includes adequate physical activity.

Current scientific thinking on nutrition is not based on rigid diet plans and self-denial. It is based on eating foods that are tasty and good for you and avoiding foods that are detrimental to your health. It involves eating in moderation, with sensitivity, pleasure and *kavanah* (thoughtfulness).

1

The following information teaches nutrition basics – carbohydrates, fats and proteins, and why some types of these are good for you and others are not. These pages are also filled with advice on planning, shopping and cooking. And, to help get you started, I have shared more than one hundred of my favorite recipes.

With the information included in this book, you will be well equipped to make healthy food choices and prepare nutritious meals for you and your family.

Food for the Soul addresses nutrition and health from a Jewish perspective. The nutrition information is universal, but tailored to our specific needs – *kashrut*, lifestyle, *Shabbat* and holidays, fast days and our own culture of food. The profound insight of our sages regarding physical health, food and spirituality is a gift for us to embrace as we consider our personal health and diet.

La'briut u b'teavon: "To your good health and enjoyment!"

— ACKNOWLEDGMENTS —

The expertise and talents of many gifted people were involved in helping to write this book. With much gratitude, I thank all of you for your time and generosity:

Batya Blitstein, PhD, for reviewing the material relating to eating behaviors and psychology.

Aryeh Bodenheimer, noted scholar, teacher and writer, for reviewing, translating, locating and recommending Jewish references.

Shragit Greenberg, MD, for insight on eating behaviors and *kashrut*.

Neal Hendel, distinguished jurist and educator, for research, review and suggestions relating to Judaism and vegetarianism.

Deena Nataf and family for recipe testing, editing suggestions and ongoing encouragement.

Rav Yosef Weiss, for patiently explaining *halachic* issues and solutions concerning insects.

Rabbis and students of *Kollel Beit Moriah*, for help with *halachic* sources; Rav Shimon Cohen, *Rosh Ha'Kollel*, Rav Avraham Vazana, RA"M *Ha'Kollel*, Rav Tzafir Chariv and my husband David and his *chevrutot* Eliyahu Fainer, Moshe Fruchter, z"l, Chaim Mackler and Moshe Luwisch, PhD.

For encouragement, suggestions, advice and assistance: Doron Degen, Michal Finkelstein, Rebecca Goldsmith, Yossi Klein Halevi, Arthur Kurzweil, Yair Liel, MD, Edna Oxman and Rav Aharon Rabenstein.

Smadar Belilty, Dorit Raviv and the Gefen staff for all of your help.

3

My editor, Taryn Levanony, for your patience and sensitivity.

The following staff members of Ben-Gurion University of the Negev and Soroka University Medical Center, Beer Sheva, Israel, for reviewing, editing and valued insights:

Yaakov Henkin, MD: Department of Cardiology, Associate Director for Academic Affairs, Medical School for International Health.

Danit Shachar, PhD: Faculty of Health Sciences, the S. Daniel Abraham International Center for Health and Nutrition.

Ze'ev Silverman, PhD: Chairman, Zlotowski Center for Neuroscience, Associate Professor and Chairman, Department of Morphology, Faculty of Health Sciences.

Goldie Stampfer, for first encouraging me to teach nutrition and cooking.

My dear Beer Sheva students, organized by Chaya Aft.

Judy Slyper, who patiently filled in gaps of my Jewish education.

My teachers and mentors – from grade school to university, Hebrew school to *Midrasha*, and the medical and business worlds; your intellectual and spiritual gifts, patience and guidance all contributed to the writing of this book.

The hundreds of young people who have touched my life. Your gifts of love, learning, laughter and gratitude will always be cherished.

Becki Cohn-Vargas, Judy Jackson, Barbara Winn and Neva Yarkin – devoted friends who have been especially supportive throughout the years.

My mother Dorothy, who has always enjoyed being in the kitchen, and at whose side I first learned to cook. Her mother, my grandmother Helen, z"l, who preferred reading to cooking; many hours at the library with her contributed to my love of reading and writing.

My father Leon, z"l, whose intense love for Israel inspired me to make *aliyah*. His mother, my grandmother Rose, z"l, unschooled but pious; she instilled in me the love of Jewish tradition and an understanding of *kashrut*.

My sons Yoav, Elan and Oren, who maintain a sense of humor, in spite of having a dietitian for a mom; you are a continual source of pride and joy. My daughter-in-law Tali and granddaughter Karen, for bringing more happiness into my life.

To my two wonderful friends, Suretta Geller and Sophie Stern: to me you are family. It is with much gratitude that I thank you both for your ready advice and tireless encouragement.

CHAPTER 1

Diet and Health: The Jewish Connection

"Since maintaining a healthy and sound body is among the ways of God – for one cannot understand or have any knowledge of the Creator if one is ill – therefore, you must avoid that which harms the body and accustom yourself to that which is health-ful and helps the body become stronger." (Rambam, *Hilchot De'ot* 4:1)

"The more we increase knowledge, increasing spiritual illumi-nation and a healthy physicality, so will this wondrous (divine) light shine in us, a lamp on the path of our life." (Rav Kook, *Orot Ha'emunah* p. 80)

Our sages recognized the connection between eating and dis-ease long before modern man documented it scientifically. Now it is common knowledge that heart disease, hypertension, Type 2 (adult-onset) diabetes, and strokes may be caused or exacerbated by our eating habits. Current evidence also suggests that among diet-related factors, overweight and obesity increase the risks of several types of common cancers.

Nearly 30% of all adults and 20% of children in the US are overweight. In Israel, as well, obesity has become a serious health issue. While we do not have statistics for the Jewish population in the US, our emphasis on food and eating, plus anecdotal evidence, suggests that our obesity and disease rates are similar to the popu-lation at large.

Judaism recognizes the association between proper nutrition and good health.

Changes in eating and exercise habits have played a major role in the fattening of our society. We have access to an incredible array of relatively inexpensive food choices. More and more of the food we eat is highly processed and refined. Fewer meals are eaten at home, and snacking is a routine part of our lives. Portion sizes are out of line with our energy expenditure, and our physical activity has significantly decreased. Simply put, we are eating more, our food choices are less healthy and we are exercising less.

Poor eating habits, an abundance of processed foods and lack of exercise contribute to obesity and diet-related diseases.

HEALTH IN THE JEWISH TRADITION

"He said, If you listen diligently to the voice of *Hashem*, your God, and do what is just in His eyes, give ear to His commandments and observe all His decrees, then any of the diseases that I placed upon Egypt I will not bring upon you, for I am *Hashem* your Healer." (*Shemot* 15:26)

"I, *Hashem*, am your healer, and I teach you the Torah and the *mitzvot* in order that you may be saved from these diseases – like the doctor who says to a person: Do not eat this thing lest it bring you into the grip of such-and-such an illness." (Rashi, *Shemot* 15:26)

"You may not in any way weaken your health or shorten your life. Only if the body is healthy is it an efficient instrument for the spirit's activity.... Therefore you should avoid everything which might possibly injure your health.... And the law asks you to be even more circumspect in avoiding danger to life and limb than in the avoidance of other transgressions." (Rav Samson Raphael Hirsch, *Horeb* 62:428)

Our tradition is rich in sources concerning the importance of maintaining physical well-being. The Rambam, Ben Ish Chai, Seforno, *Kitzur Shulchan Aruch*, *Kaf Hachayim* and *Mishnah Berura* addressed issues of diet and health in their writings. Numerous references noting the importance of guarding our health are found in the *Tanach* as well. Commentators including Joseph Albo, Baruch Halevi Epstein (*Torah Temimah*) and Samson Raphael Hirsch wrote about the connection between the body and the soul, between physical and spiritual health.

Our tradition emphasizes the connection between physical and spiritual health.

In *Sefer Devarim* (Deuteronomy), the Jewish people are described as being "fat, thick and corpulent." The once upright nation became "fat and kicked" (*Devarim* 32:15). Rav Hirsch explains this verse to mean that food eaten in excess of our needs is stored in the body as moral as well as physical fat. We sink ("kick") spiritually as well as physically when we become obese.

Another correlation between physical and spiritual health is made by Joseph Albo:

"One should have the intent that his body be whole and strong, in order for one's inner soul to be upright so that [it will be able] to know God." (Joseph Albo, *Sefer Ha'ikarim* 3:2)

Clearly, directives concerning the relationship between physical and spiritual health are plentiful in our tradition.

MEDICINE AND FAITH

"A person should direct his heart and the totality of his behavior to one goal, becoming aware of God, blessed be He. The way one rests, rises, and speaks should all be directed to this end. Similarly…one should take care to eat and drink only in order to be healthy in body and limb. Therefore, one should not eat all that the palate desires like a dog or donkey. Rather one should eat what is beneficial for the body, be it bitter or sweet. Conversely, one should not eat what is harmful to the body, even though it is sweet to the palate." (Rambam, *Hilchot De'ot* 3:2)

"There are two reasons to avoid eating harmful foods: First, to prevent the food from causing physical harm. Second, to humble the *yetzer hara* [evil inclination] and break his cravings…because certainly a person must be careful not to eat foods which he knows are bad for him." (Ra'avad, *Ba'alei Ha'nefesh*)

One may ask about our personal obligation to maintain good physical health. After all, as people of faith, should we not rely on God for good health? We pray each day for God to give us good health and heal our illnesses.

Refaenu Hashem v'nirafeh: "Heal us, *Hashem*, so that we will be healed…" *V'ha'aleh aruchah u'marpeh l'chol tachaluenu*: "bring cure and healing for all our illnesses" (*Shemoneh Esrei*, traditional Sephardic text).

The Chazon Ish explained the possible conflict between maintaining one's own physical health as opposed to relying on God to deliver good health:

"I consider the physical effort to maintain good health to be both an obligation and a *mitzvah*. It is one of the requirements dictated by the Creator for self-perfection…. However, the ways of the Divine may bypass natural laws as well as the efforts man puts unto using them. What is needed is the correct balance. Deviation from the true path is not acceptable – whether it is to rely on the level of faith which I have honestly reached, or to believe too much in the natural order." (Chazon Ish, letter 136)

"Today, one should not rely on a miracle. A sick person is required to act according to the ways of the world and call a doctor." (Birkei Yosef, *Yoreh De'ah* 336:2)

In fact, the Jewish view is one in which faith and modern medical knowledge complement one another. We request God's help in granting us good health while we seek the best possible answers from contemporary medicine.

Judaism views modern medicine and faith as complementary in maintaining good health.

We know a great deal about the relationship between diet and health; a wealth of practical nutrition information is available to us. In addition, our tradition encourages us to lead a healthy lifestyle. By heeding the advice of our sages and adapting sound nutrition and lifestyle practices, we can achieve better health and reduce the incidence of obesity and nutrition-related diseases in our community.

GIVING SIGNIFICANCE TO EATING

"You shall not eat any abomination." (*Devarim* 14:3)
"The righteous man eats to satisfy his soul." (*Mishlei* 13:25)
Baruch atah Hashem, al ha'aretz v'al hamazon: "Blessed are You Hashem, for the Land and for the food." (*Birkat Hamazon*)

The mundane act of eating is elevated to a spiritual level in the framework of *kashrut*. While the Rambam suggests that foods forbidden by the Torah are unhealthy (*Moreh Nevuchim* 3:48), the majority of our sages explain *kashrut* as *mitzvot* for the soul, rather than the body.

As the above *pasuk* in *Devarim* continues, forbidden species are described as *tamei* – impure. Abarbanel notes that the Torah uses the word *tamei* to refer to spiritual, as opposed to physical defilement (see Abarbanel's summary on *Parashat Shemini, Vayikra* 11).

"You shall not eat any abomination" is interpreted by Rav Chaim of Chernovitz as an admonition against unlimited feasting and eating only for the sake of immediate pleasure. "This type of eating should be abominable and disgusting to oneself, as if the animal instinct had come to the individual."[2] In other words, we are taught to elevate eating to a higher level – we should "eat to live" rather than "live to eat."

Eating is elevated to a spiritual level in Judaism.

In *Vayikra* (Leviticus), the laws of *kashrut* are followed by the verse: "For I am *Hashem* your God – you are to sanctify yourselves and you shall become holy, for I am holy" (*Vayikra* 11:44). Although the laws of *kashrut* are *chukkim*, "statutes that our tradition maintains were given to us without a rational reason," they serve to introduce holiness into the mundane act of eating. By observing the laws of *kashrut*, we bring spirituality and *kedushah* (holiness) to the otherwise purely physical act of eating.

As Jews, how do we become elevated to holiness through *mizvot* pertaining to eating? We request God's help, as expressed in the Friday night *Shemoneh Esrei: Kadeshanu b'mitzvotecha*: "Sanctify us through Your *mitzvot*," but we also have a personal obligation to seek holiness through mindful observance of the *mitzvot*.

Our table is considered an altar – we wash ritually before eating, make a *brachah* (blessing), salt our bread and end our meal with *Birkat Hamazon*. The ritual slaughter of animals teaches us compassion, and the strict guidelines of *kashrut* separate us from the world at large, reminding us that we belong to a special community of our own.

We approach eating in a dignified, thoughtful manner. In all of our behavior relating to food (purchasing, preparing and eating) we are reminded that we are living according to God's laws, with the aim of becoming holy. Since our tradition also encourages us to maintain good physical health, it follows that mindfully observing the *mitzvot* would naturally lead us to observe sound nutrition practices as well.

USING THE DISCIPLINE OF *KASHRUT*

"These are the creatures that you may eat from among all the animals that are upon the earth." (*Vayikra* 11:2)

For generations, our sages have puzzled over the meaning of the laws of *kashrut*. The Torah does not give us a clear explanation for *kashrut*. In fact, keeping kosher is a *mitzvah,* given to us by God, with no apparent reason. For some, reasons may be irrelevant. They simply accept the *mitzvah* and incorporate it into the fabric of their lives. For others, moral or spiritual meaning derived from the *mitzvah* acts to enhance its effect.

Many of us accept *kashrut* without question – it's a given that has been ingrained. We don't think twice about waiting between a meat and a milk meal or using separate eating utensils, and food restrictions do not faze us. We wouldn't even consider eating non-kosher food. We integrate *kashrut* into our lives just as we integrate other *mitzvot* – they are intricate parts of our lives that define us as Jews.

I lived in a community where *kashrut* was unfamiliar, even among Jews. Growing up, my friends were amazed at the complicated set of rules governing what I ate. They saw it as terribly restrictive, requiring a good deal of willpower and self-control.

But I just took it for granted. It didn't seem hard or unusual to me – it was just something our family did.

In fact, observing the laws of *kashrut* requires a tremendous amount of discipline. For those struggling with weight loss or poor eating habits, we can apply the same type of discipline to help learn new, healthier eating strategies.

**The self-control and discipline required
to observe *kashrut* can be used to
help change eating behaviors.**

Picture yourself sitting in an airplane. There is a mechanical problem and your flight is delayed by several hours. You didn't pack any food. After all, it's only a short flight and you expected to be at your destination by dinner. But you're starting to feel really hungry.

Would you eat the non-kosher snack offered by the flight attendant? Of course not!

How can you apply the ingrained discipline required to observe *kashrut* to other areas of eating?
Think about another situation: You've been invited out for *Shabbat* dinner. The food is delicious and you've eaten a reasonably-sized portion of everything. Even though you feel quite satisfied, your host insists that you have a second serving of brisket.

While keeping in mind your goal of losing another few pounds, transfer the discipline of observing *kashrut* to the present situation. Politely refuse the second serving. If necessary, explain that you are feeling quite full and are saving room for a little dessert. Compliment your host on her cooking or change the subject completely, if necessary. But stick to your resolve.

If you observe *kashrut*, you already possess an enormous amount of willpower. Expand upon this asset in other areas of eating that you would like to change.

Start with one eating behavior at a time.
Here are some examples:

- One serving portion is what I need to maintain my weight; I will not take seconds.
- When I'm thirsty, water is the healthiest thirst quencher; I will not drink sweetened beverages.
- Eating breakfast is important to my health; I will be sure to eat breakfast every day.
- I understand that chocolate is high in calories; I will enjoy just one small square a day.
- Late at night I tend to snack heavily; I will not eat after 8 P.M.

CHAPTER 2

Jewish Women: Setting the Tone with Food

"All that is sacred to the establishment of the Jewish home, the rearing and education of the children, and the kashrut and holiness of the home, the sanctity of the Shabbat – all this and more God has entrusted into the hands of the Jewish woman." (Rabbi Menachem Schneerson)³

"In all my days I have never referred to my wife as ishti, my wife. Rather, I refer to my wife as beiti, my home." (R. Yossi, *Shabbat* 118b)

Jewish women have their hands full. Even though many of us work at jobs outside of the home and enjoy the cooperation of our husbands and children, our home is still our primary domain. We take responsibility for a clean and orderly house and for the education and discipline of our children. *Shalom bayit*, a peaceful, harmonious home with Jewish values, is our lofty goal. Following in the path of our matriarch Sarah, we attempt to imbue the material world with spirituality and Godliness – to create a sanctuary within our homes.

Feeding ourselves and our families is part of this challenge. We set the nutritional tone when we decide on menus, shop for food and prepare a never-ending array of meals and snacks. Whether we eat in shifts or as a family, sitting or standing, quickly or leisurely – we set the mood and create the environment surrounding eating behaviors.

Women are most likely to influence family eating behaviors and food choices.

THE EATING ENVIRONMENT

"They shall make a Sanctuary for Me, so that I may dwell among them." (*Shemot* 25:8)
"Drawing out of a meal prolongs a man's life." (*Brachot* 54b)

God gave us *mitzvot* relating to food in order to create a connection between the dinner table and the Divine. With large families, busy schedules and hectic lives, it is not always easy to create this sense of spirituality at our tables. We are usually most successful during *Shabbat* and holidays. Striving for calm, relaxing and enjoyable meals can bring us closer to this ideal every day.

Set the dinner table in advance, or give this job to one of your children. Have all of the food ready and placed on the table before starting to eat. If you are serving dessert, have it close to or on the table as well. Wait for everyone to be seated before serving and eating. With young children, it is especially helpful to say the appropriate *brachah* together before eating. Make it a special point not to get up from the table during your meal. This may sound unusual and unnecessary, but it can go a long way in creating a calm and relaxing atmosphere. It is a powerful example to children when their parents sit comfortably through a meal rather than jump up and down to serve food, answer the phone or get up before everyone is finished eating.

Make a conscious effort to sit at the table during the whole meal and relax with your family.

EATING AS A FAMILY

There are many benefits to eating meals together. It may be the only time when most (or all) of us are together to share the day's proceedings, make future plans and discuss Torah and current events. What better time to model good eating habits and polite behavior than at the dinner table?

Children and teenagers who eat regular meals with their families have been shown to eat more fruits, vegetables and calcium-rich foods and less fried food, soda and trans fat than those who rarely eat together. Improved behavior and school performance has also been noted in teenagers who eat dinner with their families.

Most interesting is a study showing that children between the ages of 9 and 14 years who ate dinner regularly with their families were less likely to be overweight than their peers who never, or rarely, ate with their families. Additionally, as the study progressed and the children who rarely had family meals became teenagers, it revealed that they were less likely to eat dinner with their families and more likely to gain weight.[4]

Think about how enjoyable it feels when your family eats together on *Shabbat* and holidays. Try to recreate that feeling during the week by eating at least one meal a day together.

> **Eating meals together has nutritional, social and educational benefits.**

EATING FOR YOURSELF

Eating the food left over on our children's plates is a practice that is especially common among women. I had thought that this habit was a relic of my mother's generation – as survivors of war and the Great Depression; they knew poverty and hunger firsthand. They felt genuine guilt about wasting anything.

When I noticed a friend finishing her children's food at our *Shabbat* table, it took me by surprise – she is in her late twenties, college educated, having grown up in relative comfort in France before making *aliyah*. After I discreetly assured her that it did not bother me to throw out food, she was taken aback, unaware that she had even been doing this.

We now know that this is a common eating behavior among women, regardless of age, education, culture or religion – another bad habit contributing to overweight and obesity.

Here are a few suggestions to help curb this kind of detrimental eating:

- Serve your children small portions to begin with. If they are still hungry, they can have more.
- Serve yourself reasonably sized portions, using the guidelines found throughout this book.
- If you are trying to lose weight, resolve to eat only what is on *your* plate.
- Train yourself to throw out the food left on anybody else's plate.

FOOD AS A VEHICLE TO HOLINESS

"This is the great gift of the *Halachah*: To turn everything into a moment of eternity. To do the finite and to discover the infinite. To match the material with the holy. To reveal God's concern with man by calling on man to leave the world of the average and turn a simple deed into a moment of Divine revelation." (Rabbi Nathan Lopes Cardozo)

The Japanese have a ceremony for preparing tea and the Ethiopians have a ceremony for making coffee. Each involves elaborate rituals requiring time, focus and attentiveness. They oblige one to slow down and remain in the present moment. They bring a sense of tranquility and holiness to the realm of food preparation.

Baking challah is a similar experience. As we knead and braid the dough, we acknowledge the holiness of our task. We set aside a portion of challah with the belief that God is our provider. As one of the three *mitzvot* given especially to women, preparing challah is more than just baking bread – it is a spiritual endeavor requiring attention and awareness.

By taking a step back and slowing down, you can achieve a similar level of spirituality while cooking and eating. When you approach cooking with calmness, a positive attitude and *kavanah* (thoughtfulness), it becomes a creative pleasure and a gift of love. If you feel yourself rushing, feeling tense or anxious while cooking or eating, take a few deep breaths, relax and concentrate on the creative and sacred aspects of your actions.

> **Slow down and consider the spiritual and creative aspects of cooking while you are at work in the kitchen.**

A HEALTHY RELATIONSHIP WITH FOOD

"In Hebrew, the word for bread is *lechem*. This root is closely related to *lacham*, which means to wage war.... Eating is seen as the battleground between the physical and the spiritual." (Rabbi Aryeh Kaplan)[5]

Millions of women are on diets to lose or maintain their weight. Although concern over body image is usually associated with younger women, women of all ages are affected. A study of women between the ages of 61 and 92 years identified weight as their greatest concern.[6] Eating disorders such as compulsive overeating, anorexia and bulimia nervosa are widespread, affecting all segments of the Jewish community. If you or someone you know suffers from an eating disorder, it is essential to seek treatment from a qualified medical professional.

Signs and symptoms of eating disorders may include:
- Eating very large portions, even when you are not hungry.
- Feeling depressed, guilty or embarrassed after overeating.

- Eating very quickly and to the point of feeling uncomfortable.
- Preoccupation with weight, food and dieting.
- Intense fear of weight gain or being "fat."
- Feeling "fat" when not overweight.
- Dramatic weight loss.
- Obsessive exercise.
- Repeated episodes of bingeing and purging.
- Feeling depressed, anxious, out of control or hopeless.

If eating is supposed to be pleasurable, why are so many of us engaged in a personal war with food?
Many of us feel overburdened – overtaxed with family and social obligations that do not allow us time to nurture or listen to ourselves. You may never even think about how you feel when you grab something to eat between meals, in the car or at night. Are you really feeling hungry? Or are you feeling anxious, stressed, irritable, tired, lonely or depressed?

Self-esteem and a healthy attitude towards food are the foundations of making peace with your eating habits.

Just as you eat to nourish your body, you eat to nourish your soul. When your soul is at peace, you are better able to make peace with your body and your relationship with food. Judaism stresses the spiritual dimension of food and eating. By internalizing this spirituality, you can come closer to an enjoyable, relaxed and purposeful outlook towards nourishing your body and soul.

Here are some suggestions that may help you reach this goal:
- Before you begin to eat, think about how you feel emotionally and physically.
- Be "in the moment" by eliminating distractions and

concentrating on where you are and what you are doing now.

- Put aside everything else in your life, for just a moment, and consider just your own feelings.
- Concentrate on your *brachah* and its importance in connecting the physical with the spiritual act of eating.

CHAPTER 3

Eating for Optimum Health

"[A] Land of wheat, barley, grape, fig and pomegranate; a Land of olive oil and date honey." (Devarim 8:8)

The Land of Israel was renowned throughout the ancient world for these seven species enjoyed by our ancestors. Whole grains, fresh and dried fruits, olive oil and red wine – all with health benefits that we are only now discovering.

It can be confusing to know what to eat. What are we to believe from the countless magazine, newspaper and Internet articles about nutrition? Who should we believe among the many nutrition "experts" giving advice? Even the latest research studies often seem to contradict one another – one day chocolate is bad, the next day it's good.

Given the complexities of nutrition research, it may be years until we have answers to our diet and health-related questions. Yet, there is sufficient evidence from large, well-controlled, long-term studies to suggest ways of improving our diets.*

Here are my recommendations:
- Maintain a healthy weight.
- Eat between five and nine servings of vegetables and fruit every day.

---

* A physician should be consulted before making any major changes in your diet or exercise routine, especially if you have a medical condition that requires specific diet or exercise restrictions. Speak to a registered dietitian (RD) for more personal advice regarding nutrition.

- Substitute whole grains for refined grains.
- Limit your intake of sugar and highly processed foods.
- Replace saturated and trans fats with monounsaturated and polyunsaturated fats.
- Eat more fish, legumes and nuts and less red meat.
- Exercise regularly.

MAINTAINING A HEALTHY WEIGHT

"More people die from overeating than from starvation." (*Shabbat* 33a)

"Overeating is like poison to the body. It is the main source of all illness. Most illnesses which afflict a man are caused by harmful foods or by his filling his belly and overeating, even of healthful foods." (Rambam, *Hilchot De'ot* 4:15)

Nearly two-thirds of adults in the US are overweight, and one third of them are obese.[7] According to the World Heart Federation Fact Sheet, 2002, the prevalence of overweight American children has doubled in the past 30 years, from 15% to 32%. The figures in Israel and much of the rest of the world are alarming as well. Unfortunately, the statistics are getting worse, not better.

Obesity increases the risk of developing serious health conditions, including coronary heart disease, Type 2 diabetes, hypertension, gallbladder disease, arthritis, stroke and several types of cancer. Obesity-related diseases profoundly shorten life span[8] and cost an estimated $100 billion annually in the US.[9] The good news is that even modest weight loss, as little as 5% to 10% of your original body weight, can reduce your risk factors for these diseases.

Weight loss can help lower blood pressure, reduce blood sugar levels, improve cholesterol levels and increase energy levels.

How do you know if you are overweight or obese? What should

your ideal body weight be? Although we do not have precise answers to these questions, a number called Body Mass Index (BMI), based on height and weight, can help you determine if your weight is within a healthy range.

You can determine your BMI on the following web site, sponsored by the US Department of Human Services and the National Institutes of Health: www.nhlbisupport.com/bmi/

If your BMI is between 25 and 30, you are considered overweight. You are obese if your BMI is over 30. The higher the BMI, the greater the risk of developing serious illnesses such as diabetes, cancer and cardiovascular disease. Your goal should be to keep your BMI under 25 (please note that healthy BMI recommendations for the elderly are higher; see below).

The shape of your body can also influence your risk for disease. People who carry more fat in their abdominal area ("apple-shaped") are at greater risk than those whose fat is located primarily in their hips and thighs ("pear-shaped"). In fact, a recent study of men and women from around the world showed that waist-to-hip ratio was a stronger indicator of heart attack risk and actual heart attacks than BMI. Those with wider hips and slimmer waistlines were less likely to suffer a heart attack than those with large waistlines.[10]

With aging, BMI becomes less valuable as a measuring tool and waist-to-hip ratio is more useful. Although a higher BMI is often recommended for people over the age of 70, it is more important to emphasize exercise to maintain lean body mass rather than to increase BMI.

You can calculate your waist-to-hip ratio by dividing your waist measurement (in inches) by your hip measurement. Men should aim for a ratio of 0.90 or less. A healthy ratio for women is 0.80 or less.

> ## Your waist-to-hip ratio can also help determine risk factors for weight-related diseases.

Why is it that some people seem to eat whatever they want and never gain weight while others are constantly dieting and are still overweight?
There is no simple answer to weight management. Your weight depends on the number of calories you consume and the number of those calories your body stores and burns. Why do some people store more calories than they burn? The answer is likely related to genetics, environment and stress, or a combination of these. Regardless of your inherited genes (which influence but do not determine your size and shape), eating less and exercising more is the only way for most of us to lose weight.

> ## Eating less and exercising more is the best way to lose weight.

Generally, I do not recommend specific diets for weight loss. Most diets are short-term solutions for a long-term problem. My question for you is "what happens when you go off the diet?" The most successful weight-loss strategies include eating and behavior changes that you can incorporate into your life. In other words, lifestyle changes, not diets, are the key to weight loss and maintenance.

LIFESTYLE CHANGES THAT CAN HELP YOU LOSE WEIGHT

Learn to Eat "Mindfully"
Improving the way we eat goes hand-in-hand with improving what we eat. Sit comfortably, relax and say each *brachah* with *kavanah*.

Eat slowly and chew thoroughly while enjoying the taste and texture of your food. Using chopsticks might help you to slow down and eat smaller bites. Put all of the food on the table before you sit down so that you can stay seated until you have completely finished eating. Resolve not to answer the telephone while you are eating. (And please, try not to eat while you are driving!) Focus on the pleasure of eating without distractions.

It takes your stomach twenty minutes to signal your brain that it is full, so pay attention to how your stomach feels as you are eating and stop when you feel comfortably satisfied. Learn to recognize how you feel before you feel "stuffed" and stop eating then. This takes practice, but is well worth the effort.

> "One should not eat until his stomach is full. Rather, he should stop when he has eaten close to three quarters of full satisfaction." (Rambam, *Hilchot De'ot* 4:2)

Fortunately, Jewish tradition offers us tools to eat mindfully. We are taught to consider food as more than just fuel for the body. Our concepts of *tzniyut* (modesty) and *kavod* (honor) remind us of the importance of modesty and self-respect in every facet of our lives. When we respect ourselves, we are more likely to eat in a way that preserves our good health.

Practice Portion Control

Learn what a normal portion is and measure your food until you are comfortable with what a portion looks like. Just like we learn to identify a *kezayit* in order to say a *brachah achronah*, we should learn to recognize standard portion sizes for the sake of our waistlines.

> "If one eats less, one will taste more." (Chinese proverb)

Make it easier to stick with smaller portions and avoid second helpings by starting your meal with a large salad or a vegetable-rich soup. Rather than serve "family style" by putting all of the food in serving dishes on the table, try pre-portioning plates in the kitchen. You can then control serving sizes and avoid the temptation of multiple servings.

Be aware that restaurant servings are usually far too large. Don't hesitate to share an entrée, and do not be embarrassed to order an appetizer, soup and/or salad as your main course. When my husband and I share an entrée, one of our favorite restaurants automatically divides our meal and presents it on two separate plates. We order one dessert and two spoons.

Water, Water, Water

Fluid intake is essential for maintaining good health, and it fills us up so that we are less likely to overeat. Add a twist of lemon to a glass of water or try clear sparkling water for variety. Unsweetened herbal or green tea is a nice change as well.

Stay away from fruit drinks and sweetened sodas as "every-day" beverages. They can add a good many calories, with no nutritional benefit. Although a small glass of pure fruit juice is fine, you are better off eating the whole fruit, which will fill you up and contribute fiber to your diet. If you have a weakness for fruit juice, try diluting half a glass of juice with sparkling water to make a full glass.

Reduce Temptations

Stock your refrigerator and pantry with healthy, low-calorie food, and avoid prepared foods that are high in sugar, fat and salt. A good choice of snack foods might include apples, whole-grain crackers and almonds. Try low-fat yogurt or frozen yogurt with fresh fruit for a refreshing snack. Why tempt yourself with cookies, ice cream and potato chips?

Before you leave for the grocery store, make a list of what you need. Since a healthy diet relies heavily on vegetables and fruit, start your shopping in the produce department. Use your list, but always be aware of additional seasonal produce that looks especially good and may be on sale. By shopping the perimeter of the store, you can avoid most of the prepared foods, sweets, snacks and soft drinks that the food industry wants you to buy. Do not fall prey to fancy packaging, advertisements, coupons or sales. Stick to your list and do not buy anything that might be an unhealthy temptation.

Get Organized/Plan Ahead

With some advanced planning, you can avoid relying on high-calorie convenience foods. Most of us are so busy, we hardly have time to sit down and eat, let alone plan what we will eat. And, when we are really hungry, we don't have the patience to start thinking about what would be best to eat. It's human nature to resort to what is easiest – zap the frozen pizza in the microwave!

Writing a menu for the week can be a big help. Although I enjoy cooking, I am often too busy to think much about what to cook. If you take the time to write a menu, it's one less thing to think about when everyone is hungry. Even if you don't follow your plan, at least you have it as backup when life gets especially hectic.

Cook smart for *Shabbat*. Plan a healthy menu and cook extra food for the coming week. Two chickens do not take much more time to prepare than one. Cook them together and save one for a mid-week meal. Make extra vegetables and use them in a soup later in the week. Take advantage of the time you have in the kitchen by preparing more than what you need for *Shabbat*, with the idea of saving time later on.

Keep It Simple

Some people find it easier to eat less if they have fewer foods to choose from. That does not mean limiting your diet to any one food or food group, as we need a variety of foods for the various nutrients they provide. It just means simplifying your meals and the choices you give yourself. You may find it easier to practice

self-control when you prepare a meal of baked fish, a steamed vegetable and salad than if you turn the fish into a casserole and serve
it with numerous vegetables and salads.

Think about the last *simchah* you attended and you will understand the concept. If the food was served as a buffet, you will
no doubt recall how people filled their plates to capacity. Who
wouldn't want to taste a little of everything? With so many choices,
it is very difficult to refrain from overeating.

Write It Down

Keep track of everything that you eat for a week or two. Include
portion sizes, time of day and where you are when you eat. Also
helpful is to note how you feel when you eat (for example, fam-
ished, exhausted, anxious). This simple exercise will help you to
be more aware of what you are eating so that you can determine
your nutritional strengths and weaknesses.

Children often enjoy keeping a food diary as well. A valuable
and fun family project is to keep track of how many fruits and
vegetables everyone eats each day. You can make a simple chart
with the days of the week and each person's name. Let everyone
make a check mark each time they eat a fruit or vegetable, with
the goal of at least five servings each day. This type of "game" can
be an opportunity for nutrition education and motivation for the
whole family.

Hitting the Scales

There is probably no reason to weigh yourself more than once a
week, although some people rely on frequent weigh-ins to catch
small weight gains early and correct them. It is not unusual, especially for women, for weight to fluctuate, even from day to day. Keep
in mind also that quick weight loss is often a loss of water weight
and not a permanent loss of fat, whereas long-term weight loss is
often slow and steady. If constant weigh-ins produce anxiety and
lead to obsessive behavior, such as skipping meals and excessive

workouts, you are better off relying on the fit of your clothes and how you look and feel.

Get Moving

Make exercise a regular part of your daily routine. Since weight loss occurs when we burn more calories than we eat, it makes sense to "combine tactics" by eating less and exercising more. And the benefits of exercise go beyond weight loss: regular exercise has been shown to reduce the risk of heart disease, high blood pressure, osteoporosis and diabetes. In addition, exercise increases energy levels and endurance. Regular exercise can positively affect mental health as well by easing tension, stress and anxiety.

Be sure to consult your physician before beginning an exercise program. Expect to start slowly, perhaps with a 10-minute walk several times a week, increasing the time and pace gradually. For maximum benefit, most experts recommend exercising at least 30 minutes a day, four to six times a week.

For weight loss you may need to increase the time and frequency. There are many choices, including public and private programs, videotapes that you can follow at home and of course walking. Brisk walking is safe, easy, effective and free – it's a great way for most people to incorporate exercise into their lives. Keep in mind that the best exercise is the exercise that you will do regularly.

Looking for Exercise Ideas?
- Climb the stairs instead of using the elevator.
- Park your car as far as possible from your destination and walk briskly.
- Rake the leaves and shovel the snow rather than use motorized equipment.
- Keep tennis shoes handy for a short "power walk" during a break in your day.
- Try bike riding; it's an activity you can enjoy with the whole family.
- Consider forming a walking group.

- Use a treadmill or stationary bicycle while reading or watching television.

**Table 1: How to Burn 150 Calories –
Activities Based on a Body Weight of 150 Pounds**

Walking	2 miles per hour	38 minutes
Walking	4.5 miles per hour	20 minutes
Jogging	5.5 miles per hour	12 minutes
Biking	6 miles per hour	38 minutes
Biking	12 miles per hour	22 minutes
Gardening		30–40 minutes
Washing windows or floors		60 minutes
Raking leaves		35 minutes

Harvard Health Beat, August 2005, www.health.harvard.edu/healthbeat

Be Patient
Losing weight and maintaining a healthy weight can be a life-long challenge. Many of us have experienced the ups and downs of weight loss and the unhealthy "yo-yo" phenomenon of losing weight, gaining it back and then endlessly repeating the cycle. Be patient with yourself and with those who you are trying to help. Keep in mind that slow gradual weight loss is more likely to produce long-term results. And if your efforts reach a slow or difficult point, don't be too hard on yourself. Take pride in what you have accomplished.

The Bottom Line

Eat "mindfully."

Practice portion control.

Drink plenty of water.

Reduce temptation.

Plan ahead, for meals and snacks.

Simplify your food choices.

Keep a food diary.

CHAPTER 4

Deciphering Food Labels

Kosher consumers have a head start on reading food labels. With nearly a thousand kosher symbols and certifying agencies worldwide, we are used to finding and evaluating kosher certification symbols on product labels.

As health-conscious consumers, our challenge is to understand and interpret nutrition labeling and health claims. With package labels often appearing more confusing than helpful, it is easy to ignore them completely. Taking the time to understand labels will enable you to make healthier food choices for you and your family.

Generations ago, product labels barely identified the contents of food and beverage packages. In the early 1900s, the US federal government was authorized to regulate the safety and quality of food. Over time, the Food and Drug Administration (FDA) required ingredient listing on food packaging, as well as net weight and contact information of the manufacturer. With time, further nutrition information was included and labeling became more complex. In 1994, new label requirements went into effect in an effort to make it easier to choose healthy foods. The new requirements feature a box on the side or back of the package entitled "Nutrition Facts."

MAKING SENSE OF "NUTRITION FACTS"

Here is a sample label for macaroni and cheese, taken from the FDA's web page on understanding the Nutrition Facts label.

Figure 1: Example of Nutrition Facts Label

Nutrition Facts

Serving Size 1 cup (228g)
Servings Per Container 2

Amount Per Serving	
Calories 250	Calories from Fat 110

	% Daily Value*
Total Fat 12g	18%
Saturated Fat 3g	15%
Trans Fat 3g	
Cholesterol 30mg	10%
Sodium 470mg	20%
Total Carbohydrate 31g	10%
Dietary Fiber 0g	0%
Sugars 5g	
Protein 5g	
Vitamin A	4%
Vitamin C	2%
Calcium	20%
Iron	4%

* Percent Daily Values are based on a 2,000 calorie diet. Your Daily Values may be higher or lower depending on your calorie needs.			
	Calories	2,000	2,500
Total Fat	Less than	65g	80g
Sat Fat	Less than	20g	25g
Cholesterol	Less than	300mg	300mg
Sodium	Less than	2,400mg	2,400mg
Total Carbohydrate		300g	375g
Dietary Fiber		25g	30g

USFDA Center for Food Safety and Applied Nutrition

Serving Size and Servings per Container: Start at the top of the label, with the serving size. Although this amount reflects what is typically eaten by many people, it is determined by the manufacturer, and may not reflect a healthy portion size. Servings per container are based on serving size.

Is your serving size the same as the one on the label? You may need to adjust the nutrient and calorie values based on what is a realistic serving size for you.

Calories and Calories from Fat: Calories provide a measure of how much energy your body gets from food. The label lists calories according to the serving size listed. Calories from fat are listed to help you meet recommendations of eating no more than 30% of your total daily calories from fat. For example, if you eat 2,000 calories in one day, no more than 600 of those calories should come from fat.

The calorie listing on the label can help you manage your calorie and fat intake.

Percent Daily Value: The right-hand column of the label lists % Daily Value*. As the asterisk indicates, these values are based on a 2,000-calorie diet. They tell, in percentages, how much of a certain nutrient you will get by eating one serving of the food. Since most of us do not eat exactly 2,000 calories a day, percent daily value is most useful for determining if a food is high or low in certain nutrients.

If a food has more than 20% of the percent daily value, it is considered high in that nutrient, while 5% or less is considered low.

Total Fat, Cholesterol and Sodium: Total fat, measured in grams, indicates the amount of fat in one serving of the food. Listings for saturated, polyunsaturated, monounsaturated and trans fat may appear below the listing for total fat. Cholesterol and sodium, measured in milligrams, are listed under the fat information.

Look for products that are low in total fat, saturated fat, trans fat, cholesterol and sodium.

Total Carbohydrate: Listed in grams, this number combines several types of carbohydrates, including starch, sugar and dietary fiber. Specific figures for dietary fiber and sugar are often listed under total carbohydrate.

Check labels for products that are high in dietary fiber and low in sugar.

Protein: The amount of protein in a product is listed in grams. Unless there is a claim for protein, such as "high protein," a percent daily value is not required on the label.

Since most Americans get more than enough protein, this number is usually not very important.

Vitamins and Minerals: Vitamins A and C, calcium and iron are listed by percentage daily value on the Nutrition Facts label, since many people do not get an adequate intake of these nutrients. If a product is especially high in other nutrients, they may be listed here as well.

INGREDIENT LABELS

Most labels list ingredients in descending order by weight. This can give you an idea of how much of a particular ingredient the product contains. For instance, if a cereal lists four ingredients and sugar is the first, you can expect the cereal to be high in sugar. If it lists the ingredients as whole wheat, wheat bran, sugar and salt, the amount of sugar in the cereal will be lower.

Reading ingredient labels is especially important if you or someone in your family suffers from a food allergy or sensitivity. In most cases, ingredients are fairly easy to identify. But as advanced technology produces more sophisticated food products, it can be difficult to pronounce, let alone understand, what some ingredients really are. This is especially true of highly processed foods. It is best to consult a dietitian if you are unsure of any particular ingredient.

Check the first few ingredients on a label to determine the main or most prominent ingredients in the product. Does it sound healthy?

Phrases such as "no sugar added," "light" and "cholesterol free" can be confusing.

Here are some common terms and their specific meanings:

No Sugar Added	No sugars have been added during processing
Sugar, Fat or Sodium Free	Less than 0.5 grams per serving
Reduced Calorie, Sugar, Fat or Sodium	At least 25% less than the traditional food
Low Calorie	40 calories or less per serving
Low Fat	3 grams or less of fat per serving
Low Sodium	140 mg or less per serving
Light or Lite	Contains ⅓ fewer calories or half the fat of the traditional food OR the sodium content is 50% less than the traditional food
High Fiber	5 grams or more of fiber per serving
Low Cholesterol	20 mg or less of cholesterol and 2 grams or less of saturated fat per serving

These terms can be helpful, but sometimes misleading as well. For instance, a product can be cholesterol free but still high in fat (such as salad dressing or cookies made with vegetable oil). Similarly, a product with no added sugar may naturally contain a high amount of sugar (such as dried fruit).

> **These phrases can help you choose foods that meet specific nutritional needs, but do not necessarily mean that a particular food is good for you.**

HEALTH CLAIMS

The FDA has approved numerous health-related food claims. Although the standard used to validate these claims is "significant scientific agreement," there remains disagreement among health professionals regarding the accuracy and impact of these claims. Here is an example of a recently approved statement that may appear on qualifying soy products:

> "Diets low in saturated fat and cholesterol that include 25 grams of soy protein a day may reduce the risk of heart disease. One serving of [name of food] provides _____ grams of soy protein."[11]

There are similarly approved health claims for sodium and hypertension; dietary fat and fiber and cancer; saturated fat, cholesterol and fiber and coronary heart disease; and calcium and osteoporosis. Some of these claims require qualifying statements such as "Individuals with high blood pressure should consult their physician."[12]

Are consumers reading the fine print of qualifying statements on package labels? Should food companies be giving dietary and health advice? Are health claims confusing and/or misleading? And do these claims actually change eating behaviors? Unfortunately, we do not have definitive answers to these questions. As an educated consumer, try not to rely heavily on product health claims. Check the Nutrition Facts label, read the product ingredient list and stick to foods that are minimally processed.

FOOD ALLERGEN LABELING

Packaged foods under FDA regulation are required to list "major food allergens" on their labels. These allergens include milk, eggs, fish, tree nuts (such as walnuts, almonds and pecans), peanuts, wheat and soybeans. If food allergies are a concern, examine labels carefully. Manufacturers may list allergens in parentheses following the common name of the food in the ingredient list. Or, you may find them next to or after the ingredients in this format: "Contains wheat, milk and soy."

FOOD LABELING IN ISRAEL

In Israel, the Ministry of Health sets down numerous regulations concerning product labeling. Manufacturers are required to print nutrition information on all packaged food. Nutrients are listed per 100 grams of the product and may be listed by serving size as well. Total calories, carbohydrates, protein, fat and sodium are required on the label. If the product contains more than 5 grams of fat, saturated fat and cholesterol values must be given as well.

As in the US, ingredients are listed in descending order.

The Bottom Line

Use the Nutrition Facts label as a guide to calories, fat, carbohydrates and sodium.

Read ingredient labels to determine a product's main components.

Do not purchase a product solely on the basis of its health claim.

CHAPTER 5

Fat Facts: Sorting out the Good and the Bad

CHOOSING GOOD FATS AND AVOIDING BAD ONES TO IMPROVE YOUR HEALTH

For more than twenty years, many of us have successfully reduced the amount of fat in our diets. The percentage of fat in the average American diet actually decreased from more than 40% to 34% between the 1950s and the early 1990s.[13] We have followed the advice of experts who believed that we could reduce the incidence of coronary heart disease, cancer, diabetes and obesity by eating less fat and cholesterol. Low-fat desserts, egg substitutes, snacks made with "fake fats," fat-blocking diet pills and a myriad of low-fat diets have been developed to help us achieve this goal. Why then, after all of this effort, are we no better off in our battle with heart disease? How can we explain that Type 2 diabetes is on the rise, and more people than ever are overweight and obese?

Part of the explanation may be that while we can successfully reduce fat calories from our diet, we too often replace those calories with refined carbohydrate calories. In addition, portion sizes have grown larger and we have become even more sedentary. Another piece of the puzzle has to do with the type of fats that we have been eating.

Reducing total dietary fat and substituting it with refined carbohydrates does not significantly protect against coronary heart disease. A more successful strategy is to change the type of fats and carbohydrates that we eat.

WHY WE NEED FAT

Fat plays an important role in our diet. A small amount of fat can enhance the flavor of foods and provide a feeling of fullness. Dietary fat is a source of fuel for the body. It is essential for cell, muscle and nerve function, blood clotting and hormone production. Our bodies also require a certain amount of fat to absorb the fat-soluble vitamins A, D, E and K.

In order for fats to achieve these tasks, they must travel from the digestive system to the cells. This is accomplished by small fat-transporting particles comprised of fat and protein called lipoproteins. A number of these lipoproteins, including HDL (high-density lipoprotein), LDL (low-density lipoprotein) and triglycerides, play an important role in the development of heart disease.

HDL = High-Density Lipoprotein = "Healthy" or Good for Heart Health
LDL = Low-Density Lipoprotein = "Lousy" or Bad for Heart Health

CHOLESTEROL AND BLOOD LIPIDS: KNOW YOUR NUMBERS

Cholesterol is a waxy, fat-like substance produced by the liver and present in foods of animal origin. It is carried in the bloodstream via lipoprotein particles such as HDL and LDL to cells throughout the body. A small amount of cholesterol is synthesized by the body to make cell membranes and nerve sheaths, and for the production of hormones. When excess cholesterol travels through the bloodstream, it often ends up deposited in arteries, including coronary and cerebral arteries. There it contributes to narrowing and blockages, known as atherosclerosis, which can result in heart disease or stroke.

Excess cholesterol in the bloodstream can block arteries and lead to coronary artery disease.

Just as you cannot feel whether your blood pressure is high or low, you cannot know if your cholesterol levels are normal without a blood test. A lipid or lipoprotein profile measures total cholesterol and triglycerides as well as the amount of cholesterol in LDL and HDL particles. LDL is the main source of cholesterol buildup in the arteries. HDL helps prevent arterial cholesterol buildup and removes excess cholesterol from the arteries back to the liver, a process called "reverse cholesterol transport." Triglycerides are the main constituents of fat tissue, and increased amounts in the blood can also damage arteries.

Blood lipid levels are measured in milligrams per deciliter, or mg/dL. According to current recommendations of the National Cholesterol Education Program (National Institutes of Health), desirable total cholesterol for adults is less than 200 mg/dL. LDL should be as low as possible, preferably below 130 mg/dL. Since HDL helps to protect against heart disease, high levels, ideally above 55 mg/dL in women and above 45 mg/dL in men, are best. Normal triglyceride levels are 200 mg/dL or less.*

HDL and LDL levels are affected by numerous factors including

---

* Please note that these figures are under frequent review and could change. The desirable levels are also affected by the presence of additional risk factors for heart disease. Consult your physician regarding the results of your blood lipid test. Because blood lipids are only a part of the total picture, it is important that you speak with your physician regarding specific concerns that you may have about heart disease.

age, gender, weight, physical activity, diet and genetics. As we age, cholesterol levels rise. This is especially true for women beyond the age of menopause, when previously normal cholesterol levels may rise significantly and the risk for heart disease increases. In fact, coronary heart disease is the number one killer of women in the US. Being obese is a risk factor in itself for heart disease, and losing weight can often help lower total and LDL cholesterol levels and raise HDL cholesterol levels. Regular physical activity can also help you lose weight and improve your cholesterol profile.

Age, gender, weight, diet, genetics and exercise can affect your HDL and LDL levels.

Foods that have a positive effect on cholesterol levels:
Fruits, vegetables, whole grains, legumes, olive oil, nuts and fish.

Foods that have a negative effect on cholesterol levels:
Fatty meats, organ meats, high-fat cheese and dairy products, butter and margarine, bakery and snack foods made with partially hydrogenated fats.

A (VERY) LITTLE CHEMISTRY

Chemically speaking, fats are composed of fatty acids: chains of carbon atoms attached to hydrogen atoms. They differ from one another in the length and pattern of the carbon chains and the number of hydrogen atoms attached to them. Dietary fats contain a mixture of saturated, monounsaturated and polyunsaturated fatty acids. I will refer to fatty acids simply as fats.

Some fats contribute to clogged arteries and other fats help keep arteries clear.

Saturated fat: This is fat in which the carbon chain is completely filled (saturated) with hydrogen atoms. These fats are found mainly in meat and dairy products and are often solid at room temperature. Think of the fat on leftover brisket or chilled chicken soup, a stick of butter and cheese. (Exceptions include palm and coconut oils, which contain saturated fats even though they originate from plants.) Saturated fat increases levels of LDL and HDL cholesterol, though the increase in HDL is not significant enough to recommend them. *High saturated fat intake is associated with an increased risk of heart disease.*

Monounsaturated fat: Contains one (mono) double-bond in the carbon chain. Most monounsaturated fats are liquid at room temperature. Oils such as olive, canola and peanut are high in monounsaturated fat, as are avocados and many nuts. The effect of these on blood lipids is positive. *These fats can lower LDL and raise HDL cholesterol, which is beneficial for the heart.*

Polyunsaturated fat: Contains two or more (poly) double-bonds of carbon and is also liquid at room temperature. There are two main types of polyunsaturated fat: omega-3 and omega-6. (Omega refers to the position of the first double-bond in the chain.) They are referred to as "essential fatty acids" since they are essential for good health and the body does not synthesize them. Therefore, we must rely on dietary sources.

Omega-3: Found in oily, cold-water fish such as salmon and sardines, as well as canola oil, walnuts and ground flax seeds. *It has been found to be important in protecting against heart disease* by thinning the blood to prevent clotting (blood clots within arteries are the main cause of most heart attacks), reducing inflammation (which also plays a role in the development of heart disease) and lowering blood triglyceride levels. In addition, omega-3 may play a role in preventing or alleviating autoimmune disorders, Crohn's disease, several types of cancer, mild hypertension and rheumatoid arthritis.[14]

Omega-6: Found in vegetable oils such as corn, soybean, safflower and sunflower, as well as meat, poultry and dairy products. *It plays a protective role against heart disease by lowering* LDL *cholesterol.*

There has been an ongoing discussion on the ideal ratio of omega-3 and omega-6 fats in the typical American diet. In the past, omega-3 was much more abundant and omega-6 was less prevalent in our diet. This ratio has changed over the years and some scientists point to a subsequent rise in heart disease with this change. Others note the benefits of omega-6 fats and caution against cutting them out of the diet. A prudent approach is to increase your intake of omega-3 while reducing, but not eliminating, omega-6.

Trans fat: Occurs naturally in beef and dairy products, and is also created chemically by adding hydrogen to polyunsaturated oils. The oil is transformed into a more stable liquid (partially hydrogenated) or solid (fully hydrogenated), with chemical properties entirely different from the original oil. Partially hydrogenated oils are abundant in processed foods, and account for most of the trans fat in our diets. *Trans fat poses a higher risk of heart disease than saturated fat since it raises bad* LDL *cholesterol and lowers good* HDL *cholesterol.*

HOW TO AVOID UNHEALTHY FATS IN YOUR DIET

Saturated fat: Associated with an increased risk for heart disease. It is neither possible nor desirable to eliminate all such fat, since many foods containing good fats (mono- and polyunsaturated) contain some level of saturated fat as well. But there is a great deal that we can do to decrease our total consumption of unhealthy saturated fats.

Reducing dietary saturated fat is an important step towards heart health.

Table 2: To Trim or Not to Trim?

	Calories	Fat	Saturated Fat
Chicken breast, 3 ounces			
With skin	170	7	2
Without skin	120	1.5	0.5
Beef pot roast, 3 ounces			
With fat	260	18	7
Visible fat trimmed	180	7	3

Adapted from USDA Handbook 8-5 and research conducted
by Safeway in cooperation with the USDA

Start by reducing your intake of red meat, perhaps at first to once a week. When you do eat meat, choose lean cuts, and remove any visible fat. Choose fish and poultry more often than red meat, and remove the skin from chicken. During the week, use meat as you would use a condiment – in small portions, together with larger portions of vegetables and grains. Explore tofu, wheat protein (seitan or gluten) and the many *kosher* vegetarian-meat products. There are many nonfat and low-fat dairy products to choose from, including milk, yogurt, cheese and frozen desserts.

For more creative meal planning ideas and suggestions on how to limit the amount of high-fat meat in your diet, see chapter 7.

Hydrogenated fat: I rarely suggest that a healthy person entirely avoid any particular food or ingredient. My preference is to encourage healthy choices, such as vegetables, fruits, whole grains and legumes. However, one ingredient prevalent in many kosher products demands our urgent attention.

Partially hydrogenated vegetable oil is used extensively in commercial baked goods, prepared foods and restaurant cooking. *Parve* "ice cream," nondairy creamer, solid (stick) margarine and solid baking fat (such as Crisco) are often mainstays in *kosher* kitchens. These products contain a large amount of trans fat, which we now know is highly detrimental to heart health.

In addition to providing a *parve* alternative to butter, these fats impart crispness to baked goods and creaminess to frostings, fillings and spreads. To the delight of bakers and food processors, they also extend the shelf life of baked goods. Since many of these fats do not contain dairy products, they are used extensively to create kosher, *parve* products.

When hydrogenation was developed, we did not know how trans fat affected blood lipid levels. In fact, it was believed that margarine was a healthier alternative to butter. But we now know that hydrogenated and partially hydrogenated fat are damaging our health as well. Research has confirmed that trans fat clogs our arteries, and clogged arteries increase our chance of having a heart attack, a stroke or both. In addition, trans fat from hydrogenated oils appears to make blood platelets stickier, increasing the risk of clot formation inside the blood vessels.

Diets high in trans fat contribute to clogged arteries and heart disease.

The Nurses' Health Study* found that women who ate the most trans fat were twice as likely to develop heart disease as women who ate the least amount of trans fat. In addition, a significant increase in risk for diabetes was shown in women whose trans fat intake was higher. A study of men in Holland showed a higher incidence of heart disease among those who had eaten more trans fat than their counterparts.[15]

---

* The Nurses' Health Study and the Nurses' Health Study II are among the largest long-term studies investigating the risk factors for major chronic diseases in women.

Metabolic studies as well as population studies point to the adverse effects of trans fat on blood lipids. Scientists estimate that approximately 30,000, and up to 100,000, premature coronary deaths per year could be prevented if partially hydrogenated fat were replaced with natural vegetable oils in the United States.[16]

Fortunately, the FDA now requires that trans fats be listed on nutrition labels. Unfortunately, the regulations stipulate that foods containing less than 0.5 grams of trans fat per serving can claim that they contain zero grams of trans fat. Theoretically, these "zeros" could add up to an intake of several grams of trans fat a day, especially if your idea of a serving is more than that of the manufacturer.

Many large companies have reformulated their products, reducing or eliminating trans fat. This is a good start that should be encouraged, but as always, it is important to read the fine print. In some cases, for instance, newly formulated trans fat-free foods actually contain more total fat than their original version!

Read product labels carefully and avoid foods containing trans fat.

At home, we should stop using *parve* products such as stick margarine, shortening and nondairy creamers, which contain trans fat. Olive or canola oil can often be substituted for stick margarine or shortening in baking. Choose soft tub margarine instead of stick margarine for spreading on bread, or better yet, dip your bread into extra-virgin olive oil or *techinah*.

Table 3: Substitutes for *Parve* Products that are High in Trans Fat

Parve products that are high in trans fat	Substitutes
Nondairy creamer	Soy creamer, soy, rice and almond beverages
Nondairy sour cream	Soy-based products
Parve cream cheese	Avocado or soft tub margarine
Parve frozen desserts	Fruit sorbet, ices, frozen soy and rice desserts
Stick margarine	Olive or canola oil, soft tub margarine, low-trans fat margarine or nut spreads

Kosher bakeries present a challenge as well. Many of them rely on prepackaged mixes that contain partially hydrogenated fat. We need to bring this matter to bakeries' attention, and encourage them to seek healthier alternatives. At the same time, we should be thinking of the larger health picture, and request that our bakeries provide whole-grain breads, high-fiber muffins, and fewer high-fat, high-sugar choices. We must reassess our reliance on commercially-prepared baked goods and snacks, and seek healthier alternatives for ourselves and our families.

In many areas health departments have urged (or, in the case of New York City, even mandated) restaurants to stop using trans fat. Kosher consumers need to address the use of trans fat in kosher restaurants, schools and catering companies. It may not be easy to change tried-and-tested recipes that have been popular for decades. New versions may not have the same taste and texture as those we have come to enjoy. But, with new product development, innovative recipes, awareness and education, we can eliminate trans fat, improve our health and still enjoy the foods we love.

Encourage kosher bakeries, restaurants and caterers to replace trans fat with healthier alternatives.

Use the list below as your guide. When hydrogenated fat cannot be avoided, choose products that list these ingredients at the end of the ingredient list. (Remember, manufacturers are required to list ingredients in order of their predominance.)

KOSHER FOODS THAT MAY CONTAIN TRANS FAT

In the grocery section: Packaged cookies, cake, crackers, candy, snack food, potato chips, solid fats such as Crisco, cake, cookie, muffin and quick-bread mixes, biscuit and pancake mixes, ready-made pie crust, canned frosting, microwave popcorn, powdered nondairy creamer, flavored coffee, instant cocoa mix, salad dressing, ramen noodles, soup cups, breakfast/granola bars, breakfast cereal, peanut butter, chocolate and nut spreads.*

Refrigerated: Stick margarine, some tub margarines, nondairy creamer.

Frozen: Frozen pastry dough, pastries, pie crust and pies, cake, precooked potato products, *parve* "ice cream," whipped dessert toppings, waffles, fish sticks, pizza.

Bakery: Cookies, cakes, pies, pastries, doughnuts.

Restaurants: Fried foods, *parve* desserts.

THE GOOD FATS: MONOUNSATURATED AND POLYUNSATURATED

Monounsaturated fats provide the double benefit of lowering "bad" (LDL) and elevating "good" (HDL) cholesterol. The best dietary sources are olive oil, canola oil, peanuts, natural peanut butter and peanut oil, avocados and most nuts. If you refrigerate a bottle of

---

* This is by no means a complete listing. Since some companies are reformulating their products with less or no trans fats, read product labels carefully.

olive oil you will notice that, like most monounsaturated oils, it is liquid at room temperature and begins to solidify when chilled.

Extra-virgin olive oil is an especially good source of mono-unsaturated fat. It is also high in antioxidants and vitamin E, and is extremely versatile in the kosher kitchen. Choose from a wide variety of flavorful extra-virgin olive oils to use as a dip for bread, in place of margarine. Use olive oil to sauté chicken, beef, fish and vegetables. Onions for soup or stews can be browned in olive oil as well. Use it to make an omelet or scrambled eggs. Olive oil makes wonderful salad dressing and can even be used in baking.

Canola oil, derived from the rapeseed plant, is also high in monounsaturated fat. It is generally less expensive than olive oil, and is tasteless; use it for baking when olive oil might not be appropriate because of its stronger taste.

Improve your family's health by substituting olive and canola oil for margarine.

Foods containing omega-3 fatty acids are especially important for good health. The best sources for these are oily, cold-water fish such as sardines, herring and salmon. Other sources are ground flax seeds, walnuts, canola oil and nonhydrogenated soybean oil. Several studies have shown that the omega-3 fats in fish oil protect both men and women from sudden cardiac death.[17] In general, fattier fish have the highest content of omega-3 fats. Salmon rates high, followed by mackerel, tuna, trout, sardines and herring.

Salmon makes a lovely *Shabbat* and holiday entrée. There are many other kosher fish now available, so be creative and try something new occasionally. If you make your own gefilte fish, consider a variation popular in the Pacific Northwest Jewish community: add ground salmon to the mixture for a delightful taste.

Fish should be included twice a week in your diet. If you find it difficult to include fish in your diet, consider fish-oil capsules as an alternative. Or eat walnuts and ground flax seed regularly. Purchase whole flax seeds and grind a small amount of them at one time. An electric coffee grinder works well for this. Since flax seeds are high in fat, keep them refrigerated to avoid rancidity. A tablespoon or two added to hot or cold cereal or yogurt every day should give you a fair amount of omega-3 with a bonus of good quality fiber as well.

Since omega-3 fatty acid supplements may increase the blood-thinning effects of medications such as warfarin (Coumadin) and aspirin, consult your physician before taking them.

> **Read the label: Product labels can be deceptive. "Cholesterol free" does not mean "fat free." Vegetable oil or salad dressing labeled "cholesterol free" is virtually meaningless as vegetable products do not contain cholesterol.**

Is Butter Better?

Without a doubt, butter tastes better than margarine. While butter does not contain the trans fat present in stick margarine, it is high in saturated fat and high in cholesterol, and thus its use should be limited. For those who insist on the taste of butter in dairy recipes, use it sparingly: combine it with canola oil in baking, and add just a teaspoon to flavor sauces or soups. Whenever possible, use olive and canola oils; think of butter as a flavoring, to be used like spices or herbs.

Substituting oil for butter:
Oil = 100% fat   Butter = 80% fat
1 cup butter or margarine (2 sticks) = ¾ cup oil

Cooking tip: To intensify the taste of butter, heat it in a small saucepan over low heat. Cook, swirling the pan occasionally, until it becomes a nutty brown color, about one minute. Pour the butter into a small bowl to cool. This browning technique allows you to significantly reduce the amount of butter in a recipe while still providing the rich buttery taste.

NATURAL FAT SUBSTITUTES

Most of us are familiar with reduced-fat versions of common foods: kosher fat-free and low-fat dairy products, baked goods and salad dressings have been available for quite some time. It is even possible to find a number of reduced-fat hard cheeses.

I often recommend "natural" fat substitutes such as apple sauce, prune or date puree, and mashed bananas as a substitute for part of the fat in homemade baked goods. Grated carrots, zucchini and beets work in some recipes as well. These add moisture and flavor (as well as fiber, vitamins and minerals) that fat would otherwise contribute to cakes and cookies. Since fruit substitutes are fairly sweet, the amount of sugar in the recipe can often be reduced.

COMMERCIAL FAT SUBSTITUTES

In an attempt to eliminate fat altogether from certain foods, manufacturers have developed a number of fat substitutes. These commercial products, used in various baked goods, snacks and prepared foods, are meant to mimic the taste and texture of fat without the calories. They are made from pectin, gums and grains as well as chemically modified carbohydrate, protein and fat particles.

It is important to realize that fat-reduced foods are not necessarily lower in calories than their full-fat counterparts. The prospective danger is that we think we're eating fewer calories, so we compensate by eating more. Although fat substitutes may offer more fat-reduced food choices, they do not seem to be particularly effective on their own as a strategy for weight loss. Smaller portion sizes and physical activity are more likely to impact weight than fat-modified foods.[18]

STORE-BOUGHT, LOW-FAT BAKED GOODS: DON'T BE FOOLED!

We used to think that fat in particular was to blame for our expanding waistlines and increase in heart disease. The theory was that if we reduced the amount of total fat in our diets we would lose weight and reduce our risk of heart disease. Bakeries responded with low-fat and fat-free products, and consumers gobbled them up. In fact, we gobbled up so many of them that within a few years our waistlines got even thicker!

Most people assume that if a food is low in fat, it is also low in calories. We may not realize that when fat is taken out of a product, sugar is often added to improve the taste. The resulting product may be low fat, but it is not necessarily low calorie. In addition, sugar produces a quick rise in blood sugar which causes us to feel hungry again soon after eating, so we are likely to eat more.

Read the Label

Taking time to read and understand package labels is essential. When you compare products, check the serving size, as well as total calories, fat and carbohydrates. Here are some examples of how serving size makes all the difference in popular brands of regular and "light" or fat-free versions of cookies and cake.

Reduced-fat cakes, cookies and pastries often have the same or even more *total* calories and carbohydrates than their full-fat versions.

Regular version cookie, serving size: 1.2 ounces		
Calories: 160	Fat: 7 grams	Carbohydrates: 24 grams
"Light" version cookie, serving size: 0.8 ounces		
Calories: 100	Fat: 2 grams	Carbohydrates: 20 grams
Notice that the serving size for the "light" version is 0.8 ounces – almost half an ounce less than that of the regular cookie. When you compare an equal serving size, the "light" version has almost as many calories and fat, and more carbohydrates than the regular cookie, as shown here:		
"Light" version cookie, serving size: 1.2 ounces		
Calories: 148	Fat: 5 grams	Carbohydrates: 30 grams

USDA National Nutrient Database for Standard
Reference, Release 17 (2004)

Regular version butter pound cake, serving size: 2 ounces		
Calories: 210	Fat: 9 grams	Carbohydrates: 30 grams
Fat-free version butter pound cake, serving size: 1.5 ounces		
Calories: 130	Fat: 0 grams	Carbohydrates: 30 grams
Here again, the serving size for the fat-free cake is half an ounce less than the full-fat version. When an equal serving size is analyzed, we see that the calorie difference is minimal and the fat-free version contains more carbohydrates than the regular cake.		
Fat-free version butter pound cake, serving size: 2 ounces		
Calories: 173	Fat: 0 grams	Carbohydrates: 40 grams

George Weston Bakeries, Consumer Services
Department, August 15, 2005

There are many alternatives to commercially prepared, reduced-fat baked goods. Choose fresh fruit, nuts, popcorn and pretzels for snacks. Consider serving baked goods only on *Shabbat* and holidays. With little effort, you can bake your own healthier desserts that your family is sure to enjoy. A number of recipes are included in this book.

But Does Fat Really Matter?

The following headline in the *New York Times* caught many of us by surprise: "Low-Fat Diet Does Not Cut Health Risks, Study Finds."[19] The article describes several large, well-designed studies published in the prestigious *Journal of the American Medical Association*, which question the efficacy of a low-fat diet in reducing the risk of breast and colon cancer, heart attack and stroke. Researchers from the Women's Health Initiative studied nearly 49,000 post-menopausal women. They found similar rates of breast and colon cancer, as well as heart disease in women who followed a low-fat diet as compared with those who didn't. An impressive study, with surprising results! It almost sounds like an invitation to eat a few doughnuts or indulge in an ice cream sundae.

But many health professionals took a closer look and asked additional questions:

- What is the effect of specific kinds of fat on health? This study looked at overall fat intake, without differentiating between "good" and "bad" fats.
- Participants in the study consumed a diet containing 29% of calories from fat. Was this consumption low enough (as some experts believe it wasn't) to significantly reduce health risks?
- Was this a matter of "too little, too late"? The average age of the study participants was 64 years. Would the results have been different if a low-fat diet was started at an earlier age?
- Were the women followed long enough? Very minor health benefits were seen among women eating the low-fat diet for

eight years. Could more significant results be achieved over a longer period of time?

- The study participants were healthy postmenopausal women. Would a low-fat diet be beneficial for younger women or women who already have heart disease or cancer? What about men?
- How do exercise and weight loss affect health? Could the benefits of a low-fat diet be canceled by being overweight and sedentary? The study did not take these factors into account.

Reading the headlines, one may be tempted to believe that dietary fat really does not matter. Although this study should be taken seriously, it is critical to look beyond the bold print and ask questions that may not be apparent at first sight.

The Bottom Line

Choose extra-virgin olive oil, canola and nut oils.

Eat fish, especially fatty fish, twice a week.

Reduce your intake of high-fat meat and dairy products.

Avoid foods containing hydrogenated oils.

High, Low, Simple, Complex: Making Sense of Carbohydrates

Bagels, rice, popcorn, apples, noodles, potatoes, milk, candy, lentils and doughnuts – a diverse and abundant group of foods with one thing in common: they all contain carbohydrates. They provide us with most of our calories, help regulate blood sugar, and can be a good source of vitamins, minerals and fiber. Like fats, though, not all carbohydrates are created equal. Some carbohydrates are highly desirable for maintaining ideal weight and good health, while others may increase our risk of obesity and disease.

A LITTLE CHEMISTRY

Sugar, starch and fiber are the main types of carbohydrates. Chemically they are formed by chains of various sugar molecules arranged in different lengths and shapes. Sugars are formed from fairly short, simple chains, while starches and fibers are made from longer, more complex-shaped chains. These structural differences prompted the terms "simple" and "complex" to categorize carbohydrates. Simple carbohydrates are sugars and complex carbohydrates are mainly starches and fiber.

GLYCEMIC INDEX AND GLYCEMIC LOAD

Carbohydrates are somewhat more complicated than this, however. Two newer concepts attempt to define or classify carbohydrates based on how quickly they raise blood glucose levels. The *glycemic index* measures how fast and how far blood glucose rises after we eat foods containing carbohydrate. Foods that are more viscous and absorbed more slowly after ingestion cause a slower rise in blood glucose levels and have a low glycemic index. Starchy foods that are digested more rapidly, causing blood glucose to rise quicker, have a high glycemic index.

Glucose is given the arbitrary figure of 100. Foods with a ranking higher than 60 are considered high glycemic index foods. A ranking between 45 and 60 is considered moderate and less than 45 is low. These ratings are based on a 50-gram portion of carbohydrate, which is not always a realistic amount of food. For instance, raw carrots have a relatively high glycemic index, but a low percentage of carbohydrate. You would have to eat about a pound and a half of them to get 50 grams of carbohydrate. Glycemic index is also affected by the mix of foods that you eat at one time – the protein, fat and carbohydrate in your meal all work together to impact blood glucose levels.

Table 4: Estimates of Glycemic Index and Glycemic Load in Various Foods

Food	Amount	Glycemic Index	Glycemic Load
Baked Potato	1 small	90	20
White bread	1 slice	70	10
Carrot	½ cup cooked	70	4
Apple	1 medium	40	6
Spaghetti	½ cup cooked	40	6
Lentils	½ cup cooked	30	4
Peanuts	1 ounce	14	1

Glycemic load assesses the impact of specific amounts of dietary carbohydrate on blood sugar, giving us a more realistic measure that takes into account the actual amount of food being eaten. A high glycemic load is considered to be 20 or higher, a medium glycemic load is between 11 and 19, and a low glycemic load is 10 or less.

WHAT HAPPENS WHEN YOU EAT A BAGEL?

For a better understanding of these concepts, let's take a look at how the body metabolizes carbohydrates in food.

When you eat a bagel, or another food containing carbohydrates, your body metabolizes the sugar and starch in the food, reducing them to simple sugar molecules. The sugar molecules are converted into glucose, which is used as fuel for our cells. The exception is the carbohydrate in fiber, which cannot be broken down into sugar molecules and passes through the body largely undigested.

As glucose enters our bloodstream, cells in the pancreas secrete insulin, a hormone that allows cells to absorb it. As glucose is absorbed into the cells, the level in the bloodstream returns to normal, and insulin production decreases. In other words, insulin acts as a signal to the cells to accept incoming glucose while regulating the level of glucose in the bloodstream.

WHAT CAN GO WRONG: INSULIN RESISTANCE

In recent years, we've seen an alarming phenomenon – an enormous number of people whose system for metabolizing carbohydrates has gone awry. Their cells do not react properly to the incoming signal to accept glucose – they resist the "nudge" from insulin to "open up" and take in the glucose. The resulting "insulin resistance" causes a high level of glucose to remain in the blood. In response, the pancreas works overtime to pump out more insulin in an effort to get glucose into the cells. With time, the overworked pancreas gets worn out and slows or even stops its production of insulin. This condition can lead to obesity, high cholesterol levels and Type 2 (non-insulin-dependent or adult-onset) diabetes, whose prevalence has reached epidemic proportions in recent years. Especially disturbing is the significant increase in the number of children and teenagers now being diagnosed with insulin resistance and diabetes.

Insulin resistance and Type 2 diabetes have reached epidemic proportions.

Insulin resistance is influenced by weight, activity level, diet and genetics. The heavier you are, the harder it is for your body to properly metabolize glucose. Since exercise increases the amount of muscle in the body, and muscle handles glucose and insulin much more efficiently than fat, increasing physical activity leads to better glucose metabolism as well. Consuming a large quantity of high glycemic index foods can stress the blood sugar-insulin regulating system and increase the risk of insulin resistance. We know that some people are more sensitive than others and that genetics play a role in this reaction.

WHAT CAN YOU DO?

The Diabetes Prevention Program was the first clinical trial to show that diet, exercise and losing a modest amount of weight can actually prevent or delay the onset of diabetes in people at risk. More than 3,000 people took part in the trial. All of them had high blood glucose levels and were overweight, and most of them had a family history of Type 2 diabetes. Participants were assigned to one of three groups: (a) a lifestyle modification program (a healthy diet designed for moderate weight loss and 30 minutes of exercise five days a week); (b) treatment with the medication Metformin (used to lower blood sugar); and (c) treatment with a placebo. After nearly three years of follow-up, the results were exciting: When compared with the people receiving a placebo, the lifestyle modification group showed a 58% reduced risk of getting diabetes, while those taking medication reduced their risk by just 31%.

> **The message is clear: Although you cannot change your genes, you can reduce your risk of developing insulin resistance and diabetes with easy-to-do, inexpensive lifestyle changes.**

Carbohydrates have an important place in a healthy diet. The trick is to differentiate between carbohydrates that are good for you and those that are not.

SUGAR – LIMIT YOUR INTAKE

Various estimates suggest that Americans eat an average of 20 teaspoons of *added* sugar a day. That works out to about 10% of our total daily caloric intake. And that does not include sugar occurring naturally in foods such as fresh fruit and juices. Given our love of sweet snacks, juice drinks, soda and desserts, this is not very surprising.

Table 5: Sources of Additional Sugar

Major Sources of Added Sugar	(Percentage of Total Sugar Consumed)
Sweetened soft drinks	33%
Sugar and candy	16%
Cake, cookies, pies, pastries	13%
Fruit drinks	10%

Guthrie and Morton 2000

Like other carbohydrates, sugar is converted into glucose and used by our bodies as fuel, which is not bad in itself. It has become problematic, however, because we consume too much of it. And too much sugar, along with too much fat, has led to our overweight and obesity crisis.

Besides making us fat and increasing triglyceride levels, sugar fills us up with "empty" calories, leaving little room for more nutrient-dense, healthier foods. This is especially true for children. It is easy to understand why a child would not be hungry if he or she has eaten a candy bar or drunk a can of soda before dinner. In fact, data shows that people who ate the most added sugar had the highest overall caloric intake with the lowest intake of vitamins, minerals and essential nutrients.[20] Excess sugar can contribute to dental caries, and if we are genetically prone, can also lead to insulin resistance, which is often a precursor of Type 2 diabetes.

For optimum health and weight control, limit your intake of sugar.

IT'S STILL SUGAR

Sugar comes in many forms. Granulated white and brown sugar is frequently used in home cooking, while dextrose, fructose and corn syrup are more often used in processed foods.

High fructose corn sugar is an inexpensive sweetener created by treating corn syrup with an enzyme that converts some of its dextrose to fructose. It is used in soft drinks as well as many other processed foods and beverages. It is estimated that approximately one-third of our added sugar intake comes from soft drinks sweetened with high-fructose corn sugar.[21] Like all sweeteners, it has no nutritional value other than to provide calories.

Types of Sugar Found In Various Food Products
On product labels, the amount of sugar is listed under carbohydrates. In addition, all of the following are sugars in one form or another. Look for them in the list of ingredients: brown sugar, cane sugar, corn sweetener, corn syrup, dextrose, fruit juice concentrate, fructose, glucose, high-fructose corn syrup, honey, invert sugar,

lactose, maltose, malt syrup, molasses, raw sugar, sucrose, sugar and maple syrup.

But Is It Natural?

The simple answer is that sugar is sugar is sugar. Brown sugar is white sugar mixed with molasses, a liquid sweetener derived from sugarcane juices. Maple sugar is derived from maple trees and rice syrup is processed from rice. Numerous other "natural" sweeteners can be found in health food stores.

Honey contains antioxidants, but only in small quantities – enjoy it in moderation as a sweetener, but do not count on it as a significant source of nutrients. Be sure to avoid feeding honey to infants under the age of one year, as it contains bacterial spores that can produce botulism poisoning. Unlike in older children and adults, the digestive system of infants has not yet developed beneficial bacteria that can prevent botulism poisoning.

Sugar Substitutes

With so many people trying to cut calories and reduce their carbohydrate intake, it is no wonder that manufacturers have come up with a variety of sugar substitutes. Here is a brief overview of some of them:

Sugar alcohols: These include sorbitol, xylitol, mannitol and hydrogenated starch hydrolysates. They do not raise blood sugar levels as rapidly as sugar, although some of them, due to their bulk, may provide nearly as many calories as sugar. They may cause diarrhea, gas and bloating, but are generally considered safe.

Sucralose: Known commercially as Splenda, it is 600 times sweeter than sugar. Although it is produced by combining sugar with chlorine, it no longer resembles sugar after its chemical alteration. It is heat stable and does not have an aftertaste, making it a popular sugar substitute in the food industry. Sucralose is relatively new on the market and we do not have data on its long-term use, but presently it is considered safe.

Aspartame: Includes Sweet 'N Low blue packet, Equal, NutraSweet and others. This is a synthetic combination of amino acids. Because it is intensely sweet, it can be used in very small quantities to sweeten foods. People with phenylketonuria, a rare metabolic disorder, should avoid aspartame. Some people claim that aspartame causes headaches. Increased cancer risk has not been proven. It is probably safe in moderation.

Acesulfame K: Sold as Sunette and Sweet One, this is a synthetic chemical that is not metabolized by our bodies. The FDA considers it safe, though many believe that it deserves further, more intensive testing.

Stevia: An herbal sugar substitute sold in health food stores as a dietary supplement. Although it has been used for years in Japan and South America with no apparent side effects, it has not been tested or approved by the FDA.

Saccharin and *Cyclamate:* Includes Sweet 'N Low, Sugar Twin and others. These are two synthetic sweeteners. Some studies suggested evidence of cancer risk in heavy users, but the FDA has concluded that it is safe.

Neotame: A newer sweetener that is a synthetic combination of amino acids. Because it is far sweeter than other products, it is more cost-effective and is expected to be widely used in food products. Animal and human studies have not raised safety concerns, although there are no long-term studies of its use.

Tagatose: Includes Naturlose and Gaio tagatose. This is another new product similar in structure to fructose. Although it is chemically derived from lactose or whey (milk derivatives), it has been certified kosher *parve*. Since most of it passes through the body unabsorbed, large intakes may cause gas, bloating and nausea. Otherwise, it appears to be safe.

It would be wise to consider how the various sugar substitutes might interact with each other to affect our health as they become more commonplace in prepared food. An occasional spoonful of aspartame in your coffee might be harmless, but combined with sucralose in cereal, acesulfame in yogurt and sorbitol in chewing gum, there could be health implications that we are currently unaware of. Hopefully, researchers will address this issue in the near future.

In evaluating sugar and sugar substitutes, keep in mind that sugar itself is a completely safe product. It only becomes problematic when we eat too much of it. We have no evidence that sugar substitutes curb cravings for sugar, help us eat fewer calories or assist in weight loss. On the contrary, many of us figure that if we use sugar substitutes we can eat an extra cookie or two! I recommend avoiding artificial sweeteners and using sugar in limited quantities.

Limit your intake of sugar and sugar substitutes and get the bulk of your carbohydrate calories from fruits, vegetables and whole grains.

Save cookies, candy and cake for *Shabbat*, holidays and special occasions. Reserve soft drinks for a special treat, perhaps once a week for *Shabbat* dinner or lunch. During the week, serve fruit for dessert and popcorn, pretzels or nuts for snacks. Try not to purchase ready-made baked goods, since once they are in the house it is hard to resist temptation. If you enjoy baking, look for recipes with a healthier profile: fruit compotes and crisps, pudding made with skim or low-fat milk and cookies containing whole grains, nuts and dried fruit. In many recipes, you can reduce the amount of sugar and fat and substitute whole-grain flour for all-purpose flour and still enjoy tasty results. Suggestions for adapting your own favorite recipes are found throughout this book.

THE STAFF OF LIFE: WHOLE GRAINS

"Now you, take for yourself wheat, barley, beans, millet, and spelt: put them into one vessel and prepare them as food for yourself." (*Yehezkel* 4:9)

A grain of wheat or barley picked directly from the field is a nutritional powerhouse. As an intact or whole grain consisting of bran, germ and endosperm, it contains high-quality protein, fat, carbohydrate, vitamins, minerals, antioxidants and fiber.

When wheat is processed and refined, the outer bran and germ are removed, shedding many of its valuable nutrients and fiber. The same is true for other grains, including rice, oats, barley and corn. In some cases, the grain is "enriched" after processing by adding B vitamins and iron. Although this enrichment is helpful, it does not restore the fiber and other nutrients lost in the refinement process.

Most of the nutrients and fiber in grains are in their outer bran and germ.

A major difference between whole and refined grains is in how they are metabolized. Refined products are digested and converted to glucose quickly, causing blood sugar to rise and then drop again fairly rapidly. In contrast, since fiber slows the absorption of carbohydrates, whole grains take longer to digest and break down. The result is a slower, more regulated rise in blood sugar. Practically, we feel fuller and the return of hunger is delayed.

Whole Grains and Health

Large studies have shown that diets rich in whole grains can protect against diabetes and heart disease.[22] They may also play a role in protecting against certain types of cancer. Constipation, a major gastrointestinal complaint, is often relieved by eating a diet high in fiber from whole grains. And even more good news – an increased intake of whole grains may help to reduce long-term weight gain.[23]

We do not completely understand how whole grains work to produce these health benefits, though we suspect that there may be additional nutrient components in the intact grain that have yet to be discovered. We do know that whole grains give us a feeling of fullness, so we tend to eat fewer calories. Additionally, whole grains seem to work best as a complete unit: the bran, germ and endosperm do not produce the same nutritional benefits when separated from each other.

Aim for at least three servings of whole grains every day.

Fiber Facts

Fiber is the indigestible portion of carbohydrates. It was once referred to as "roughage." Since it passes through the body without providing nutrients, its value was thought to pertain only to digestive health. We now know that fiber has additional health benefits as well.

There are two main types of fiber, each with its particular benefits. *Soluble fiber*, which partially dissolves in water, becomes sticky when ingested and binds excess cholesterol in the intestine. *Insoluble fiber* does not break down in water. As it moves slowly through the digestive system, it helps regulate blood glucose levels by delaying the absorption of sugars and fats. Insoluble fiber acts like a sponge by soaking up water and expanding as it moves through the digestive system. This action can help reduce the risk of developing intestinal disorders such as constipation, diverticulitis and hemorrhoids.

Types of fiber:

Soluble Fiber	Insoluble Fiber
Oats	Whole grains
Legumes	Seeds
Nuts and Seeds	Carrots
Apples	Tomatoes
Strawberries	Zucchini

In large studies of men and women, a high fiber intake (particularly fiber found in whole grains) was linked to a significantly lowered risk of coronary heart disease.[24] As discussed earlier, Type 2 diabetes risk is increased with the consumption of high glycemic index foods such as white bread, refined cereal and potatoes, which cause blood sugar levels to rise quickly. Fiber also plays a role, with a high fiber intake protecting against the development of Type 2 diabetes.[25]

Weight can be influenced by fiber intake as well. Individuals consuming a high-fiber, low-glycemic index diet showed less weight gain and greater weight loss in a number of studies.[26]

Diverticulitis is a common inflammatory disease of the colon affecting the middle-aged and elderly. Dietary fiber, especially the insoluble fiber found in whole grains, has been found to reduce the risk of developing this serious condition.[27] One of the most common gastrointestinal complaints, especially among the elderly, is constipation, which can often be relieved with an increased intake of fiber. If you are not used to eating much fiber, increase your intake gradually rather than all at once. Since water absorbs fiber, be sure to drink more water as you increase your fiber intake.

Eating plenty of fiber can decrease your risk for developing coronary heart disease, Type 2 diabetes, diverticulitis and constipation.

Current recommendations call for adults to consume between 25 and 30 grams of dietary fiber each day. However, most Americans average less than half of that amount. Increasing your intake of whole grains, legumes, nuts, vegetables and fruits is the best way to increase the fiber in your diet.

Table 6: Good Sources of Fiber

Food, standard serving size	Dietary fiber, grams
100% Bran cereal, ready-to-eat, ½ cup	9
Lentils, cooked, ½ cup	8
Chickpeas, cooked, ½ cup	6
Rye crackers, 2	5
Bulgur wheat, ½ cup cooked	4
Sweet potato, cooked, 1 medium	4
Spinach, cooked, ½ cup	4
Prunes, stewed, ½ cup	4
Pear, raw, 1 small	4
Figs, dried, ¼ cup	4
Whole-wheat spaghetti, ½ cup cooked	3
Almonds, 1 ounce	3

USDA National Nutrient Database for Standard Reference, Release 17 (2004)

Real Whole-Grain Ingredients

By carefully reading package labels, you can learn to distinguish between products containing whole and refined grains. True whole-grain products list the main ingredient as whole wheat, whole rye, whole oats, brown rice or another whole grain. Ingredients are listed on the package label by their prevalence. When whole grains are listed first or second on the label, chances are that they are present in a significant amount. Be aware that when wheat flour is listed as an ingredient, it may mean whole or refined flour, so look carefully for the word "whole" wheat. The phrases "stone-ground," "multi-grain," "100% wheat," and "contains bran" may not necessarily mean that the product is whole grain.

Checking the fiber content on the package label is another way of knowing whether you are getting a whole-grain product. It should be listed by weight (grams of fiber) and percentage (Percent Daily Value). Some products now include a whole-grain health claim approved by the FDA: "Diets rich in whole-grain foods and other plant foods and low in total fat and cholesterol may help reduce the risk of heart disease and certain cancers." These foods are required to contain 51% or more whole grains by weight and be low in fat.

Choosing Healthy Breakfast Cereals

It's not hard to confuse the grocery store cereal aisle with the candy aisle. Once you bypass the sugar-coated concoctions (mainly on the middle and lower shelves, at the eye level of the youngsters they are meant to appeal to), check the package label for the following:

Less than 12 grams of sugar.

200 calories or less per serving.

The first ingredient should be a whole grain.

5 grams or more of fiber per serving.

Read the Label

Do not assume that dark-colored bread is whole grain. Many loaves contain caramel color or molasses to give the appearance of being whole wheat or rye. Ask to see the ingredient label if the bread you buy is not prepackaged.

If tasty whole-grain bread is not available in your community, consider purchasing a bread machine and making your own. These machines are now relatively inexpensive, and will pay for themselves in a short time. There are many delicious whole-grain bread recipes available, and the technique is fairly simple: put the ingredients into the bread pan and let the machine do the work! Even whole-wheat challah is easy to make. I like to prepare challah dough in the bread machine on Thursday, give it a slow second rise overnight in the refrigerator, and shape and bake it on Friday. There is nothing nicer than the aroma of fresh-baked challah to welcome *Shabbat*.

Enjoy the Variety
Many whole-grain products can be found in the supermarket. Brown rice, oats, bulgur and cracked wheat, barley, kasha, popcorn and whole-grain cereals are commonplace. Even whole-grain pastas and crackers can be found in most major grocery stores. For more variety, consider shopping at a health food or specialty store, where many of the products have kosher certification.

Store whole grains in airtight containers in a cool dry place. Since they contain a small amount of fat, they can go rancid more quickly than refined grains. In warm climates, extend their storage time by keeping them in the refrigerator or freezer.

> **A variety of whole grains to try: barley, brown rice, bulgur wheat, cracked wheat, wheat berries, triticale, rye, kamut, kasha (buckwheat groats), oats, millet, quinoa, teff, corn, spelt and amaranth.**

Cooking with Whole Grains
The usual method of preparation is to rinse the grain in a strainer, add it to boiling water and simmer until most of the liquid is

absorbed. The ratio of grain to liquid varies, but is usually one part grain to two or three parts liquid. Cooking times vary as well, and other cooking techniques can be used.

Whole grains often take longer to cook than refined grains. For instance, white rice may cook in 15 to 20 minutes, while brown rice can take 30 to 45 minutes. When time is a critical factor, you can soak grains for several hours to reduce the cooking time.

Whole grains are very versatile. Cook more than what you need, and enjoy the leftovers throughout the week. Leftover brown rice can be stir-fried with vegetables for a quick meal. Add grains to soups, stews and casseroles. Tasty patties and vegetable or meat loaves can benefit from the addition of whole grains. Even salads can be made from grains – try *tabouli* made with bulgur, barley or wheat berries and salads based on brown rice with added vegetables, fruits and nuts.

Try to include one whole-grain food with every meal.

It Doesn't Have to Weigh a Ton: Baking with Whole-Wheat Flour

Try substituting whole-wheat pastry flour for half or all of the flour in your cookie recipes. This works especially well with chocolate chip, oatmeal, spice and peanut butter cookies, where the difference in taste may not be noticeable. Muffin recipes also take well to the addition or substitution of whole grains, as do yeast and quick breads, pancakes and waffles. A few tablespoons of gluten flour (available in health and natural food stores) added to whole-wheat yeast dough will produce a lighter loaf of bread.

Table 7: White and Whole-Wheat Flour – Here's the Difference

	Whole-Wheat Flour, 100 grams	White Flour, 100 grams
Dietary Fiber	12 grams	3 grams
Calcium	34 milligrams	15 milligrams
Magnesium	38 milligrams	22 milligrams
Potassium	405 milligrams	107 milligrams

Agricultural Research Service Nutrient Database
for Standard Reference, Release 17

It's Easy to Incorporate Whole Grains:

Breakfast
Oatmeal, shredded wheat, bran flakes or other whole-grain cereal
Whole-grain muffin
Pancakes or waffles made with whole-grain flour
Whole-grain toast with fruit spread or nut butter

Lunch
Tuna sandwich made with whole-grain bread
Spaghetti sauce with whole-grain pasta
Corn or whole-wheat tortilla with beans, vegetables and low-fat cheese
Mushroom barley soup

Dinner
Brown rice or bulgur wheat
Kasha or barley
Fresh or frozen corn or polenta
Whole-grain pasta with vegetables or a sauce

Snack
Popcorn
Baked tortilla chips
Whole-grain crackers or pretzels
Cookie or muffin made with whole-grain flour

How much is a serving?

1 slice bread
½ bagel (3″ diameter)
1 muffin (2½″ diameter)
1 cup of ready-to-eat cereal
½ cup cooked cereal, grain or pasta
2 cups popcorn

The Bottom Line

Eat at least three servings of whole grains every day.

Avoid refined grains.

Limit sugar and sugar substitutes.

CHAPTER 7

Choosing Protein: High or Low, Animal or Vegetable?

Compared with what we know about fat and carbohydrate, we know relatively little about protein and its relationship to health. We do know that protein is essential for healthy growth, tissue repair, immune function and a variety of hormones and enzymes that are essential for good health. Hair and skin are composed mainly of protein, as are muscles, bones and hemoglobin in blood.

Protein molecules are composed of various building blocks called amino acids. There are approximately twenty different amino acids that combine in the body to form an endless variety of protein particles. (Think of amino acids as letters of the alphabet and proteins as words.) About half of these amino acid building blocks can be synthesized in the body. The remaining amino acids, called *essential* amino acids, must be obtained from food. Animal protein is a source of "complete" protein, containing all of the essential amino acids, while vegetable protein (except for soy) is "incomplete," or lacking in some of the essential amino acids. Since we do not store amino acids, and the process of forming protein particles in the body is ongoing, we need a daily supply of dietary protein to maintain and repair body functions.

ARE YOU GETTING ENOUGH PROTEIN?

Growing children, pregnant and nursing women, and people who are recovering from illness or injury need extra protein in their diets. But the rest of us will do just fine on 40 to 60 grams of protein a day, or 10% to 20% of our daily caloric intake.

Use this formula to calculate your specific daily protein requirement:
Weight in pounds ÷ 2.2 = weight in kilograms
Weight in kilograms × 0.8 = daily protein requirement

Most of us get enough protein without even thinking about it. For example, you will get 56 grams of protein by eating the following:

Breakfast: 1 cup of yogurt = 12 grams
Lunch: 3 ounces tuna = 20 grams
Dinner: 3 ounces chicken breast = 24 grams

When you add in the protein from vegetables, grains, eggs, nuts and dairy products that you eat throughout the day, it is easy to get more than enough protein to meet your needs.

> **Most of the protein in a healthy diet should come from plant sources, low-fat dairy, fish and poultry.**

HIGH PROTEIN FOR WEIGHT LOSS

The popularity of high-protein diets for weight loss has soared. There are several possible reasons for their apparent success. High-protein foods are digested slowly, causing us to feel satiated for a longer time. And when we feel full, we are less inclined to eat as much and as frequently. In addition, protein tends to elevate blood sugar at a slow, steady rate, avoiding the hunger that often occurs after eating simple carbohydrates, which raise and then drop blood sugar quickly.

Although high-protein, low-carbohydrate diets may initially work more quickly than low-fat diets, their long-term effectiveness has not been confirmed. Studies so far seem to indicate an initial, quicker weight loss with a high-protein diet, but equal weight loss compared with other diets after a year or more.

IT'S A PACKAGE DEAL

Protein in food is not an isolated element. It comes in a "package" of sorts – and the different parts of the package have an influence on health. The protein in beef, for example, comes with saturated fat and cholesterol, which are detrimental to health. On the other hand, the protein in legumes comes with very little fat and a good amount of beneficial fiber and micronutrients. Since animal and vegetable proteins by themselves have similar health effects, our goal is to choose, as often as possible, protein that is part of a healthy "package." Here are some examples:

Protein in a Healthy Package	Protein in an Unhealthy Package
Fish, poultry (skin removed)	Fatty, untrimmed beef, lamb
Skim or low-fat dairy products	Whole-milk (full-fat) dairy products
Beans, nuts, whole grains	

THE MEAT OF THE ISSUE

"Do not be among the guzzlers of wine, among the gorgers of meat." (*Mishlei* 23:21)

When I was growing up, dinner was based on a "main course" of protein, complemented by a vegetable and starch. My mother had a schedule: meat meals on Monday, Wednesday and *Shabbat*, dairy meals on Tuesday and Thursday and leftovers on Sunday. Due to the high cost of kosher meat, we "stretched" it to the maximum. Most of our meat meals were chicken. We ate red meat occasionally, and prepared it with economy in mind. Beef stew was cooked with a small amount of beef and a large amount of vegetables. Meatloaf was based on ground beef mixed with grated onion, potato and carrot. On the infrequent occasions that we ate brisket or roast beef, our serving sizes were moderate so that we could get an additional meal or two from the leftovers later in the week. This eating model helped keep us fairly slim.

Today, many of us eat meat fairly regularly. Lunch might include a sandwich with cold cuts or a hamburger, with meat for dinner as well. We often cook beef for *Shabbat* and holiday dinners and include it in our *cholent* for lunch. Our portion sizes have grown as well. For example, the "normal" hamburger has grown by more than one ounce in the past twenty years.[28] An ounce may seem insignificant, but it adds nearly 100 calories (plus more saturated fat) to the hamburger.

Meat is a good source of quality protein, iron, zinc, vitamin B12 and other important nutrients, but its high saturated fat and cholesterol content is detrimental to health, and we should be careful not to eat too much of it.

Choosing meat wisely:
- Select meat with the least amount of visible fat. Trim off as much fat as possible.
- Choose the leanest ground beef available, and drain off the excess fat after cooking.
- Remove the skin from chicken before cooking or making soup. Your butcher may be willing to do this for you. This works well when cooking chicken in a sauce. For roast chicken, leave the skin on but remove it before eating.
- Skinless, boneless chicken and turkey breast are low in fat and easy to prepare in a variety of ways. Our favorite *Shabbat* dinner includes chicken breasts sautéed lightly in olive oil and cooked in a sauce that varies from week to week.
- Chill meat and soups made with meat or poultry and skim off the hardened fat.

- Avoid high-fat processed meat such as hot dogs, bologna and salami. There are a number of reduced-fat kosher products available. Use chicken, turkey or the wide variety of vegetarian substitutes for sliced meat. With added sliced tomato, cucumber and lettuce, these work especially well for sandwiches.
- Liver is very high in cholesterol. If chopped liver is a family favorite, make it a once-a-month special treat, and limit serving sizes to three ounces.

Choose chicken and poultry more often than red meat.

Meat in Moderation

Think of meat as a side dish, rather than as a main entrée. If you are used to eating meat for lunch and dinner, start by trying meatless lunches. Gradually reduce the number of times you eat meat for dinner as well.

Practical suggestions for reducing the amount of meat in your diet:

- Prepare a stir-fry using a small amount of beef and a larger amount of vegetables. Or toss whole-grain noodles with sliced vegetables and a small amount of cooked chicken pieces.
- Cook meat sauce for spaghetti using a small amount of ground beef, lots of tomato sauce and added vegetables, such as eggplant, zucchini and mushrooms.
- Try meat substitutes. With a similar texture to ground meat, they can be used successfully in casserole dishes, stuffed vegetables and "meatballs" cooked in a sauce. You may need to increase the seasoning in your recipe, as these products can be a bit bland. Beans and grains can also fill in for meat in dishes such as chili and tacos.

- Explore ethnic food: Sephardic Jewish cuisine, for example, makes use of a variety of grains, beans, fish and nuts. Indian, Asian, Italian and Latin American cuisines also include many meat-free dishes that can be adapted to the kosher kitchen.

Eat red meat only occasionally and in small servings.

How much is a serving?
½ chicken breast
1 chicken leg and thigh
2 slices roast beef (3 × 3 × ¼")
1 hamburger (3" diameter × ½" thick)

FISH – BEYOND GEFILTE

"This may you eat from everything that is in the water: everything that has fins and scales in the water, in the seas, and in the streams, those may you eat." (*Vayikra* 11:9)

Most of us are familiar with gefilte fish, herring, smoked whitefish, lox, and canned tuna and salmon. In fact, fish has been an integral part of kosher cuisine throughout our history. As a *parve* food, it is adaptable to dairy and meat meals, and makes a fine main course on its own. Today we are fortunate to have access to a wide variety of delicious and nutritious fresh, frozen, canned and smoked kosher fish.

Fish is an excellent protein source, with less fat and cholesterol than meat. In addition, the omega-3 fats found in fish, especially fatty fish, are highly beneficial for heart health. (See chapter 5: Fat Facts.) Omega-3 has been found to lower cholesterol,[29] decrease the risk of heart disease,[30] and help protect against sudden cardiac death.[31] Salmon, sardines, herring and mackerel are especially high in heart-healthy, omega-3 fats. Tuna and trout are good sources as well. Canned salmon and smoked salmon (lox), though high in sodium, are also excellent sources of omega-3 fats.

Try to include fish in your diet twice a week.

Safety Concerns of Fish

In recent years, there has been concern over the safety of some fish. Contaminants such as dioxins, mercury, PCBs and pesticides have washed into lakes and coastal waters, concentrating in the fatty tissue of fish. Farm-raised salmon can contain toxins as well.

In the US, pregnant women are advised to limit their intake of seafood. However, an observational study of nearly 12,000 pregnant women in the United Kingdom does not support these recommendations. The study suggests that limiting fish intake during pregnancy can actually be detrimental to a child's development. Children of mothers who ate fish more than three times a week showed a lower risk for cognitive, behavioral and developmental delays. Alternatively, children of mothers who ate the least amount of fish had the highest risk of less than optimum development.[32]

Omega-3 fatty acids, found mainly in fish, are essential for neurological development, and this benefit may outweigh any possible harm from contaminants.

In light of this, the following US government guidelines for pregnant women and young children should be taken into consideration together with ongoing research into the benefits of consuming fish.[33]

- Eat up to 12 ounces (two average servings) a week of fish low in mercury. These include canned light tuna, salmon, pollack, perch, whitefish, herring, sole, tilapia, sardines, trout, haddock and flounder.
- Limit your intake of albacore (white) tuna to 6 ounces, or one serving, per week.
- Avoid fish with high mercury content, such as king mackerel.

- Check advisories about the safety of fish caught in local lakes, rivers and coastal areas, and avoid those with high mercury content.

Choose chunk light tuna rather than white albacore tuna, which can be high in mercury.

Although it is impossible to remove mercury from fish, you can take a number of steps to reduce your exposure to other harmful contaminants:

- Grill or broil fish so that the juices run off.
- Be sure to cook fish thoroughly, and remove the fat and skin before eating.
- Try to eat a variety of fish to reduce the risk of ingesting any one particular toxin.

Nitrites, which are often added to smoked fish as preservatives, may pose a risk for cancer if consumed in large amounts.[34] If you eat lox or other smoked fish frequently, look for nitrite-free varieties or be sure to consume some form of vitamin c along with the smoked fish. Vitamin c inhibits the formation of carcinogens formed in the body from nitrites.

While harmful chemical concentrations in fish need to be taken seriously, several major studies suggest that for most people, the benefits of eating fish regularly outweigh the potential risks.[35]

How much is a serving?

½ can tuna
½ salmon steak
9 medium sardines

EGGS

"Any food that is the size of an egg, an egg is better than it, i.e., there is no food the size of an egg that is as healthful as an egg." (Rashi, *Brachot* 44b)

When I studied nutrition, it seemed that eggs, or at least egg yolks, were public enemy number one in the battle against heart disease. On one hand, eggs are close to being the perfect food nutritionally. They contain high-quality protein and a full contingent of easily absorbed vitamins and minerals. On the other hand, with 200 mg of cholesterol per yolk (the recommended total daily cholesterol intake is 300 mg), we were encouraged to limit egg consumption to once or twice a week.

We now know that for most people, saturated fat rather than cholesterol is the biggest culprit in raising blood cholesterol. In fact, much like salt and blood pressure, it seems that some people's blood lipids are sensitive to dietary cholesterol while others' are not. A large study published in 1999 showed that eating an egg a day did not increase the risk of developing heart disease or strokes in healthy people. In diabetics who ate an egg a day, there seemed to be a weak connection with developing heart disease.[36] If you are diabetic, or if your cholesterol levels are high, it might be wise to limit eggs, or at least egg yolks, to once or twice a week, or consider using egg substitutes, which work especially well in cooking and baking. For others who enjoy eating eggs, there is no reason to feel guilty about including them more often in your diet.

THE IMPORTANCE OF FOOD SAFETY

Food-borne illness results from eating food contaminated with harmful bacteria and microorganisms. Millions of people become ill and thousands die every year in the US alone from this serious public health problem.

Here are four simple steps that you can take to help prevent getting sick from food:[37]

- Wash your hands, utensils and surfaces with hot soapy water before and after preparing food. This is especially important when preparing meat, poultry, fish and eggs. Wash fruits and vegetables carefully, even if they will be peeled before eating.
- Keep raw meat, poultry, fish and eggs away from other cooked foods. Never place prepared foods on an unwashed plate or cutting board that was previously used for raw meat, poultry, fish and eggs.
- Cook food to the proper temperature, using a thermometer as a guide. Eggs should be cooked until both the yolk and whites are firm. Keep hot foods hot if you will not be serving them immediately.
- Refrigerate or freeze perishables, prepared foods and leftovers within two hours. Defrost food in the refrigerator, in cold water or in the microwave, not on the countertop. Keep a thermometer in your refrigerator and make sure that the temperature is no higher than 40 degrees Fahrenheit. The freezer should be set for 0 degrees Fahrenheit.

Safe Eggs

For years I've lectured about the importance of food safety. I don't miss an opportunity to talk about cleanliness in the kitchen: washing hands repeatedly, using separate towels for hands and dishes, changing towels daily, disinfecting sponges (see instructions below), and using a bleach solution to clean surfaces used for raw meat, fish and poultry. I advise my students to purchase a refrigerator thermometer to be sure that cold foods are kept cold and a meat thermometer to check that meat is thoroughly cooked.

You can imagine my consternation (and agony!) when I recently contracted Salmonella poisoning. The culprit was most likely a raw egg used in the salad dressing at an upscale kosher restaurant in New York.

Salmonella contamination of eggs is a genuine problem, affecting hundreds of thousands of people every year in the US with severe illness and even death. Although eggs are not the only culprit, centralized industrial egg farming is largely to blame for the increased incidence of Salmonella poisoning since the 1970s. The particular strain of bacteria common to eggs, *Salmonella Enteritidus*, accesses the egg through an infection of the hen's ovaries. The bacteria are sealed within the egg at the time it is laid, and, unless the egg has been tested, you have absolutely no way of knowing that it is contaminated.

Until the testing of eggs becomes universal, here's what you can do to keep from getting sick:
- Do not eat foods prepared with raw eggs (no homemade *parve* mousse, sorbet, truffles, mayonnaise or anything else made with raw eggs, please).
- Do not "taste test" uncooked dough or other foods containing raw eggs.
- Store eggs in the refrigerator and do not use them after the expiration date.
- Discard any eggs with a broken or cracked shell.
- If you intend to separate the egg, use an inexpensive egg separating device, not the shell.
- Cook eggs thoroughly (no runny yolks!) and refrigerate foods containing cooked eggs.

Eating Away from Home
When eating out, insist that all meat, poultry, fish and eggs are fully cooked. Don't be embarrassed to ask if raw eggs were used in any of the dishes. Most health departments advise against using fresh raw eggs, but there is no universal law prohibiting it.

Restaurants are inspected periodically in most states. Their findings, including any citations, will often be listed on the health department website. Insist on good hygiene and proper food handling wherever you eat. Unsafe food is no different from non kosher food!

If you develop severe diarrhea, chills and or stomach cramps between 12 and 72 hours after eating, you may have contracted food poisoning. Only a physician can determine for sure. If in doubt, see your doctor. Your local health department will follow through if food poisoning is diagnosed.

Sanitizing Sponges

Damp sponges and scrubbing pads provide an ideal breeding ground for germs present in most kitchens. You can kill 99 percent of harmful bacteria with a two-minute "zap" in your microwave oven.

Follow these guidelines (based on recent research):[38]

- Be sure that there are no metal parts on your sponge or scrubber.
- Moisten your sponge or scrubber with water before putting it into the microwave oven.
- Place the sponge or scrubber in a shallow bowl for ease of handling.
- Use high power and microwave for a full two minutes.
- Remove the sponge or scrubber very carefully, since it will be extremely hot.
- Depending on how often you cook, you may want to microwave your sponges and scrubbers once a day or every other day.

LEGUMES: VEGETABLE PROTEIN PAR EXCELLENCE

"Jacob gave Esau bread and lentil stew, and he ate and drank, got up and left..." (*Breishit* 25:34)

As the above *pasuk* testifies, dried beans and peas, known as legumes, have been dietary staples since biblical times. They contain more protein than any other plant food, are low in fat and high in B vitamins, vitamin E and minerals including potassium, magnesium, selenium, iron and calcium. In addition, legumes are an excellent source of soluble fiber, and can contribute to lowering cholesterol and stabilizing blood sugar.

Unlike animal protein, the vegetable protein in legumes does not contain all of the essential amino acids needed by our bodies. It is therefore wise to complement legumes with grains, nuts, seeds and vegetables to be sure that no amino acid is missing from your diet, especially if you are a vegetarian. At one time it was considered necessary to eat "complementary" protein at the same meal, but we now know that eating it on the same day will achieve the same effect.[39] If you are eating a healthy, varied diet, this should be easy enough.

Because they offer such good nutrition at a very low cost, legumes are among the most widely consumed foods in the world. Chickpeas (garbanzo beans), fava beans and lentils are popular in Sephardic cuisine, while split peas and lima beans are commonly used, especially in soups, in the Ashkenazic kitchen.

One of the first processed foods to be certified kosher, Heinz Vegetarian Beans, is a familiar legume to most of us. Now, a wide variety of legumes can be purchased dried (prepackaged or bulk) and canned. Lentils and split peas, available in many colors and sizes, cook in a short time, making them a convenient choice for meals when there is not much time to cook. Other beans require presoaking before cooking, although even this step can be shortened with the method described below. Store dried beans in a cool dark place, and try to use them within six months of purchase. The older the beans, the longer it will take for them to cook.

Legumes are an excellent and economical source of low-fat, high-fiber protein.

Most of us are familiar with using beans in soup and *cholent*, but there are endless other possibilities as well. Spreads similar to *hummus* (garbanzo bean spread) can be made from white beans or lentils. Pinto and black beans can be used in place of meat in dishes such as tacos, enchiladas and chili. Indian-style *dhal*, a deliciously spiced dish, is made with quick-cooking red lentils. Rice and lentils are combined with browned onions in the nutritious Middle-Eastern dish *mejadra*. You can also create interesting salads from legumes. In addition to the traditional three-bean salad, try mixing white beans, garbanzos or lentils with various vegetables and toss with your favorite vinaigrette dressing. Vegetarian and ethnic cookbooks are good places to look for interesting recipes using legumes.

Try to eat at least two vegetarian meals every week.

Some legumes, such as lentils and split peas, are easier to digest than others. If you are not used to eating beans, start with small portions and give your body time to get used to them. By soaking and parboiling dried beans, you can remove some of the indigestible sugars that can cause indigestion. Be sure to cook beans until they are completely soft and creamy on the inside, as this will also ensure easier digestion.

Table 8: Fiber in Legumes (per ½-cup cooked serving)

	Black beans	Chickpeas	Lentils	Lima beans	Split peas
Calories	114	135	115	108	116
Protein (grams)	8	7	9	7	8
Fiber (grams)	8	6	8	7	8

Preparing Legumes

Cooking beans is easy, though you will need to plan ahead. You can cook a large batch of beans and freeze them in smaller portions to use when you are in a hurry.

1. Sort: Pick out any stones and debris and rinse the beans in a colander.

2. Presoak: Except for lentils and split peas, beans should be soaked before cooking, unless you will be cooking them in a pressure cooker. There are two methods for soaking beans:

    Quick Method: Place the beans in a saucepan and cover them with water – 4 cups of water for each cup of beans. Bring to a boil and boil for 1 or 2 minutes, cover the pan and let them soak for 1 hour. Drain the beans and discard the cooking water.

    Long Method: Cover the beans with water – 4 cups for every cup of beans, and let them soak for at least 4 hours or overnight. In hot weather, soak beans in the refrigerator so that they will not ferment and spoil. Drain and discard the soaking water.

3. Parboil: Place the presoaked beans in a saucepan and cover with cold water. Bring to a rolling boil and boil for 10 to 15 minutes. Remove any scum that may rise to the surface of the water and discard any beans that may have risen to the top. (This step is not absolutely necessary, but may aid digestion for people who are sensitive to beans. It is also not necessary if you will be cooking beans in a pressure cooker.)

Except when you want a slightly firm texture for a salad, beans should be cooked thoroughly, until they are soft and creamy. Cooking time will vary depending on the type and age of the bean, but count on about 1½ hours. The mineral content of your water and altitude affects cooking time – high altitude and hard water can add significantly to cooking time. Do not add salt or acid ingredients such as vinegar, lemon juice or tomatoes until the beans are tender, as they can toughen the beans. Beans can be cooked on the stove, in the oven, in a pressure cooker or in a slow cooker (crock pot).

Cooking choices:

On the Stove: Drain and rinse the beans, place them in a large saucepan and cover with cold water. Add flavorings or vegetables, if desired. Bring to a boil, lower the heat and simmer, partially covered, until very soft.

In the Oven: Drain the parboiled beans and put them into a casserole dish. Add boiling water to cover, and flavorings such as celery, onion and garlic. Cover and bake at 325 to 350 degrees Fahrenheit until tender. Keep the beans simmering, not boiling, and let them cool in their liquid.

Pressure Cooker: Put soaked or unsoaked beans in the pressure cooker with seasonings (except salt) and 1 teaspoon of oil to prevent clogging the pressure gauge. If the beans have not yet been soaked, use 5 cups of water for each cup of beans. Otherwise, use 4 cups of water. Bring to high pressure and maintain for 25 minutes, unless otherwise indicated. Lower pressure and taste for tenderness.

Slow Cooker: Cover soaked beans with water (3 to 4 cups for each cup of beans) and cook on low for about 8 hours or on high for about 6 hours. Add seasonings and salt during the last hour of cooking.

Add a dish or two containing legumes to your weekly menu.

How much is a serving?
½ cup cooked dried beans
½ cup tofu
1 cup lentil or split pea soup

WHAT ABOUT SOY?

The soybean deserves a place in the kosher kitchen. From beverages to tofu, puddings and frozen desserts to roasted soy nuts, soy is nutritious as well as versatile. Soy foods contain high-quality, low-fat protein as well as calcium and omega-3 fatty acids. Some are high in fiber as well. Soy can often be used as a substitute for dairy ingredients when a *parve* product is desired or for those who are allergic or cannot tolerate dairy products. In place of red meat, it offers high-quality protein with no saturated fat.

Although research on soy foods has increased in recent years, study results have not yet given us a clear picture of all of their possible health implications. Soy shows promise in alleviating menopausal symptoms, and in playing a protective role in prostate and breast cancer.[40] It may play a role in preventing menopause-related bone loss, with less of an effect on reversing bone loss.[41]

Evidence of the heart-health benefits of soy is extensive. Soy foods have been shown to decrease total cholesterol and LDL levels while increasing HDL levels, critical factors in protecting against cardiovascular disease.[42] For this reason, the FDA has authorized a health claim for foods containing a minimum of 6.25 grams of soy protein per serving, and the American Heart Association now recommends including soy foods in a heart-healthy diet.[43] It is important to emphasize that the positive effect of soy on heart health seems to be achieved when soy protein *replaces* animal protein in people's diets. A typical high-fat diet supplemented with soy is not likely to achieve similar results.

> **Soy can be a healthy substitute for high-fat, high-cholesterol foods.**

Food or Supplement?

The main health benefits of soy are attributed to isoflavones, which are phytoestrogens that chemically resemble the hormone estrogen. These compounds seem to be most effective when consumed in soy foods, as opposed to concentrated soy protein or soy extract supplements.

Eat soy foods rather than concentrated soy supplements.

When to Be Cautious

A high consumption of soy can affect thyroid function and interfere with the absorption of thyroid medication. If your thyroid function is compromised or if you take thyroid medication, speak with your physician about possible interactions and effects of eating soy products.

Clinical studies of soy intake and breast cancer have shown conflicting results. The current recommendation for breast cancer survivors and those with a high risk of developing breast cancer is to consume only small amounts of soy foods. Women taking Tamoxifen should avoid soy foods altogether.[44] Because we do not fully understand the hormone-mimicking effects of soy isoflavones, it seems prudent to limit the amount of soy fed to children.

What Is It and What Do I Do with It?

Tofu: Made by heating, coagulating and pressing soymilk into a firm block, much like cheese is made from cow's milk. Tofu's bland taste and variety of textures make it a versatile ingredient in the kosher kitchen, especially since it is *parve.* Use soft silken tofu in salad dressings, dips, creamy sauces and desserts. When pureed, soft tofu has a texture similar to ricotta cheese, and can be used as a substitute or partial replacement in lasagna or cheese cake. Firm tofu is most often used in stir-fries, combined with vegetables and flavorful sauces or spices.

Tempeh: A fermented product produced from soybeans that is often combined with rice or other grains or beans. It comes vacuum-packed in a flat cake and can be found refrigerated near other soy products, usually in health or whole food stores. Its firm, chewy texture lends itself to sandwiches and stir-fries. It can also be crumbled or cubed and used in vegetable stews and casseroles.

Miso: A thick fermented paste made of cooked soybeans, salt and often rice or barley. It is used extensively in Japan, especially in soups and sauces as well as a condiment. It is particularly high in sodium.

Soy Sauce: A brown liquid made from fermented soybeans that is used as a flavoring in many Asian cuisines. Because it is very high in salt, I recommend using it sparingly or using a low-sodium variety.

Soybean Oil: The most frequently consumed oil in the US. It is low in saturated and monounsaturated fat and high in polyunsaturated fat.

Tempeh, miso and soy sauce are low in isoflavones compared with other soy products. Soybean oil does not contain isoflavones.

Soymilk: Extracted from cooked ground soybeans. It can be purchased refrigerated or vacuum (aseptic) packed and comes in various flavors and fat content. Purchase soymilk that is fortified with calcium and vitamin D, especially if you are using it in place of cow's milk. Look for aseptic packaged soy milk fortified specifically with calcium carbonate, as other forms of calcium are not as easily absorbed in the body. Also, be sure to shake the carton vigorously before pouring, as the added calcium tends to settle to the bottom of the carton. You may want to try several brands to find the one that suits your taste. Reduced-fat soymilk is often tastier than nonfat versions, and fresh products tastier than aseptic packaged products. Soymilk is *parve*, but may be produced on dairy equipment. Use soymilk as you would cow's milk, in recipes or with cereal or coffee.

Soymilk creamers: A healthy version of the nondairy liquid and powdered creamers that are commonly used in kosher homes and restaurants. Nondairy creamers usually contain hydrogenated vegetable oil, and should be avoided. Liquid vegetable oil, sweeteners, thickeners and flavoring are added to soymilk to produce a rich, creamy product that can be enjoyed in coffee.

Soy-based vegetarian products: These include veggie burgers, "hot dogs," deli slices and soy-based products that resemble ground beef. They can be found in the refrigerator or freezer section of your grocery or whole foods store, and many of them are *parve.* In Israel, frozen soy-based patties are available in a variety of flavors and are extremely popular. Some brands are exported to the US and may be found in kosher markets. Be aware that like many processed foods, they are often high in sodium. These products are convenient for occasional last-minute meals.

Frozen soy desserts: Another way to include soy in your diet. Check the label carefully, as some frozen desserts are *parve* and others are not. Look for low-fat healthy brands that do not contain partially hydrogenated fats.

Soy nuts: Soybeans that have been soaked and roasted, either in oil or by dry-roasting. You may find them salted and flavored. Eat them as a snack or sprinkled over salads for a little crunch. Like nuts, they are calorie dense and should be enjoyed in small quantities.

Soy additives: A variety of soy derivatives are used as fillers and additives. Soy protein concentrate, soy protein isolate or textured soy protein may be added to ground meat as an extender, made into meat-like products or used in baked goods and other processed foods.

How much is a serving?
1 cup soy milk
½ cup tofu
½ cup tempeh
¼ cup soy nuts

PROTEIN FROM WHEAT

Seitan or "wheat meat" is a protein-rich food made from the gluten of wheat. It has been used in Asia for hundreds of years and is used today in many kosher vegetarian and dairy restaurants as a meat substitute. Its slightly chewy, firm texture and mild taste lends itself to any number of recipes, including stir-fries, stews, casseroles, tacos and sandwiches. Low in fat and convenient to use, it can be found in the refrigerated section of health or whole food stores. In Israel it can be purchased frozen, flavored as *schwarma*. If ready-made kosher seitan is not available in your area, you can buy packaged wheat gluten powder in a box and prepare it easily by mixing it with water. Vegetarian cookbooks are a good source of recipes using seitan.

Three ounces of seitan provides 314 calories, 64 grams of protein, 12 grams of carbohydrate and less than 2 grams of fat.

NUTS AND SEEDS

Packed with vitamins, minerals and fiber, nuts and seeds are also a good source of plant protein. Although nuts are high in fat, most of that fat is healthy mono- and polyunsaturated. (Brazil nuts are an exception, with a high percentage of saturated fat.) Walnuts are a good source of heart-healthy omega-3 fatty acids. Many studies have supported the finding that eating nuts regularly can lower your risk of heart disease.

For a healthy snack, eat nuts in place of highly processed snack foods.

Use them in cooking and baking for added nutrition and crunch. Sprinkle nuts or seeds on salads and soups, in place of croutons. Experiment with natural nut butters such as almond and cashew in addition to peanut butter on sandwiches. *Techinah* (ground sesame seeds) thinned with water, lemon juice and garlic makes a delicious and healthy salad dressing as well as a sauce for steamed vegetables.

Because of their high fat content, nuts and seeds are prone to spoilage. Buy them from a store where the turnover is good and keep them in a cool dry place. For extended storage, nuts should be kept in the refrigerator or freezer. Be sure that nuts smell fresh before using them. (Rancid nuts will have an "off" smell similar to oil paint.) Avoid highly salted nuts and those prepared with added oils or sugar coatings.

Lightly roasting nuts brings out their flavor. Either heat shelled nuts in a dry skillet over medium heat, stirring constantly, or bake them in an oven at 325 degrees Fahrenheit for 3 to 15 minutes, depending on the size and type of the seed or nut. They should look and smell lightly toasted.

As healthy as they are, keep in mind that nuts are high in calories and should be enjoyed in moderation. To avoid adding extra calories to your diet, eat them in place of, rather than in addition to, other foods. An ounce (about a handful) of nuts or seeds is a good amount to eat daily.

Table 9: What's in an Ounce?

One ounce (raw shelled)	Amount	Protein	Calories
Almonds	23 whole	6	164
Cashews	12 whole	5	157
Hazelnuts	21 whole	4	178
Pecans	20 halves	3	196
Peanuts	20 whole	7	161

Pistachios	49 whole	6	158
Pumpkin seeds	3 tablespoons	7	153
Sunflower seeds	3 tablespoons	6	164
Walnuts	14 halves	4	185

USDA National Nutrient Database for Standard
Reference, Release 17 (2004)

JUDAISM AND VEGETARIANISM

"God said, "Behold, I have given to you all herbage yielding seed that is on the surface of the entire earth, and every tree that has seed-yielding fruit; it shall be yours for food." (*Breishit* 1:29)

"Every moving thing that lives shall be food for you; like the green herbage I have given you everything." (*Breishit* 9:3)

The laws of *kashrut*, including *shechitah* (ritual slaughter), remind us that all life is sacred and not to be taken casually. Prohibitions against harming animals are found throughout the Torah and Jewish literature. They include prohibiting animals to work on *Shabbat* (*Shemot* 20:10), relieving the suffering of an animal, even if it belongs to an enemy (*Shemot* 23:5), feeding your animal before yourself if it is dependent on you for food (*Brachot* 40a, based on *Devarim* 11:15) and forbidding the killing of a cow and her calf on the same day (*Vayikra* 22:28).

At the same time, Judaism also maintains that animals are meant to serve mankind. The Rambam describes four levels in the hierarchy of creation, each level deriving sustenance from the level beneath it. The lowest level is the silent, inanimate realm of earth, rocks and minerals. Level two is vegetation – plants that receive their sustenance from the earth. The animal world is level three and humans, who derive nourishment from plants and animals, are on the highest level.

In Chasidic thought, when a person eats with proper *kavanah*, his or her eating meat serves to elevate the innate sparks of *kedushah* that resided in the animal's soul. The food becomes an element of the person, both physically and spiritually. Therefore, the chicken that is eaten on *Shabbat* is considered to be a fortunate chicken!

Judaism accepts vegetarianism for health and ethical reasons and permits eating meat with proper mindfulness.

Rav Avraham Yizchak Hacohen Kook considered God's permission for us to eat meat after the flood as a temporary concession to our basic weakness and imperfection. In his view, humanity fell from its initial moral state after the flood. When we reattain an elevated level of morality, at the time of the restoration of the *Beit Hamikdash* in Jerusalem, we will naturally revert to being vegetarians.

Rav Chaim David HaLevi, former chief rabbi of Tel Aviv, believed that plant sacrifices, rather than animal sacrifices, would be offered in the Third Temple (*Aseh L'cha Rav* vol. 9, p. 120–121).

As is well known, the current chief rabbi of Haifa, Rav Sha'ar Yashuv Cohen, is a committed vegetarian.

EATING MEAT ON *SHABBAT* AND FESTIVALS

Although the Rambam seems to have encouraged eating meat on *Shabbat*, Rabbi Akiva taught that one should not go out of his way to purchase meat for *Shabbat* if he could not afford it.

Is eating meat on *Shabbat* a requisite for fulfilling the commandment of *Oneg Shabbat*? Many authorities seem to agree that eating meat on *Shabbat* is not essential, especially if a person believes that non-meat meals are healthier, more enjoyable and ideal. According to this view, *Oneg* (delight or pleasure) assumes personal preference when it comes to food.

Just as we serve our fanciest food to honored guests, we strive to give *kavod* (dignity) to *Shabbat* by serving our very best food – the best according to our own ideals. And if meat is not considered an ideal food, it would not seem to be a necessary component of *Shabbat* meals.

If meat or poultry are currently an integral part of your *Shabbat*, but you are trying to reduce the amount that you eat during the week, you might consider serving meat only on *Shabbat*, while featuring leaner vegetarian and fish dishes during the rest of the week.

How should a vegetarian relate to *V'samachta b'chagecha*, "experiencing joy on the festivals" (*Devarim* 16:14), when the Talmud suggests that "there is no joy without meat and wine" (*Pesachim* 109a)? A number of sages felt that the obligation to eat meat on festivals was no longer in effect after the destruction of the *Beit Hamikdash*: "Only wine is essential to *simchah*" (ibid.).

Here again, we need to consider the matter of "joy" on a personal level. If eating meat is not your ideal – if it does not make you feel joyous, it would not seem to be a necessary part of your holiday menu.

Vegetarianism and Health

Lower rates of heart disease, Type 2 diabetes and hypertension have been reported in vegetarians. Reduced intakes of saturated fat, cholesterol and animal protein plus higher intakes of carbohydrates, fiber, vitamins, minerals, antioxidants and phytochemicals are added benefits of a healthy plant-based diet.

If you choose a vegetarian diet, concentrate on protein from legumes and nonfat or low-fat dairy products, complex carbohydrates, a variety of vegetables, nuts and seeds to ensure an adequate intake of proteins and essential nutrients. Getting sufficient calcium may be difficult for vegetarians, especially those who do not eat dairy products. (See the section on milk and diary products for good sources of calcium, and consider a supplement if necessary.)

A well-planned vegetarian diet can be delicious and healthy.

Since vitamin B12 occurs in meat, poultry, fish, eggs and dairy products, deficiencies can be common in vegetarians, especially those who are strict vegans (vegetarians who avoid all animal-derived foods). Fortified breakfast cereals and vitamin B12 supplements are recommended. Omega-3 fatty acids, which are highly beneficial for heart health and are most commonly found in fish, can be obtained by eating ground flax seed or flax oil.

The Bottom Line

Choose most of your protein from plants, fish, poultry and low-fat dairy sources.

Eat lean red meat occasionally, and keep serving sizes small.

Include fish in your diet several times a week.

Legumes, including soy, are an excellent low-fat source of protein.

Soy may not be recommended for everyone.

Nuts and seeds are healthy snack foods when eaten in moderation.

Well-planned vegetarian diets can be healthy and delicious.

CHAPTER 8

L'chaim! Drinking for Your Health

Fluids are essential for good health and well-being. Since fluids are used continuously for vital metabolic functions affecting all of our body's cells and organs, they must be constantly replenished. The amount of liquid you need depends on a number of factors, including your activity level, your diet and the weather. Very active people need to drink more than people who are sedentary. If you eat a lot of fruits and vegetables, which have high water content, you may need to drink less. And if you live in a hot, dry climate you will need to drink more than if you live in a cooler, more humid climate. Most of us are familiar with the recommendation to drink eight glasses of fluid each day, but that amount may be more than necessary for some people and not enough for others.

WATER – THE FIRST CHOICE IN BEVERAGES

The beauty of water is that it has no calories or additives and if it comes from your tap, it is the most inexpensive beverage available. Most public water supplies are safe. Request a report from your local municipality if you are unsure of the quality of your tap water, and consider a filtering system if necessary. Depending on the filtering system you choose, it may be necessary to change the actual filter on a regular basis to ensure that your water is free of contamination. Bottled water may not offer any special benefits, and may in fact be nothing more than tap water packaged in a fancy bottle.

I recommend water as the beverage of choice with meals (except when milk is appropriate, especially for children) and whenever you are thirsty. For a nice change, try plain or lightly flavored unsweetened sparkling water. Fill a glass pitcher with water; add thinly sliced lemons or oranges and/or fresh herbs such as mint or lemon balm for a classy, refreshing presentation. Teach your children to drink water at an early age, and they will be less likely to crave sweetened sodas and juice drinks.

Make water the beverage of choice for you and your family.

PURE FRUIT AND VEGETABLE JUICES

Juices made from 100% real fruit or vegetables, with no added sweeteners, can be part of a healthy diet, providing important vitamins, minerals and fluid. A small glass of pure orange juice for breakfast can give you a good amount of vitamin C (and calcium if you choose calcium-fortified juice) to start the day.

Table 10: Juice and Fruit – Compare the Calories

One medium size *orange*	69 calories
One cup (8 ounces) *orange juice*	110 calories
One medium size *apple*	72 calories
One cup (8 ounces) *apple juice*	117 calories

USDA National Nutrient Database for Standard Reference, Release 17 (2004)

Notice that I recommend a *small* glass of juice with breakfast, and not unlimited juice throughout the day. Think about how many pieces of fruit it takes to produce a cup of juice and you will realize how many more calories you are getting by drinking juice rather than eating a whole piece of fruit. And it is so easy to gulp down a glass of juice – much faster than peeling an orange or chewing an apple, so it is easy to drink a large quantity without thinking too much about the extra calories. Since most of us would do well to reduce our calories, choose whole fruit rather than juice whenever possible. Remember too that you are getting valuable fiber from the whole fruit that juice usually does not provide.

> ## As an alternative to sweetened beverages, fill one-third of a glass with pure fruit juice. Pour in plain soda water to the top and enjoy!

SOFT DRINKS AND FRUIT-FLAVORED BEVERAGES

Not that long ago, children and teenagers drank nearly twice the amount of milk as soda. Now the figures are reversed, as soft drink consumption has doubled in the past 25 years. In fact, the major source of added sugar in the American diet, more than 30%, comes from sweetened soft drinks. Considering that a 12-ounce can of soda contains an average of 8 teaspoons of sugar (plus artificial flavor, color and often caffeine), it is easy to understand why it should not be a regular part of anyone's diet.

> ## Eliminate soft drinks and fruit-flavored drinks from your diet.

In addition to "empty," nonnutritive calories that most of us don't need, soft drinks fill us up so that we are less hungry for nutritious food. For some reason, many of us regard calories from beverages differently than food calories. Instead of drinking soda in place of other foods, we drink it in addition to other foods, adding extra calories and increasing our chance of gaining weight.

Fruit-flavored juices, drinks and "punches" are basically sugar water – highly sweetened, flavored and colored drinks that sometimes contain a small amount of fruit juice and added vitamins. Play close attention to ingredient labels when you are buying juice to be sure you are getting 100% fruit juice and not a fruit drink.

Like soda, fruit drinks are a prime source of "empty" calories. They promote tooth decay and weight gain while filling us up so we are not hungry for healthy foods. There is strong evidence that increased consumption of soft drinks and sugared juice drinks contributes to weight gain and increased incidence of Type 2 diabetes, a virtual epidemic in our communities today.[45]

If you or your children are big consumers of soda and fruit drinks, try making them a once-a-week *Shabbat* treat, rather than an everyday beverage.

TEA – A REFRESHING ALTERNATIVE

"Boil water, infuse tea, and drink. That is all you need to know." (Sen no Rikyu, sixteenth-century Japanese tea master)

Among the Chinese, Japanese and the British, tea has long been the esteemed beverage of choice. After water, it is undoubtedly the most popular drink in the whole world. Some of our ancestors drank it black with a sugar cube between their teeth, while others enjoyed it steeped with fresh mint leaves. Most of us grew up thinking of it as a rather lackluster beverage produced from a tea bag. Yet, in recent years, tea has become a gourmet specialty drink – an endless variety of tea from around the world is now available to us.

Tea leaves contain flavanoids – antioxidant compounds that block the destructive process of oxidation in our cells. Other chemical substances in tea, such as caffeine, fluoride and phytoestrogens, may also be responsible for its posited role in increasing bone density, preventing tooth decay, increasing cognitive function and assisting in weight maintenance.

Research is still in its infancy, but whether tea proves to have health benefits or not, it is a delicious, refreshing and enjoyable low-calorie beverage.

A Tea Primer

All tea originates from leaves of the tea plant. The leaves are steamed, rolled and dried to produce *green tea*. Tea leaves that have been fermented first and then dried become *black tea*, whereas partially fermented tea leaves are known as *oolong tea*.

There are many varieties and blends of green, black and oolong teas, and they can be purchased loose or in tea bags. Be sure to check for kosher certification on any tea containing added flavorings. *Herbal tea* is really not tea at all, but the leaves, flowers or roots of various plants. Although soothing and sometimes therapeutic, herbal teas do not contain the same beneficial flavanoid compounds found in real tea.

Brew your tea for about three minutes to release its valuable flavanoids. The highest concentrations of flavanoids are found in brewed hot tea, as opposed to iced and instant preparations.[46] Stay away from presweetened tea mixes, which offer little more than a high dose of sugar. Decaffeinated tea contains 10% to 20% fewer flavanoids than regular tea. If caffeine is problematic for you, stick with green tea, which usually contains less caffeine than black. Research has shown that adding milk to tea does not interfere with flavanoid absorption.[47]

If fresh, high-quality tea is not available in your community, I suggest exploring the wide variety of tea from around the world that can be ordered from kosher-certified companies like Rishi Tea (www.rishi-tea.com) and Stash Tea (www.stashtea.com).

COFFEE – NOT NECESSARILY BAD AFTER ALL

If you enjoy coffee, you may feel better knowing that drinking a moderate amount of coffee may not be detrimental to your health.

Several studies suggest that coffee may play a role in preventing a number of diseases including Type 2 diabetes, liver disease and Parkinson's disease.[48]

Coffee consumption does not seem to raise the risk of developing cardiovascular disease or cancer. It can help improve short-term memory, decrease fatigue and improve mental functioning and reaction time.

We are all familiar with coffee's best-known ingredient, caffeine. However, coffee contains other chemical compounds as well. Like tea, fruits and vegetables, coffee is a rich source of antioxidants. One newly identified group of substances in coffee, called quinides, appears to improve the ability of the liver to metabolize glucose, which can stabilize blood sugar. This may explain the mechanism at work in reducing the risk of diabetes. Scientists are also exploring potential anti-cancer compounds found in coffee.

Three or four cups of coffee a day may be perfectly safe for your health.

When to Avoid Caffeine

Caffeine is a stimulant that can raise blood pressure, induce heart arrhythmias, anxiety and headaches, and exacerbate gastrointestinal and urinary disorders. Premenstrual syndrome (PMS) may be adversely influenced by caffeine. Additionally, caffeine may interfere with sleep and relaxation in some people, but not in others.

Children, teens and the elderly may be especially vulnerable to the adverse effects of caffeine. According to current recommendations, pregnant and breastfeeding women should limit their intake of caffeine to 300 milligrams or less per day.

Although research has shown that moderate caffeine intake does not significantly affect calcium absorption, adding several tablespoons of milk to your coffee should compensate for any potential calcium loss.

Read labels carefully and avoid coffee beverages that contain added sugar and fat. Flavored coffee drinks (mixes and those at coffee shops) may be very high in calories. Skip the flavored syrup and whipped cream and opt for coffee with skim or low-fat milk, a small amount of sweetener, and a dash of cinnamon or cocoa if you like.

Avoid high-fat, high-calorie coffee drinks.

Caffeine Confusion

Dietitians and physicians often advise people to eat or drink "in moderation." What this means in practical terms is often left to individual interpretation. In the case of caffeine, a moderate intake is considered to be about 300 milligrams a day or approximately three to four cups of coffee.

One problem is that the caffeine content of coffee and tea varies widely. Here are the results from 400 one-cup samples of coffee and tea prepared by consumers in the United Kingdom and analyzed for caffeine:[49]

Ground coffee: 15–254mg

Instant coffee: 21–120mg

Black tea: 1–90mg

Green tea, depending on the type and brewing method, has been found to contain anywhere from 8 to 100mg of caffeine per cup.

Chocolate contains a small, rather insignificant amount of caffeine.

Twelve ounces of cola may contain between 0 and 60mg of caffeine.

Read product labels carefully, as extra caffeine is added to some cola and non-cola soft drinks, making them especially inappropriate for children.

Caffeine Abuse

"Energy drinks" are beverages that may contain vitamins, minerals, herbs, amino acids, sugar and a large amount of caffeine. (Sports drinks, on the other hand, are often used by athletes and contain electrolytes such as sodium, potassium and chloride. These are intended to replenish nutrients that may be lost with intense physical exertion.)

The popularity of "energy drinks" as well as diet pills containing caffeine has become problematic in recent years, especially among young people who may be ingesting dangerous amounts of caffeine. Caffeine abuse can cause insomnia, tremors, nausea and vomiting, and can lead to serious illness.

ALCOHOL

"And wine…gladdens the heart of man." (*Tehillim* 104:15)
"Go eat your bread with joy and drink your wine with a glad heart, for *Hashem* has already approved your deeds." (*Kohelet* 9:7)

Our tradition encourages a moderate consumption of alcohol on joyous occasions. *Shabbat*, holidays, weddings and festive meals usually include at least a bottle of wine on our tables. With the increasing availability and wide variety of high-quality kosher wine, it may be more commonplace to serve wine with weekday meals as well.

While moderate drinking offers benefits to the heart and circulatory system and seems to play a protective role against Type 2 diabetes[50] and gallstones,[51] heavy drinking is a major cause of death throughout the world. Alcohol can disrupt sleep and interact dangerously with a variety of medications. Heavy drinking can damage the heart, liver, pancreas and brain. It can harm a fetus and contribute to violent behavior. Its negative effect on judgment and coordination is implicated in close to half of all traffic accidents.[52]

Women in the Nurses' Health Study who drank two or more drinks a day had a slightly increased chance of developing breast cancer compared with women who did not drink.[53] But this increased risk seems to be offset by an adequate daily intake of the B vitamin folic acid.[54] Results from the same study suggest that older women who drink up to one alcoholic drink a day have less mental decline than women who abstain from alcohol.[55]

Given that heart disease, and not breast cancer, is the number one killer of women, the choice, at least for women, to drink or not to drink a glass of wine with dinner needs further consideration.

Alcohol and Heart Health

Compared with nondrinkers, men and women who consume one to two alcoholic beverages a day have a lower risk of coronary heart disease and stroke, and their overall mortality rate is lower as well. This applies to people who do not have heart disease as well as to those who do or are at risk for heart disease.[56] This may partially be explained by the fact that moderate amounts of alcohol raise HDL ("good") cholesterol.[57] Alcohol affects blood clotting as well, possibly preventing the formation of clots that can block arteries. A small study of women with heart disease who drank at least half a glass of wine a day showed an increase in their heart rate variability, a marker of the interval between heartbeats that has been associated with heart health.[58] Researchers are working on additional theories to explain the alcohol-heart health connection.

To Drink or Not to Drink: Weighing the Benefits and Risks

In general, the risks of drinking moderate amounts of alcohol exceed the benefits until middle age. Women who are pregnant or trying to conceive and children and teenagers should avoid alcohol altogether. Young men, who are more likely to suffer from alcohol-related accidents and less likely to be worried about heart disease, might do well to limit their intake. For men and women over the age of 50 or 60, moderate alcohol intake may offer some protection against heart disease. But if you are a woman who is at risk for breast cancer, if you have a history (or family history) of alcoholism, take medications that interact with alcohol or suffer from a medical condition that precludes alcohol consumption, these factors outweigh the possible benefits to your heart.

Since alcoholic beverages mainly supply calories with few essential nutrients, there is probably no reason to begin drinking, especially if you are overweight. And if you are in good physical condition, maintain a healthy weight, exercise, eat properly and have no family history of heart disease, it is probably not necessary to add alcohol to your diet for heart health. If you already drink, or plan to begin, women should limit their intake to one drink a day and men to no more than two drinks a day.[59] Be sure to include at least 600 micrograms of folic acid in your diet. Because alcohol affects everyone differently, consult with your health professional for personal advice on the benefits and risks associated with drinking alcohol.

Moderate drinking is defined as no more than one drink a day for women and no more than two drinks a day for men.

How much is a serving?		
Beverage	Serving Size	Calories
Beer, regular	12 ounces	144
Wine, white	12 ounces	100
Wine, red	15 ounces	105
Wine, sweet dessert	3 ounces	141
Distilled spirits, 80 proof	1.5 ounces	96

MILK AND DAIRY PRODUCTS

"But it shall be that from the abundant production of milk he will eat cream…and honey." (*Yeshayahu* 7:22)

I grew up drinking milk with cereal for breakfast, with a sandwich for lunch, and with dairy dinners several times a week. It was understood that children drank milk as a beverage – and in those days, milk was delivered in bottles to your door and came in one full-fat variety. With time, we learned that saturated fat was harmful to heart health and low-fat and fat-free dairy products were introduced. I still remember mixing various amounts of full, low-fat and nonfat milk until I was able to drink "straight" nonfat milk. Now, of course, we can choose from a full range of flavorful reduced and nonfat kosher dairy products.

But is milk really good for you, as the advertisements proclaim? Can it help prevent osteoporosis? What about its effect on heart health and cancer? And what if you cannot comfortably digest milk?

Calcium and Bone Health

"Then *Hashem* will guide you always, sate your soul in times of drought and strengthen your bones." (*Yeshayahu* 58:11)

Most of us are familiar with the role of calcium in building and maintaining strong bones and teeth. In fact, 99% of the calcium in our bodies is stored in our bones and teeth. The remaining 1% is found in blood and tissues where it is essential for proper blood clotting, cell metabolism, muscle contraction and nerve impulse transmission.

The calcium needed by the body is obtained in two ways. One is from eating foods containing calcium. However, when blood levels of calcium drop too low, the body obtains calcium in another way – by mobilizing it from our bones. Normally, the "borrowed" calcium is replaced later on, but it is not a simple matter of eating more calcium to make up for what was lost.

Osteoporosis

Bones are continually being broken down and built up as calcium is removed from them and then added back in a process called remodeling. Provided there is sufficient calcium intake and adequate physical activity, bone production exceeds destruction in the first two to three decades of life. After the age of 30, the destruction of bone usually exceeds its production. With age, bones become less dense due to an increased rate of bone loss. In the first three to five years after menopause, women have an increased loss of bone as estrogen production decreases. Men lose bone later in life as their testosterone levels drop.

When bone destruction is greater than bone production, bones become weak and less dense, leading to osteoporosis (literally, porous bones). It is estimated that 10 million Americans have osteoporosis, and another 34 million have low bone mass (osteopenia), placing them at risk for osteoporosis.[60] Bone fractures resulting from osteoporosis affect 1.5 million people a year, with over 300,000 hospitalizations due to hip fractures alone.[61]

Heredity, small physique and physical inactivity all play a role in bone loss, as do inadequate calcium intake, excessive alcohol consumption and cigarette smoking. Women who are constantly dieting to stay slim may not be getting adequate nutrition and are at risk for osteoporosis.

The incidence of osteoporosis can be reduced by attaining peak bone mass during the first thirty years of life and limiting bone loss after that time.[62]

Slim, inactive women are at greater risk for developing osteoporosis.

Building Strong Bones during Childhood

Because 90% of bone mass is established as teenagers finish their growth spurt (at around the age of 17), it is vital that adequate bone development occur by that time. The importance of bone development in children and teens is essential for healthy bones later in life. By eating and drinking foods rich in calcium and by being physically active, proper bone development is most likely to be achieved early in life. A high intake of fruits and vegetables during childhood and adolescence may also increase bone density, as reported in a study of teenage girls.[63]

Most children and teenagers do not get enough calcium and exercise to protect against osteoporosis later in life.

Unfortunately, most children and teenagers do not get enough calcium to achieve the maximum bone density necessary to protect against osteoporosis. Also, physical activity among children has decreased considerably, putting them at added risk for osteoporosis later in life. A study of 50 Orthodox teenaged boys and girls from Brooklyn found significantly low bone mineral density and low calcium intake.[64] Without compromising our strong tradition of learning, we need to encourage regular exercise and sufficient calcium intake to ensure good bone health in our youth.

Adequate calcium intake can be achieved by adding low-fat dairy foods, milk, calcium-fortified foods and other foods rich in calcium to children's diets. And again, it cannot be overemphasized; children should get plenty of physical activity, including weight-bearing exercise.

Serve milk and high-calcium foods to your children for breakfast, with dairy meals and as snacks.

How Can I Limit Bone Loss?

As adults, we face the challenge of bone loss due to age, genetics, hormonal changes and physical inactivity. Although we have no control over most of these factors, there are several lifestyle changes that we can make to preserve the health of our bones.

Exercise

Exercise puts stress on our bones and causes them to retain and possibly gain strength. Weight-bearing exercise includes dancing, jogging, stair-climbing, weightlifting, aerobics and, most basic of all, walking. These types of exercise also increase the strength of our muscles and improve balance, helping us to avoid falls that may produce fractures.

Calcium

Adequate calcium intake is essential for reducing the risk of osteoporosis. If getting enough calcium from food is difficult, consider taking a supplement containing calcium and vitamin D. Look for a supplement with added magnesium if calcium alone causes constipation. For optimal absorption, spread your calcium intake throughout the day. If you take supplements, take no more than 500 to 600 milligrams of calcium at one time, with food.

Table 11: Recommended Daily Calcium Intake

Age (years)	Calcium (mg/day)	Dairy Servings*
1–3	500	3 servings**
4–8	800	3 servings
9–18	1,300	4 servings
19–50	1,000	3 servings
51 +	1,200	4 servings

Dietary Reference Intakes for Calcium. The National Academy of Sciences (NAS) 1997

* The recommended dairy servings are based on the NAS calcium recommendations. A serving size of dairy equals 1 cup (8 ounces) of milk, 1 cup of yogurt and 1 to 1.5 ounces of cheese.

** Serving sizes for children ages 1 to 3 are two-thirds the adult size. For example, a serving of milk for kids ages 1 to 3 is 6 ounces, rather than the 8-ounce size for older kids, teens and adults.

Vitamin D

The body uses vitamin D to better absorb calcium. Vitamin D is found in some foods as well as in fortified milk and vitamin supplements. You may have heard vitamin D referred to as the "sunshine" vitamin, since our skin produces it when exposed to sunlight. If you live in northern areas (above 40 degrees latitude), the winter sun will not be strong enough to promote the formation of vitamin D. Wearing sunscreen also prevents the formation of vitamin D, but do not forego this important protection against skin cancer. Recent studies point to the long-term benefits of vitamin D on bone health rather than its ability to prevent fractures later in life. The recommended intake for adults is a minimum of 1,000 IU (international units) daily. The US government has set the safe upper limit for vitamin D as 2,000 IU a day.

Vitamin A

An excess intake of preformed vitamin A (also known as retinol, and found in animal foods and vitamin supplements) seems to play a negative role in bone remodeling – the ongoing building up and breaking down of bones. Avoid multivitamin supplements containing preformed vitamin A. Beta-carotene, another form of vitamin A found in fruits and vegetables, does not have the same negative effect on bones.

In Table 11 RDAs for vitamin A are listed as micrograms (mcg) of Retinol Activity Equivalents (RAE) to account for the different biological activities of retinol and provitamin A carotenoids [1]. Table 11 also lists RDAs for vitamin A in international units (IU), which are used on food and supplement labels (1 RAE = 3.3 IU).

Table 12: Recommended Dietary Allowances (RDAs) for Vitamin A

Age (years)	Children (mcg RAE)	Males (mcg RAE)	Females (mcg RAE)	Pregnancy (mcg RAE)	Lactation (mcg RAE)
1–3	300 (1,000 IU)				
4–8	400 (1,320 IU)				
9–13	600 (2,000 IU)				
14–18		900 (3,000 IU)	700 (2,310 IU)	750 (2,500 IU)	1,200 (4,000 IU)

NIH Office of Dietary Supplements

Vitamin K
Research studies, including the Nurses' Health Study, suggest that vitamin K, together with calcium, plays an important role in bone health.[65] Women whose intake of vitamin K was below the recommended daily intake had low bone density, though the same relationship was not seen in men.[66] Green, leafy vegetables such as spinach, broccoli, Brussels sprouts, kale, Swiss chard and dark green lettuce are good sources of vitamin K. One or two servings a day should be adequate for good bone health.

Caffeine
If you drink four or more cups of coffee (or other caffeinated drinks) a day, you may be at increased risk for bone fractures, since caffeine tends to promote urinary calcium excretion.

Alcohol and Smoking
Drinking more than one alcoholic beverage a day puts you at a higher risk for osteoporosis, and smoking increases the rate of bone loss.

Protein
Excess dietary protein can interfere with calcium absorption and promote calcium loss from bones.[67] Because we don't really know how much protein intake is too much, a moderate, rather than high, protein intake is advisable.

Are Dairy Products for Everyone?
While dairy products provide an excellent, convenient and relatively inexpensive source of calcium, they may not be the best choice for everyone.

Lactose Intolerance
Lactose intolerance is the inability to digest lactose, the main sugar component of milk. It results when the body produces an insufficient amount of the enzyme lactase, which breaks down lactose before it is absorbed into the bloodstream. Without enough lactase, symptoms that include bloating, gas, cramps and diarrhea may occur when dairy products are ingested. Many people develop lactose intolerance over time and may not experience symptoms until they are adults. People with lactose intolerance differ in the amount and type of dairy products they can comfortably eat. In many cases, dairy products such as yogurt and cheese are well tolerated. When eaten together with other foods, or in small quantities, dairy foods may not cause symptoms at all.

Lactase tablets are available without prescription to help in the digestion of lactose. Milk treated with lactase is fairly common as well. In Israel, strains of bacteria known as probiotics are added to some yogurt and dairy beverages and may ease symptoms of lactose intolerance in some people.[68] If you are among those who have tried and still find it difficult to digest dairy products, you should consider getting calcium from nondairy sources and supplements.

Table 13: What's in an 8-Ounce Cup of Milk?

	Calcium	Calories	Fat (grams)	Saturated fat (grams)
Whole (3.25% fat)	276	150	8	4.5
Low-fat (2% fat)	285	120	5	3
Low-fat (1% fat)	290	102	2.4	1.5
Nonfat, skim, fat-free	306	83	0	0.3

USDA National Nutrient Database for Standard
Reference, Release 17 (2004)

Saturated Fat

A high intake of saturated fat, a component of many dairy products, is a risk factor for heart disease. Although many dairy products are available in low-fat versions, many of us crave the full-fat products such as premium ice cream, cheese and butter. If full-fat dairy products are your main source of calcium, switch to low-fat or nonfat versions or look for other healthier sources of calcium.

Choose nonfat or low-fat dairy products.

Table 14: Good Dairy Sources of Calcium

Food	Calcium (mg)
Plain nonfat yogurt, ½ cup	225
Plain low-fat yogurt, ½ cup	208
Ricotta cheese, low-fat, ½ cup	335

Mozzarella cheese, part skim, 1 ounce	222
Swiss cheese, full-fat, 1 ounce	224
Cottage cheese, 2% fat, ½ cup	78

Table 15: Nondairy Sources of Calcium

Food	Calcium (mg)
Soymilk, calcium fortified, 1 cup	368
Sardines, 3 ounces	325
Tofu, firm, prepared with nigari, ½ cup	253
Salmon, red canned, with bones, 3 ounces	203
Salmon, pink canned, with bones, 3 ounces	181
Orange juice, fortified with calcium, ½ cup (per Minute Maid brand information)	175
Almonds, ¼ cup	175
Techinah, 1 tablespoon	154
Kale, cooked, ½ cup	90
Broccoli, cooked, 1 cup	62
Figs, 4 dried	56

USDA National Nutrient Database for Standard Reference, Release 17 (2004)

The Bottom Line

Choose water when you are thirsty.

Avoid soft drinks and sugar-sweetened beverages.

Eat whole fruits instead of fruit juice.

Consult your physician on the risks and benefits of drinking alcohol.

Be sure that you and your children get adequate calcium and vitamins D and K.

Choose nonfat or low-fat dairy products.

Include weight-bearing exercise in your daily routine.

— CHAPTER 9 ——————————————

Eat Your Fruits
and Vegetables

"Any city that does not have vegetables [available] in it, a Torah scholar may not reside in it." (Eruvin 55b)

Rashi explains this Gemara as follows: *"Vegetables provide a nutritious and inexpensive addition to a diet, allowing a scholar to subsist on a smaller income and devote more time to Torah study."*

Your mother was right when she told you to eat your vegetables. No other food group provides more health-promoting nutrients (with the fewest calories) than fruits and vegetables. They are loaded with vitamins and minerals, high in valuable fiber and packed with phytochemicals – plant substances shown to prevent and even reverse an array of diseases. A diet high in fruits and vegetables can lower blood pressure and reduce the risk of heart disease, cancer and stroke. Furthermore, antioxidants in produce may influence age-related cognitive function, cataracts and macular degeneration. And, eating lots of fruits and vegetables helps us to feel full, so we are less likely to overeat and gain weight.

Depending on how many calories you need, you should eat between five and nine servings of vegetables and fruits each day for optimum health.

For optimum health eat five to nine servings of vegetables and fruits each day.

Quick and easy ways to add more vegetables to your diet:
- Cut up leftover cooked or raw vegetables and add them to green salads.
- Top baked potatoes with salsa or marinara sauce rather than sour cream.
- Add cooked eggplant, zucchini, mushrooms, peppers and onions to pasta sauce.
- Enjoy carrot or tomato juice as a snack instead of a soft drink.
- Add frozen peas, carrots or corn to soups and salads.
- Order or make your own pizza with half the cheese and twice the vegetables.
- Add diced or shredded vegetables to prepared deli salads.

How much is a serving?
½ cup cut-up cooked or raw vegetable
1 cup raw leafy vegetable
½ cup vegetable or fruit juice
½ cup cut-up fresh, frozen or canned fruit
1 medium whole fruit
¼ cup dried fruit

CARDIOVASCULAR HEALTH

In the large Harvard Nurses' and Health Professionals studies, men and women who ate the most fruits and vegetables had the lowest chance of developing cardiovascular disease. In fact, even those who increased their intake of produce by just one serving significantly lowered their risk of heart disease.[69]

The DASH (Dietary Approaches to Stop Hypertension) study explored the effects of a low-fat diet rich in vegetables, fruits and low-fat dairy products, and found a significant reduction in blood pressure among those who followed the diet.[70]

Eating fruits and vegetables can protect against heart disease.

ANTIOXIDANTS

Fruits and vegetables, like most foods, are complex substances containing an array of nutrients, including vitamins, minerals, fiber and various phytochemicals. Many phytochemicals in fruits and vegetables act as antioxidants – substances that protect cells from damage caused by unstable molecules known as free radicals. Damage by free radicals can sometimes progress to the point that cells become cancerous. Although data from human studies have been inconsistent, considerable laboratory evidence indicates that antioxidants may slow or prevent this cell damage. Ongoing studies are examining the role of phytochemicals in cancer development and prevention. A likely theory is that various phytochemicals in plant foods work together synergistically to inhibit oxidative damage to cells.[71]

Even though we do not have clear-cut answers yet, evidence strongly indicates that eating a wide variety of fruits and vegetables is a good preventative health strategy. We also know that eating real fruits and vegetables, rather than taking antioxidant supplements, is the best way to protect and maintain good health.

Get the benefits of antioxidants from fruits and vegetables rather than from supplements.

EATING FOR GOOD VISION

Eating plenty of fruits and vegetables may help prevent common, age-related eye diseases such as cataracts and macular degeneration. Preliminary research suggests that the antioxidants lutein and zeaxanthin, found in dark green leafy vegetables, may play a role in protecting the eyes from age and environmental damage.[72] Other lutein-rich fruits and vegetables include mangoes, corn, sweet potatoes, carrots, winter squash, tomatoes, oranges and honeydew melon.

Eat a leafy green salad with at least one meal each day.

Terminology

Phytochemical or phytonutrient: A chemical produced by plants.

Antioxidant: A chemical compound that protects cells from the harmful effects of oxidation.

Flavanoids: Water-soluble pigments – found in plant foods – that may act as antioxidants; also known as *bioflavanoids*.

Carotenoids: Fat-soluble red and yellow pigments found in plant and animal foods.

Phytosterols: Plant compounds similar in structure to cholesterol that can block the absorption of cholesterol in the body; they are added to some margarines and oils.

Probiotic: A nonnutritive living micro-organism that may assist in digestion and immune function; some common probiotics are *Lactobacilus* and *Bifidobacterium*; they may be added to dairy products or produced as supplements.

Prebiotic: An indigestible food substance that enhances the growth of beneficial bacteria in the digestive tract.

WHAT HAPPENED TO VEGETABLES?

My mother made sure to include a fresh salad and a cooked vegetable with dinner and fruit for dessert. My lunchbox contained fresh fruit, lettuce on my sandwich and carrots and celery sticks. The abundance of good quality produce and a slim budget translated into healthy at-home meals. My own children grew up with a vegetable garden in the yard, fruit picking at local farms and an array of unusual produce supplied by community-supported agriculture.

Unfortunately, vegetable and fruit consumption has now plummeted in the US. With many women working outside of the home and shuffling busy schedules, the convenience of processed and take-out food often seems like the easiest, if not the only, solution to meals and snacks. Vegetables don't seem to fall into the "quick and easy" category, as they usually require some degree of preparation. Just the thought of washing, peeling, cutting and cooking may seem overwhelming to many of us. In the car or at the office, it's easier to dig into a candy bar or bag of cookies than to wash or slice a piece of fruit for a snack. Is it surprising that French fries are the most popular vegetable in the US? How is it possible to eat the recommended five to nine servings of a variety of vegetables and fruit each day?

Making It Easier
Reduce vegetable preparation time by purchasing prepackaged salad ingredients. Many brands are certified kosher. Although more expensive than regular produce, they are still less expensive than most other packaged convenience foods, and certainly healthier. Many fruits and vegetables are already "ready-to-eat," requiring just a wash or a peel. Among the easiest fruits are apples, pears, bananas, avocadoes, grapes, cherries and berries. Vegetables that require minimum preparation are cherry tomatoes, celery, cucumbers and carrots.

> ## Choose convenient prepackaged and "ready-to-eat" fruits and vegetables.

Frozen vegetables and fruit are another convenient way to save time while ensuring good nutrition. Keep a bag of frozen peas, corn and spinach in the freezer and you will have vegetable "insurance" when meal preparation time is limited. Frozen berries and cut fruit work well for last-minute desserts. When summer berries are abundant, it's easy to freeze them yourself: place them in a single layer on a cookie sheet; when they are completely frozen, store them in a freezer bag for use during the year.

Enjoy fresh, frozen or dried fruit for dessert.

You may find it easier to wash and prepare your vegetables all at once before you start cooking. I find that, especially before *Shabbat*, it is easier to wash, check, cut and refrigerate everything that I will need for cooking, either the day before or the morning before I plan to cook.

To Peel or Not to Peel
Vegetable peels are there to protect the inner, more nutritious portion of the food. Other than fiber, they do not offer special or extra nutritional value. If you buy nonorganic produce, take care to remove the peel from vegetables like carrots, cucumbers and potatoes, which may contain pesticide residues.

Sprout Safety
Sprouted seeds and beans have been a popular "health" food for years. Although they add a nice texture to salads and provide some vitamin C, folate and fiber, they can contain dangerous toxins and bacteria. Sprouts have been the cause of numerous outbreaks of food-borne illness. The FDA has been working on ways to ensure the safety of sprouts, but a sure solution has not yet been found. If you are a healthy adult and enjoy eating sprouts, buy only fresh, refrigerated sprouts. Rinse them thoroughly before using. Since cooking destroys toxins, it is advisable to eat only cooked sprouts and avoid alfalfa sprouts altogether.

Mixing Your Colors
When you eat a wide variety of vegetables and fruits, you get a good assortment of nutrients – vitamins, minerals, fiber and phytochemicals that no one type of food contains. Dark green veg-

etables contain lutein and zeaxanthin. Orange and red fruits and vegetables are high in beta-carotene, and red ones contain lycopene. Anthocyanins are phytochemicals found in blue and purple fruits and vegetables, while allicin is present in white-colored vegetables. Use color as your guide – the more varied the colors on your plate, the better off you will be.

Table 16: The Color Palette

Color: Green	
Nutrients	Vitamin K, potassium, folate, lutein, zeaxanthin
Foods	Spinach, Swiss chard, kale, broccoli, cabbage, green lettuce, Brussels sprouts, cauliflower, kiwi, honeydew melon
Color: Orange and Yellow	
Nutrients	Vitamin C, potassium, beta carotene, folate, lutein
Foods	Carrots, sweet potatoes, winter squash, cantaloupe, mangoes, apricots, peaches, oranges, pineapple, bananas
Color: Red	
Nutrients	Vitamin C, lycopene
Foods	Tomatoes, watermelon, pink grapefruit, strawberries, red pepper
Color: Blue and Purple	
Nutrients	Vitamin C, anthocyanins
Foods	Blueberries, purple grapes, beets, red cabbage, plums, blackberries

Color: White	
Nutrients	Allicin, polyphenols
Foods	Garlic, onion, leeks, pears, green grapes

Eat a colorful diet for optimal health.

Do You Need a Multivitamin Supplement?
While vitamin and mineral supplements are not a substitute for a balanced, nutritious diet, a daily multivitamin is good nutritional "insurance" – a "back-up" source of nutrients that may be missing or deficient in your diet. There are many kosher brands to choose from. Look for a basic, inexpensive one that meets USP standards and contains no more than 100% of the Daily Value (%DV) for vitamins and minerals.

Getting Your Kids to Eat Vegetables
It's hard to take children to the grocery store and avoid the hundreds of food products packaged especially to appeal to them. Food marketing to children is big business. From billboards to television, movies and books, product placement geared especially for children is everywhere. What can parents do to guide their children away from the endless aisles of processed foods and towards the colorful array of vegetables in the produce department? And just how can you get your children to eat the vegetables you buy? Here are a few suggestions:

Start with produce: When you are shopping with your children, start off in the produce department. Encourage children to explore unusual and unfamiliar fruits and vegetables, and choose something new to try at home. Talk with them about what is in season now and what might be growing on local farms. Keep in mind that most grocery stores are arranged with the healthiest products around the perimeter – produce, dairy, meat, fish and bread. Limit your time in the center aisles, where most of the highly processed foods are found. This is easier to do if you prepare a shopping list at home and discipline yourself to follow it at the store.

Family meals: Eat together as a family as often as possible. Family meals have been shown to improve children's behavior as well as their eating habits. When children see their parents eating vegetables, they are more likely to try them as well. Don't force your children to eat, and don't discuss eating at the table. Just put the food on the table and maintain a casual, relaxed mood.

Aesthetics: Use your imagination to present food in an attractive, appealing manner. A colorful platter of vegetables, for example, may catch the eye and attention of your child more than a bowl of iceberg lettuce. Turn broccoli and asparagus into finger food "trees" and arrange fruit on a plate to look like a clown or face. Most children enjoy dipping their food. Try low-fat mayonnaise mixed with ketchup or ready-made guacamole as a quick dip for carrot and celery sticks.

Sleight of hand: Children who might not eat whole vegetables and fruit may eat them when slightly disguised. While a carrot or sweet potato may not appeal to your youngster, a soup or sauce may be acceptable. Leftover cooked vegetables can easily be made into a soup or sauce by pureeing them with milk or broth. Sneak grated vegetables into meat or turkey loaf, pasta sauce and muffins. Try blending fruit with milk into flavorful smoothies.

Start a garden: You don't need a large yard to start a simple vegetable garden with your children. Even without a yard you can grow a variety of vegetables in pots on your patio or porch. Young children are fascinated as seeds become plants bearing edible food. With supervision, let them plant, water, weed, pick and eat from the garden. Somehow a cucumber or a tomato tastes better to children when they have had a part in growing it. My son Elan had his first taste of blackberries when he crawled on his own to the wild bushes growing in our yard. I wonder if he would have enjoyed them as much had he not discovered them himself.

Connect to the land: Talk to your children about the source and production of fruits and vegetables. Take them to a local farm, if possible, where they can see for themselves where their food comes from. Community-supported agriculture and farmer's markets are other ways for children to experience hands-on contact with the food they eat.

Get cooking: My own connection with food began in the kitchen, helping to mix and stir, setting the table and eventually cooking family meals. When I taught preschool, some of the children's favorite activities involved preparing their own snacks and baking challah for *Shabbat*. Children enjoy active involvement with food preparation. Organizing ingredients, mixing, arranging food on a plate and licking the bowl can all serve to encourage children to enjoy new and different foods.

Involve children in growing and preparing fruits and vegetables.

Feeding Toddlers Safely
Young children who are just starting to eat "table food" are not always able to chew their food properly. To avoid choking, cut or finely chop their food into small, easily managed pieces.

Avoid the following foods: popcorn, nuts, raisins, grapes, hot dogs (meat or vegetarian) and large pieces of vegetables.

Vegetables, Bugs and *Kashrut*

"Every teeming creature that teems upon the ground – it is an abomination, it shall not be eaten." (*Vayikra* 11:41)
"For I am *Hashem* your God – you are to sanctify yourselves and you shall become holy, for I am holy; and you shall not contaminate yourselves through any teeming thing that creeps on the earth." (*Vayikra* 11:44)

"Insects and worms that we are unable to see with the naked eye (even though we might be able to see them using a micro-

scope or magnifying glass) are not subject to any prohibition."
(Rav Ovadia Yosef, *Yechaveh Da'at* 6:47)

God blessed us with an abundance of fruits and vegetables, which
are a particularly important part of a healthy diet. Produce is intrin-
sically kosher and *parve*, making it especially easy to incorporate
into every meal of the day. The potential *kashrut* problem arises
when various insects and worms find their way onto our fruits and
vegetables. The Torah is clear in stating that insects, at least those
visible by the naked eye, are not kosher.

Insects that are visible to the naked eye are not kosher.

The Pesticide Problem
Crops throughout the world are treated with pesticides to control
insect infestation and ensure a plentiful yield. We now know that
pesticides used to kill bugs can be harmful to people as well. The
USDA has limited the use of some of the most potent chemicals on
produce, and is encouraging the use of alternative methods of pest
control. In order to minimize the harmful effects of pesticides, a
whole industry of organically grown produce has been developed.
I encourage eating organic and locally raised produce whenever
possible. For the kosher consumer, this poses a potential problem:
healthier, pesticide-free fruits and vegetables are more likely to be
infested with insects.

Pesticides or Bugs – What a Choice!
I believe that it is possible to eat a wide variety of health-promoting
vegetables and fruits while strictly observing the laws of *kashrut*
regarding insects.

Previous generations of pious and observant Jews ate their
fruits and vegetables straight from the garden or farm. They had

their share of insects and worms, without benefit of modern pest control. Most likely, they washed and checked for bugs without worrying excessively about those that were not visible to the eye in daylight.

Today, some of us have the luxury of rabbinically supervised crops that have been specially grown and checked for insects. This is a welcome convenience, but choices are often limited, the cost may be prohibitive and pre-checked produce is not widely available.

Washing produce carefully can remove most insects. It is also important for food safety – harmful pesticide residues and bacteria can also be removed with a good washing.

Here is a basic approach to washing and checking vegetables and berries for insects:

- Smooth-skinned fruits and vegetables, winter squash and melons that do not require soaking should be thoroughly washed and checked before cutting and eating to remove any insects, dirt and pesticide residue.
- Leafy and cluster vegetables such as dark green or red lettuce, Swiss chard, spinach, various cabbages, broccoli and cauliflower should be separated from their stem, rinsed and soaked in a large basin or sink of cold water. Add salt or vinegar to the water to loosen any insects and dirt that may be attached to the vegetables. Use a large amount of salt or vinegar – when you dip your finger into the solution and taste it, you should be able to detect a strong taste. (For example, a sink full of water may require up to a cup or more of vinegar or up to ½ cup or more of salt.) Swirl the vegetables around in the water and let them soak for a minute or two. Lift them from the water, wash each leaf and cluster separately and carefully inspect for insects in a well-lit area.*

---

* These instructions were recommended by Rav Yosef Weiss, Chief Kashrut Inspector, Machzikei Hada'at Belz, Jerusalem, September 15, 2005.

There are various *halachic* views concerning the inspection of produce for insects. Consult your rabbi for specific details.

The Bottom Line

Eat five to nine servings of vegetables and fruit every day.

Choose a variety of colorful fruits and vegetables.

Encourage your children to eat plenty of fruits and vegetables.

CHAPTER 10

A Dash of Salt

"Three things are bad in excess but fine in moderation: yeast, salt and refusal." (Brachot 34a)

Corned beef, pastrami, lox and pickles – some of our favorite deli foods, are loaded with salt. While salt (sodium chloride) is essential for the healthy functioning of our bodies, an excess intake can contribute to high blood pressure (hypertension) in people who are "salt sensitive." Stomach and colorectal cancers have also been associated with a high consumption of salt.[73] High blood pressure (hypertension) is a risk factor for coronary heart disease, stroke, congestive heart failure and kidney disease. It affects more than one of every three middle-aged and elderly Americans.

The DASH (Dietary Approaches to Stop Hypertension) studies examined the effect of diet on blood pressure. Its impressive results showed that hypertension could be reduced with a diet low in total fat, saturated fat, cholesterol and sodium, emphasizing low-fat dairy foods and fruits and vegetables rich in potassium.[74]

Weight loss, a diet high in potassium-rich fruits and vegetables and low in sodium can often lower blood pressure.

WHERE DOES ALL OF THIS SALT COME FROM?
Most of us would do fine getting about 1 gram (1,000 mg) of sodium a day. But our average daily intake can reach up to 5 grams, or nearly 4 teaspoons, of salt a day.

Salt occurs naturally in many of the foods we eat, including eggs, fish, dairy products, soft water and even vegetables. However, almost 80% of the salt we eat comes from processed foods[75] such as canned soups, sauces, vegetables and fish; salad dressings; frozen meals; and snack foods such as potato chips, crackers and pretzels. Powdered soup and broth mixes, instant noodle cups and packaged macaroni and cheese are high in sodium, as are smoked and cured fish and meats such as hot dogs, salami, corned beef, herring and lox. Even ready-to-eat cereals can contain high amounts of sodium. Check product labels carefully and avoid foods high in sodium. Choose healthier, low-sodium alternatives whenever possible.

Healthy young adults should consume no more than 2,300 mg of sodium, or about 1 teaspoon, of salt each day. Middle-aged, older adults and those with hypertension should restrict sodium intake to no more than 1,500 mg of sodium a day.[76]

Table 17: Salt in Processed Foods

Food	Sodium (mg)
Dill pickle, 1 large (4″)	1,731
Smoked salmon (lox), 3 ounces	1,700
Instant soup mix, 1 cup prepared	1,484
Corned beef brisket, 3 ounces	964
Pasta or spaghetti sauce, ½ cup	601
Beef hot dog, cooked	600
Macaroni and cheese, 1 cup	561
Cottage cheese, 2%, ½ cup	459

Food	Sodium (mg)
Canned red salmon, ½ can	457
Raisin bran cereal, 1 cup	362
Canned corn, ½ cup	351

USDA National Nutrient Database for Standard
Reference, Release 17 (2004)

Reduce the sodium in your diet by avoiding processed foods.

ADDING OUR OWN SALT

We get another 11% of our sodium when we add salt while cooking and at mealtimes.[77] Since many of us are so used to the flavor of salt, it can be difficult to cut back, so try doing it gradually.

Here are some suggestions:
- Reduce or eliminate the salt called for in most recipes. Except for yeast breads, where salt is essential for proper rising, you can reduce by half the salt in baked goods.
- Use spices, herbs, salt-free seasoning blends, lemon juice and vinegar as flavorings instead of salt.
- Look for sodium-reduced salad dressings, or make your own with olive oil, vinegar and spices.
- Use fresh or frozen vegetables instead of canned whenever possible.
- Look for pasta and marinara sauces that are low in sodium. Or combine a jar of bottled sauce with a can of salt-free tomato sauce and add herbs for extra flavor.
- Rinse canned foods, such as vegetables, beans, tuna and salmon, to remove some of the salt.

- Limit your use of condiments such as ketchup, mustard, barbeque and soy sauce.
- Keep the salt shaker off of the dining table. Offer fresh ground pepper, a salt-free seasoning mix or a squeeze of lemon as flavor enhancers.

Table 18: Read the Sodium Label

Phrase	What It Means per Serving
Sodium or salt free	Less than 5 mg of sodium
Very low sodium	35 mg or less of sodium
Low sodium	140 mg or less of sodium
Reduced or less sodium	At least 25% less sodium than the regular version
Light in sodium	50% less than the regular version
Unsalted or no added salt	No salt added to the product during processing

Sodium in Kosher Meat

Kosher meat and poultry, having been salted as part of the koshering process, are naturally high in sodium. If you eat a healthy diet that includes fresh (not smoked, cured or pickled) meat only occasionally, and if your blood pressure is normal, the sodium in kosher meat should not be a problem. Just be sure not to add additional salt or high sodium seasonings during cooking. Chicken soup, for instance, needs no added salt if a variety of fresh vegetables and herbs are added to the broth.

When hypertension is a problem, you may want to boil your meat and discard the cooking water, which contains most of the sodium. Broiling also eliminates much of the sodium in kosher meat.[78]

POTASSIUM

While too much dietary sodium can raise blood pressure, a high potassium intake works to lower it. A diet high in potassium can blunt the effect of salt on blood pressure, may reduce the risk of kidney stones and possibly decrease bone loss. For people taking diuretics or drinking a large quantity of coffee, extra potassium is especially important, as these cause potassium to be excreted in the urine. While bananas have long been recommended as a good source of potassium, many other fruits, vegetables, beans and nuts are also good sources. If your diet includes between five and nine servings of vegetables and fruits a day, as well as legumes and nuts, you will probably attain the recommended adult intake of 4,700 milligrams of potassium a day quite easily.

If you suffer from diabetes or kidney disease, consult your physician or dietitian before significantly increasing your intake of potassium.

Table 19: Potassium Content of Foods

Food	Potassium (mg)
Potato, 1 small, baked (2 × 5″)	610
Sweet potato, 1 medium, baked (2 × 5″)	542
Lima beans, ½ cup	477
Winter squash, ½ cup, cooked	448
Banana, 1 medium (7″)	422
Cantaloupe, 1 cup diced	417
Lentils, ½ cup cooked	365
Avocado, ½ cup slices	354

Food	Potassium (mg)
Prunes, 4 dried	244
Garbanzo beans, ½ cup cooked	238
Orange juice, ½ cup	236
Broccoli, ½ cup cooked	229
Figs, 4 dried	228
Almonds, 1 ounce (23 nuts)	206
Tofu, ½ cup	150
Walnuts, 1 ounce (14 halves)	125

USDA National Nutrient Database for Standard
Reference, Release 17 (2004)

The Bottom Line

Use a minimum amount of salt in cooking and at the table.

Avoid eating high-sodium processed foods.

Eat an abundance of fruits, vegetables, legumes and nuts.

Childhood Obesity

The prevalence of overweight and obese children and teenagers has doubled in the last two decades, leading to an increase in high blood pressure, high cholesterol and Type 2 diabetes, diseases previously occurring primarily in adults. Overweight adolescents have a 70% chance of becoming overweight or obese adults, with the percentage increasing when one or more of their parents is overweight.[79] In addition to health risks, overweight and obese children may experience poor self-esteem, depression and social isolation.

The roots of this critical problem begin at an early age, when eating and physical activity habits become established. In fact, a tendency towards obesity may even begin in infancy. One study suggests that breast-feeding may help reduce the likelihood of a child becoming obese by the age of three years old.[80] Another study looked at kindergarten children who participated in a school-based program that included nutrition education and daily physical activity. When compared with a control group, their body weight and overall fitness were significantly healthier.[81] It is never too early to start your child on the road to good health and nutrition.

Childhood obesity can create serious health problems.

A child's weight is determined by eating habits, exercise, genetics and lifestyle. Eating habits are influenced by parents, teachers, peers and advertisements for unhealthy food aimed specifically at children. They may also be affected by psychological factors such as anxiety or fear, hormonal imbalances or certain medications. We know that youngsters today are eating more food and more calories than youngsters did twenty years ago, with snacks and soft drinks contributing a significant amount of those extra calories.[82]

Like many adults, children have become more sedentary. Physical education programs in schools are nonexistent, infrequent or inadequate. Most children rely on buses and carpools rather than walking or bicycling to school or friends' homes.

WHAT CAN PARENTS DO?

A physician is the best person to determine whether your child's weight is healthy. A physician will consider age, growth patterns and medical or psychological conditions that could affect your child's height and weight. If he or she determines that your child is overweight or obese, you can help in many ways.

First of all, let your child know that he or she is loved and appreciated, regardless of his or her weight. Focus on your child's health and good qualities rather than on their weight. Reinforce positive eating behaviors with approval and praise, and avoid criticism and disapproval when trying to influence their eating habits. Try to alleviate as much stress as possible in your child's life. Like adults, children may use food as comfort when they hurt emotionally. Seek professional advice from a child psychologist or psychiatrist if your child seems unusually anxious or depressed.

> **Show love and acceptance, regardless of your child's weight.**

Children model their behavior on the adults around them. Be a good role model by choosing healthy foods and getting plenty of physical activity. Provide healthy meals and snacks and avoid bringing unhealthy foods into your house. When children see that their parents are making healthy choices, they are likely to do so as well.

Eating breakfast may be a significant factor in maintaining a healthy weight. A study of girls between the ages of 9 and 19 found that those who regularly ate breakfast had a lower body mass index (BMI) than girls who skipped breakfast. The researchers suggest that fiber in cereal and other healthy foods such as milk and orange juice could explain the difference. Eating breakfast may also be a reflection of healthier eating habits in general.[83]

Be a good role model for your children by eating healthy foods and exercising regularly.

Eat meals together as often as possible and strive for a calm and relaxed mood at the table. Eat slowly and don't rush through meals. Keep conversation away from food and focus on pleasant, nonconfrontational subjects. Do not coerce your child to try a particular food or bribe him or her into eating or abstaining from food. If you are serving dessert, make it as healthy as possible and serve it as part of the meal rather than a "reward" for eating or not eating something else.

When serving food to your children, give them small, manageable portions. A small but noteworthy study of preschoolers showed that children ate what they were served, regardless of portion size. They ate whatever amount was on their plate for dinner regardless of whether they had eaten a large or small breakfast or lunch. Furthermore, the study showed that children who ate snacks between meals did not eat any less at mealtime.[84] If we serve our children large quantities of food at meals and numerous snacks, they will likely eat it all and gain weight. As parents and caregivers, we need to take responsibility for the quantity as well as the quality of our children's food.

WHAT HAPPENS AT SCHOOL?
School-based nutrition and physical education programs have been successful in teaching healthy eating and exercise habits to children.

Unfortunately, many of our schools have either eliminated or reduced exercise programs, and nutrition education is rarely part of the curriculum. As parents, we can work with teachers and administrators on including such programs in our children's schools.

If your child's school serves lunch, check the menu and encourage the inclusion of healthy food choices. Vending machines in schools should provide healthy alternatives to candy bars, soft drinks and high-fat snacks. If your children bring lunch from home, give them healthy choices and let them help decide what to bring. Children can help make sandwiches and pack cut-up vegetables and fruit. You may want to write a weekly menu so that your children know what to expect in their lunchboxes.

Teachers as well as parents are powerful role models for children. They should be aware that their own eating and exercise habits will be noticed by their students. As with parents, teachers should strive to be good examples when it comes to good nutrition and physical fitness.

Suggestions for encouraging healthy eating:
- Encourage your child to eat when hungry and to eat slowly.
- Do not use food as a reward or punishment.
- Serve water to your children and limit sweetened drinks.
- Plan ahead with healthy snacks.
- Discourage eating while doing other activities, such as homework and reading.

The Bottom Line

Eat meals together as a family as often as possible.

Be a role model by eating healthy foods and exercising.

Encourage your child to be physically active.

Serve child-sized portions and limit snacking.

CHAPTER 12

Healthy Strategies
for Snacking

Snack foods or "nosh" can be part of a healthy eating plan. The key to healthy snacking is to plan ahead so you will have a variety of satisfying choices when you feel hungry. Fresh and dried fruit, nuts and carrot sticks are always good snack choices, but what about the times when you feel like cookies or potato chips?

Healthy snack foods are available, but you must do some searching for the best choices. Look for snack foods that contain healthy ingredients such as grains, seeds and nuts, and stay away from products high in sugar, fat and salt.

Snack on nuts, seeds and fruit
rather than processed foods.

Baked and low-fat potato or corn chips are a healthier choice than regular fried chips. Whole-wheat pretzels contain more fiber than those made from white flour. Look for pretzels that are low in sodium. If you do not have time to bake, a wide variety of healthier kosher cookies can be purchased, especially at stores featuring whole or healthy foods. Old-fashioned varieties such as fig bars, ginger snaps, and graham crackers are often a good choice. Choose low-fat, whole-grain varieties that do not contain trans fat.

Check the label on crackers to be sure that they are low in sodium and do not contain trans fat. Many varieties are made with whole grains and added fiber.

Frozen desserts can make a nice snack, especially in warm weather. Look for natural varieties of fruit ices or popsicles, frozen yogurt and rice and soymilk desserts. Low-fat or nonfat products can be high in sugar. On the other hand, they often contain a significant amount of valuable calcium. Consider making your own popsicles from pure fruit juice, or freeze banana halves or grapes for a simple, cost-effective and refreshing summer treat.

Keep a supply of healthy snacks in your house.

SNACKS FOR CHILDREN

It can happen in the car or at home – you are on your way home from the store or in the middle of making dinner or talking on the phone when your children start to bicker or demand your attention. It often seems that the easiest solution is to give them something to eat.

Many of us are quick to pacify tired or cranky children with food. This may seem like an easy solution at the time, but in the long run, it is best if food is not used to influence children's behavior. Early eating habits can influence a child's attitude towards food for a lifetime. With the increased incidence of childhood obesity and eating disorders such as anorexia and bulimia, we must try our best not to use food as a reward or punishment for our children's conduct.

If your children are truly hungry, keep a supply of healthy snack foods available for such occasions. If boredom is the problem, a stash of games, toys, music or books is a much better option than food.

Do not reward or punish children's behavior with food.

Healthy Snack Ideas

Fresh fruit	Leftover salad
Dried fruit	Unsweetened applesauce
Frozen fruit slices, berries or	Whole-grain crackers
banana halves	Nuts
Carrot and celery sticks	Whole-grain muffin
Popcorn, air-popped without fat	Low-sodium pretzels
Low-fat cottage cheese	Low-fat or nonfat yogurt

CHOCOLATE

For those of us with a passion for chocolate, it may be time to dismiss some of our guilt and enjoy certain types of it in moderation.

Natural antioxidants called flavanoids, found in fruits, vegetables, tea and red wine are also present in chocolate. Cocoa beans are unusually rich in flavanoids, which play a role in reducing blood clotting and coronary artery blockages. Research has also shown that the flavanoids in chocolate improve blood vessel function, increasing blood flow in the arteries.[85] Immune function and blood pressure may also be improved by eating chocolate high in flavanoids.[86]

Contrary to popular belief, chocolate does not seem to cause or aggravate acne or tooth decay. Whether it acts as an aphrodisiac or antidepressant, as many nonscientific reports have suggested, remains to be seen. There is a small amount of caffeine in chocolate, which can aggravate heartburn and acid reflux.

Chocolate gets a bad rap from its high fat content, though much of the saturated fat in good quality chocolate consists of stearic and oleic acids, which have a neutral effect on cholesterol levels.[87] Unfortunately, many of our favorite chocolate candy bars contain added milk and vegetable fat as well as a large amount of sugar. These add extra unhealthy calories and lead to weight gain, negating possible benefits of the chocolate itself. Although an ounce of dark (bittersweet) chocolate contains about 150 calories, a whole 3½ ounce bar contains over 500 calories. By eating one chocolate bar a day and not subtracting other calories from your diet, you could gain a pound of weight in one week!

> ## One ounce of bittersweet chocolate (70% cocoa) contains approximately 150 calories and 20 milligrams of caffeine.

Cocoa and chocolate products currently on the market vary widely in flavanoid content. Although it is nearly impossible to know the flavanoid content of various chocolates, we know that fermentation and roasting time, alkalizing ("Dutch process") and the addition of ingredients such as milk, all reduce flavanoid content.

Although there is much yet to be discovered, current evidence suggests that chocolate high in flavanoids may contribute to improved cardiovascular health.[88] Just keep in mind that eating too much chocolate can lead to weight gain, and thus cancel the possible health benefits.

If you enjoy chocolate, your best options are dark or bittersweet varieties, with a cocoa content of 70% or higher. Stick to a single small piece, about an ounce, several times a week as a dessert or snack.

> ## If you are not overweight, enjoy a small amount of high-quality bittersweet chocolate occasionally.

The Bottom Line

Snack on fruits, vegetables, nuts and seeds.

Choose snacks that contain healthy ingredients.

Avoid highly processed snack foods.

Keep healthy snack foods in your refrigerator and pantry.

CHAPTER 13

Shabbat: Your Extra Soul Deserves to Be Healthy

"Rabbi Shimon ben Lakish says: God gives man an enhancement of the soul on Erev Shabbat, *and on* Motzei Shabbat *it is taken away, as it says, 'And on the seventh day He made* Shabbat, vayinafash' *(Shemot 31:17), meaning that after* Shabbat, *woe, the soul is gone! Rashi explains the enhancement of the soul as increased capability for rest and happiness, an openness of the soul, so that one can eat and drink and not feel overfull."* (Bavli Beitzah 16a)

"If you proclaim the Shabbat *a delight and the holy day of* Hashem *honored...then you will delight in* Hashem." (Yeshayahu 58:13)

On *Shabbat* we are especially attentive to both our spiritual and physical needs. We nurture our soul with special *tefilot* and *kavanah*. We dress in our finest clothes, clean the house and plan a festive meal. Just as we take extra care in our spiritual and physical preparations for *Shabbat*, so too should we take extra care in tending to matters concerning our health. When it comes to food, we should do our best to nurture our extra soul and not overfeed it.

Many of us associate certain foods with *Shabbat*. It may be *cholent*, chopped liver, *bourekas* or chicken soup that brings pleasant nostalgic memories to mind. We often think fondly of the *Shabbat* meals we ate with our parents or grandparents. It is only natural to want to transmit these gastronomic memories to our own families.

Unfortunately, some of our more traditional foods are less than healthy. A typical meal of "white-bread" challah, chicken soup, chopped liver, brisket, potatoes, cooked carrots, tea and cake contains an unhealthy amount of saturated fat, simple carbohydrates and sugar. When our ancestors ate meager mid-week meals and walked to the market and back, the extra fat and calories from a *Shabbat* meal like this were probably necessary for adequate caloric intake. Today, we can hardly afford similar meals when we overeat during the week and rarely get adequate exercise. With the high level of nutrition-related diseases in our communities, it behooves us to consider healthy alternatives to high-calorie, fat and sugar-laden *Shabbat* meals.

Shabbat meals can be delicious without being high in fat, simple carbohydrates and sugar.

HEALTHIER *SHABBAT* MEALS

Delicious *Shabbat* meals can be planned around traditional foods that have been adapted to reduce fat and sugar. For instance, if your family enjoys eating chicken, remove the skin before cooking. (Your butcher may be willing to do this for you.) You can retain some of its moisture by cooking it in a tasty sauce or rolling it first in beaten egg and then in seasoned crumbs before baking. Chicken or meat soups may be prepared in advance and refrigerated so that the hardened fat can be easily removed. Better yet, choose a soup based on vegetables or legumes. Consider healthier alternatives to problematic favorites such as chopped liver and *kishkeh*. Many tasty options using vegetables, beans, grains and nuts can be found in kosher and vegetarian cookbooks. Try roasting white or sweet potatoes in olive oil – delicious and much easier, quicker and healthier than sweet kugel. Even *cholent* or *hamin* (as it is called by Jews of Sephardic descent) can be prepared with lean meat that has been trimmed of excess fat or skinless chicken. Vegetarian versions based on beans and grains are a delicious and healthy alternative as well.

PLANNING AHEAD

"Six days shall you work and on the seventh day you shall desist; you shall desist from plowing and harvesting." (*Shemot* 34:21)

The Hebrew word for plowing is *charish*. According to the Koznitzer, the first letter of *charish* – *chet* – stands for *chamishi – Yom Chamishi*, "Thursday." The second letter – *resh* – stands for *Yom Revi'i*, "Wednesday," and the *shin* for *Yom Shishi*, "Friday." He explains that this tells us that Wednesday, Thursday and Friday should be used as days to prepare for *Shabbat*.[89]

Planning ahead for *Shabbat* meals can reduce or eliminate the rushing and stress that many of us feel as candle lighting approaches. During the short days of winter this can be especially challenging, but a little organization and simplification can go a long way in assuring a calm and restful *Shabbat*.

Start by writing a menu for *Shabbat* meals, and then make a shopping list. Think of anything that can be done ahead of time – even measuring the dry ingredients for a cake or doing laundry on Thursday rather than Friday can make a big difference. If you bake your own challah, prepare the dough on Thursday evening, place it in an oiled plastic bag and refrigerate it for a slow overnight rise, to be shaped and baked on Friday.

Advance planning can help simplify *Shabbat* preparations.

If possible, plan your menu and shop for groceries on Wednesday. Look for fresh seasonal produce, keeping an eye out for unusual or exceptionally nice fruits or vegetables that will enhance your *Shab-*

bat meals. Wash lettuce and other greens when you get home. Broccoli, cauliflower, and other vegetables can be checked for insects, washed and blanched in advance as well. Sort dry peas or beans ahead of time when you have a few extra minutes. When soup is on your menu, get a head start by preparing the ingredients or the soup itself a day or two in advance.

To keep meal preparation easy, concentrate on a small number of elegantly presented dishes. For dinner, you might start the meal with a low-fat soup or a salad to tease the appetite and partially fill the stomach. Follow with chicken, turkey, fish or lean beef, a whole-grain pilaf or potatoes and a fresh cooked vegetable. Finish your meal with tea, fresh or dried fruit and nuts, or a home-baked dessert.

By considering the seasons, you will ensure freshness and flavor in your food. For instance, in the winter months, you might begin a meal with half a grapefruit or a salad of avocado and orange slices. Choose a warming soup made with lentils, garbanzos or split peas. During the summer, consider a refreshingly cold gazpacho soup made with vine-ripened tomatoes or a salad featuring greens and seasonal fresh fruit or vegetables.

Plan *Shabbat* menus that feature a small number of elegant seasonal dishes.

Use your imagination to create meals that are in tune with good health, seasonal and reasonably priced produce and the climate. A nice change from a hot lunch in mid-summer might feature cold soup, salad, a variety of thinly sliced vegetables, cooked tuna or salmon and a yogurt or mayonnaise-based dressing. Serve reduced-fat brownies, fruit and iced tea for dessert. Roast or poach a whole fillet of salmon and serve it with several salads for another refreshing *Shabbat* meal. A composed salad of tuna or salmon artfully arranged with new potatoes, fresh cooked green beans, hard cooked eggs, olives and tomato wedges makes an elegant entrée as well.

Shabbat during the Summer

> "One should not retire shortly after eating, but should wait some three or four hours." (Rambam, *Hilchot De'ot* 4:5)

Kabbalat Shabbat during the summer poses another challenge. Some communities bring in *Shabbat* early, most often to accommodate families with young children. For those who bring *Shabbat* in at its "normal" time, dinner often begins late in the evening. It then becomes impractical to take the Rambam's wise advice and wait several hours after eating before going to sleep.

Another solution is to serve a lighter fish or vegetarian dinner, rather than a heavier meat meal. It is easier to digest, less likely to produce heartburn and will leave you feeling more comfortable before bedtime.

QUANTITY CONTROL

> "Indulge not excessively in a meal which you enjoy." (*Gittin* 70a)

We all worry about having enough food for *Shabbat*. This is normal given that we can't just pop something extra into the oven during *Shabbat*. Most of us also think about feeding an extra guest or two who may show up at the last minute. Cooking extra food for the coming week is also a smart strategy.

Just keep in mind that serving an enormous quantity of food is not necessary or desirable. Set out the amount of food that you feel will adequately feed everyone and keep extra portions in the kitchen, to be served later if needed. You will be doing a favor for your family and friends who will likely find it difficult not to overeat when faced with a huge amount of food on the table.

Shabbat meals do not have to be high-calorie, multi-course affairs that challenge our willpower and our waistlines. With planning and attention to detail, they can be festive as well as nutritious.

A nice long walk can be a refreshing and relaxing part of your *Shabbat*. Walking burns calories, enhances heart and lung function, strengthens bones and lowers levels of stress and anxiety.

Here are some ideas for creating healthier *Shabbat* dinners:

Winter Shabbat *Dinner*

Before	After
Challah	Healthy Whole Wheat Challah*
Gefilte fish	Poached salmon, on a bed of greens
Chopped liver	Lentil "Chopped Liver"*
Brisket with gravy	Chicken baked with brown rice
Potato kugel	Steamed broccoli
Cabbage soup	Mixed green salad
Cooked carrots	Fresh sliced citrus fruit
Mixed green salad	Homemade Brownies*
Bakery brownies	Tea
Tea	

* Recipes marked with an asterisk (*) can be found at the end of this book.

Summer Shabbat *Dinner*

Before	After
Challah	Healthy Whole Wheat Challah*
Smoked whitefish	Roasted salmon fillets
Potato *knishes* or *bourekas*	Roasted baby potatoes
Chicken soup with noodles	Eggplant salad
Chicken schnitzel	Steamed asparagus
Mixed green salad	Israeli salad
White rice	Watermelon and cantaloupe slices
Cooked zucchini squash	Homemade Lemon Cake*
Chocolate cake	Tea
Tea	

CHAPTER 14

Holidays

"V'samachta b'chagecha…"   (*Devarim* 16:14)

Festive meals and symbolic foods are central to our holiday celebrations. What would *Rosh Hashanah* be without honey cake? On *Sukkot*, we prepare casserole dishes and stuffed vegetables. *Purim* means *hamentashen, Tu B'Shevat* means dried fruits and nuts and *Chanukah* means *latkes* and *sufganiyot* (jelly-filled doughnuts). We make picnic meals on *Lag B'Omer* and eat dairy foods on *Shavuot*. *Pesach*, of course, is the quintessential food-based holiday. Despite its many dietary restrictions, it seems as though we are constantly cooking and eating!

How can we best enjoy holiday meals and special treats while maintaining a healthy diet? And can we prevent ourselves from putting on extra pounds at these times? The best advice is to use common sense and moderation. Plan holiday meals that will not leave everyone feeling stuffed. Keep it simple and elegant.

When possible, try to adapt traditional recipes to make them lower in fat and sugar. For example, stuff summer or winter squash with a savory brown rice or bulgur filling. Homemade *hamentashen* are fun to make. Substitute half of the white flour in your favorite recipe with whole-wheat pastry flour and fill them with gently cooked, pureed dried fruit. *Latkes* and *sufganiyot* always present a challenge. In Israel, *sufganiyot* now appear in bakeries before *Rosh Hashanah* – that's more than three months of temptation! My strategy is to hold off until *Chanukah*, buy one of the best and freshest *sufganiyot* available and enjoy it with relish and without guilt. Make a similar plan with *latkes* – choose one day of

Chanukah and enjoy them in moderation, freshly cooked, with applesauce and/or reduced-fat sour cream. Prepare *Lag B'Omer* sandwiches on whole-grain bread and include a variety of vegetables and fruits to munch on. Dairy-based *Shavuot* specialties can be prepared using reduced-fat dairy products such as part-skim mozzarella and low-fat ricotta cheese.

Plan traditional holiday meals that are delicious and nutritious.

NUTRITIOUS SYMBOLIC FOODS

Most traditional holiday foods have a symbolic meaning. *Latkes* and *sufganiyot* are fried in oil, reminding us of the oil found by the Maccabees in the Temple. *Hamentashen* remind us of Haman's hat or ears, and honey symbolizes our desire for a sweet New Year.

On *Rosh Hashanah*, Sephardic Jews eat a variety of foods that symbolize our wishes for the coming year (*Shulchan Aruch Orach Chayim* 583:1). If you substitute fish for the lamb, these symbolic foods are especially nutritious. With such a healthy start to the year, we might consider this a hint as to how we should eat during the rest of the year as well!

Before the main *Rosh Hashanah* meal the following *brachot* are said (following the blessing and eating of the challah):

1. Date (*tamar*)

   Eat a date and say the blessing *borei pri ha'etz*; then take another date and recite: May it be Your will, *Hashem* our God, God of our forefathers, that they (our enemies) cease to exist (*yitamu* sounds like *tamar*).

   Take a vegetable (not one of the symbolic ones below) and recite the blessing *borei pri ha'adamah*, while having in mind the other vegetables that will be eaten.

2. Leeks (*karte*)

May it be Your will, *Hashem* our God, God of our forefathers, that they be decimated (*she'ikartu* sounds like *karte*) – our foes and our enemies and all who seek our harm.

3. Swiss chard or beet greens (*selek*)

May it be Your will, *Hashem* our God, God of our forefathers, that they be removed (*yistalek* sounds like *selek*) – our foes and our enemies and all who seek our harm.

4. Black-eyed peas (*rubiya*)

May it be Your will, *Hashem* our God, God of our forefathers, that our merits increase like *rubiya*.

5. Orange (winter) squash (*kara*)

May it be Your will, *Hashem* our God, God of our forefathers, that You tear up (*sh'tikra* sounds like *kara*) the evil edict of our judgment; and may our merits be declared before You.

6. Pomegranate (*rimon*)

May it be Your will, *Hashem* our God, God of our forefathers, that our merits be plentiful as the seeds of a pomegranate.

7. Head of a lamb or fish (*rosh*)

May it be Your will, *Hashem* our God, God of our forefathers, that we be like a head and not like a tail.

8. Apple dipped in honey

May it be Your will, *Hashem* our God, God of our forefathers, that there be renewed for us a good and sweet year, from the beginning of the year until the end of the year.

The Bottom Line

Cook healthier versions of favorite holiday recipes.

Be careful not to overeat.

Enjoy holiday treats in moderation and without feeling guilty.

PESACH – LET MY PEOPLE EAT

> "All who are hungry, let them come and eat, all who are in need, let them join in celebrating the *Pesach* festival." (*Pesach Haggadah*)
> "You shall not eat any leavening; in all your dwellings shall you eat *matzot*." (*Shemot* 12:20)

If there is one holiday that is associated primarily with food, it is *Pesach* (Passover). For many of us, the association is positive and joyful. I have fond food memories of *Pesach* as a child – my favorite ruby red dishes, the wooden bowl and chopper for making *charoset*, and happy hours with my mother in the kitchen. Later memories revolve around food as well – cooking with a dear friend for shared *Sedarim*, marrying into the Sephardic practice of eating *kitniyot*, and shopping for beautifully fresh spring produce. Even now the chores of *Pesach* cleaning are balanced with the excitement of trying new recipes, planning menus and anticipating the familiar, once-a-year holiday foods.

Planning Ahead for an Enjoyable *Pesach*

If in your mind *Pesach* means long, tedious weeks of cleaning and preparation, you will probably feel exhausted by the time you sit down for the *Seder*. The thought of taking time to plan creative and healthy meals may seem totally unrealistic or impossible. With careful planning though, you can approach the holiday with joy and relaxation.

Make your *Pesach* preparations easier with these suggestions:

- Remember that *Pesach* cleaning is not spring cleaning. Our obligation is to remove *chametz*, not cobwebs and dust. In our Beer Sheva community, we have come to expect at least one dust storm just before *Pesach* – it gives us a realistic perspective on cleaning!
- Start cleaning for *chametz* as early as possible. Begin with the areas that are farthest from the kitchen and dining room. You can start by cleaning the car, bedrooms, basement and office. Stop bringing *chametz* into these areas once they are clean. You might want to designate the cleaned areas as "*chametz* free."
- Try to include family members in *Pesach* preparations. Children will be more cooperative if they feel that they are a part of the process. You will feel less frazzled if you have the cooperation and help of your family.
- Plan your meals to use up all *chametz* that remains in your pantry and freezer. *Purim* is a good time to start using up leftover baking ingredients. Our favorite *hamentashen* filling is made from a variety of leftover dried fruits. *Mishloach manot* make creative use of foods and ingredients that we already have on hand.
- Start browsing cookbooks, and make a note of new *Pesach* recipes that you would like to try. Newspapers, magazines and the web are all good recipe sources.
- Create a week-long *Pesach* menu, incorporating old favorites and new ideas. Base your menus on fresh, seasonal produce. Try to keep your menus fairly simple.
- After planning your menu, write a shopping list. Include nonperishables, fresh and frozen foods and paper goods. Jump-start your *Pesach* shopping by purchasing nonperishables several weeks in advance.
- Right after *Pesach*, evaluate your shopping list and create a new list for next year. List the amounts that you used as well,

to take the guesswork out of next year's shopping. Make a list of recipes and menus that worked well, so that you can use them again next year.

- Plan to have everything ready a day before *Pesach* starts. My most relaxing *Seder* took place when *Pesach* began on a *Motzei Shabbat*. Then everything had to be ready before *Shabbat*. While the details of preplanning were complex, it was a joy to sit down feeling completely refreshed. It occurred to me then to act as if *Pesach* started a day early every year.

The key to enjoying *Pesach* is planning ahead.

How to Have a Life outside of the Kitchen
To make your life in the kitchen easier during *Pesach*, organize your tasks. Before getting started, make a list of what needs to be done, based on your menus. Wash and check as many of your vegetables as possible at one time, do your cooking at one time and baking at another. In this way, the equipment and ingredients you need for each type of job will be at hand.

Since sugar, potato starch, cake meal, nuts, spices and eggs are the basis for most cakes and cookies, keep all of these ingredients on the countertop while you prepare several recipes at one time. Sometimes I premeasure dry ingredients for several recipes one day and mix and bake them the following day.

Use your kitchen equipment to good advantage as well. If several recipes call for ground nuts, for example, grind them in the food processor at the same time to avoid additional cleaning chores.

Pesach cooking and baking calls for a large number of eggs. Since egg yolks are high in fat and cholesterol, you may want to substitute a portion of whole eggs with egg whites. Years ago I developed a shortcut for preparing a large number of egg whites in advance: separate a dozen or more eggs and discard the yolks; put the whites in paper cups (or use an ice cube tray) and mark the number of whites on the outside of the cup; freeze each cup of egg whites and store all of the cups in a zip-lock bag when they are solid. Defrost as many cups as you need. Just remember that two egg whites are equal in volume to one whole egg.

Consider cooking larger amounts of food in advance. For instance, for the *Seder*, I prepare a Turkish-style *charoset* that contains apples, oranges, dried fruits and nuts. A double batch prepared before the *Seder* doubles as a spread for *matzah* throughout the week. Mixed dried fruit compote can similarly be prepared early on and eaten throughout the week.

Healthy Eating during *Pesach*
One of the best ways to eat well during *Pesach* is to serve a variety of fruits and vegetables at every meal. Even without beans and peas, there are many choices, including Swiss chard, summer and winter squash, red and green cabbages, sweet potatoes, carrots, asparagus, broccoli, cauliflower, celery root, fennel, avocado, tomatoes, eggplant, peppers, leeks and artichokes. Green salad tossed with olive oil and lemon juice is a refreshing addition to any meal. Vegetable-based soups are lovely served as a first course or as a meal of their own. Many year-round soup recipes can be easily adapted to *Pesach*. Even *matzah brei* and kugels benefit from the addition of cooked vegetables such as onions, mushrooms, spinach, asparagus and broccoli. A refreshing fruit soup makes a nice starter, especially if the weather is warm. Desserts based on fruit are delicious and healthy. Sliced fresh melon, dried or fresh fruit compote and fruit salad make great desserts. Strawberries seem to be particularly tasty around *Pesach*. My mother added them to freshly picked and stewed rhubarb for a special treat.

> **Instead of eating cookies and candy,
> eat fruit for dessert during *Pesach*.**

Serve fish as often as possible. Fresh cooked fish makes an elegant, easy and healthy first or main course. One of our favorite *Seder* menus includes fresh poached salmon, roasted new potatoes and a green vegetable. Gefilte fish is always welcome at *Pesach*. I make a large batch of Sephardic-style fish balls flavored with cilantro and cooked in a tangy tomato sauce – we enjoy them hot or cold throughout the week. Bottled gefilte fish and canned tuna or salmon make nice, easy lunch meals during *Chol Hamoed*. Leftover cooked fish can be made into a salad or fish cakes for a casual lunch.

Poultry is a good choice as well. Be sure to trim the fat and remove the skin, preferably before cooking. Cook your chicken soup early, refrigerate it overnight and skim the hardened fat before serving. Choose lean cuts of beef and trim as much excess fat as possible.

Look for recipes calling for oil rather than margarine. In cooking, it is easy to substitute oil for margarine. Olive and walnut oils are the best choices for cooking, baking and salads. Peanut oil may be available as well. Avoid cottonseed oil, which is higher in saturated fat than most other oils. Kosher-for-*Pesach* canola oil is acceptable for Sephardim who eat *kitniyot*.

There are a number of healthy alternatives to spreading butter or margarine on *matzah*. My family enjoys mashed avocado (guacamole) and the bottled Israeli-made sun-dried tomato and olive spreads. Unsweetened fruit spreads are often available for *Pesach* as well. I make an extra batch of fairly thick *charoset*, which doubles as a spread for *matzah* throughout the week.

Pesach desserts are often very high in fat and sugar. When you bake your own desserts, you can usually reduce the amount of sugar in the recipe. Try baking cakes and cookies that feature ground nuts, and reduce the amount of fat by substituting two egg whites for at least some of the whole eggs in your recipes. As an alternative to baked goods, serve fresh or dried fruit and nuts for dessert. Low-fat dairy products such as yogurt or ricotta cheese served with fruit also make an easy dessert for dairy meals.

The Bottom Line

Serve fruits and vegetables at every meal.

Emphasize fish and poultry rather than beef.

Choose heart-healthy olive and walnut oils.

Enjoy nuts and low-fat dairy products.

Reduce the sugar in recipes.

Substitute two egg whites for whole eggs in recipes.

YOM KIPPUR AND OTHER FAST DAYS

"The fast of a pious man is such that eye, ear and tongue share in it, so that he regards nothing except that which brings him near to God." (*Kuzari* [Schocken translation] 3:5)

Judaism has always acknowledged the relationship between the physical and spiritual elements of life, and most of our holidays embrace both, through celebration and *tefilah*. On *Yom Kippur* and other fast days, we strive to elevate the spiritual while setting aside the physical. A sensible approach to the fast allows us to disregard, but not totally neglect, our physical needs in order to better concentrate on our spiritual ones.

To ensure an easy and safe fast, start drinking plenty of water a few days in advance, so that you will be completely hydrated. If you usually drink a lot of coffee or other caffeinated beverages, start tapering off a week or so before the fast, to minimize withdrawal headaches.

On the day before a fast, avoid eating heavily salted and fried foods. Make a point of eating foods containing complex carbohydrates and continue to drink lots of water or non-caffeinated liquids.

Dinner before a fast should begin early enough to allow for a relaxed meal. Save time for brushing teeth, blessing the children and a last drink of water before candle lighting. You might want to consider eating a mid-morning brunch that day or a hearty breakfast followed by a very light lunch or mid-day snack; that way you can start dinner early enough to avoid rushing.

The pre-fast meal should contain complex carbohydrates, a moderate amount of protein and a small amount of fat. You might serve a green salad dressed with olive oil, a light soup, chicken or turkey breast, brown rice pilaf and poached fruit for dessert. Use salt sparingly, to avoid thirst later on. Stay away from overly sweet and spicy foods, carbonated beverages and alcohol. Eating a moderately sized meal may actually make fasting easier than trying to eat enough at dinner "to cover" the next day.

When the fast is over, drink water, juice or tea and eat something fairly light. Some synagogues set out cake and beverages after Ne'ilah with this in mind. At home, a light dairy meal is most welcome. Avoid a large, heavy meal and rehydrate with plenty of water.

Be sure to consult your physician and your rabbi before deciding to fast if you have a chronic disorder such as heart disease, diabetes, ulcers or hypertension. Cancer patients and those who are seriously ill should not fast without express permission from their physician and their rabbi. Although the obligation to fast usually falls on pregnant women (Orach Chayim 617:1), it is most important to abide by the advice of your physician and rabbi. Nursing women should also seek medical and halachic advice before fasting.

CHAPTER 15

Finding Reliable Diet and Nutrition Information

Information on nutrition, food and health is everywhere. Newspapers, magazines, television, web sites, billboards, advertisements and salespeople are all eager to share their views and opinions on nutrition. New studies appear in the press almost daily, often contradicting previous studies. How are we to know what to believe and who to believe? What makes one study better or different from another? And how should we apply the latest information to our own food choices?

SCIENTIFIC RESEARCH

Today's abundance of readily available scientific research is responsible for great advances in understanding the role of nutrition in health. But there are many unanswered questions, and many contradictory research studies. Sometimes it even seems that the more we know, the more confusing it becomes.

While scientific developments advance at a rapid pace, it may take years to reach a conclusion on how particular nutrients or eating behaviors affect health and disease. Not that long ago, we advised that a high fiber intake could lower the risk of colon cancer. A low-fat diet was suggested to lower the risk of developing breast cancer. Many studies suggested that vitamin E played a protective role against heart disease and some cancers. With more recent results of larger, long-term and more accurate studies, these findings came into doubt and dietary recommendations were changed.

These reversals can be frustrating. When our health is at stake, we want to know what to do now. We want to be able to make intelligent choices for ourselves and our families based on current knowledge. While the media is often quick to report on studies that seem reliable, it is often difficult to interpret these studies, and harder still to determine their practical implications.

Good scientific research may take years to produce conclusive results.

Scientists employ a variety of methods in nutrition research. Studies may compare healthy people to people who have a particular illness (case-control studies). They may take a group of people, divide them into separate groups and feed each of them a different type of diet (randomized trial). Laboratory research on animals, cells and tissues are often the starting point of further human research.

In general, the most reliable information comes from cohort studies – those that follow large groups of people over long periods of time. The Nurses' Health Study and Health Professionals Follow-up Study that are mentioned throughout this book are cohort studies that have provided and continue to provide a wealth of information on diet and health.

DECIPHERING THE MEDIA

Media reports are often short and catchy, and their focus is usually on one particular study. An attention-getting report is often one that contradicts previous scientific research, with the consumer left not knowing what to believe. Here are some questions to ask when evaluating news stories on diet and health:

Is the report based on animal or human studies?

Although new, gene-based technology has revolutionized animal research studies, they are still often a first step, and not necessarily applicable to humans. The most reliable research studies the long-term effects of nutrition on real people.

How was diet assessed in the study?

Nutrition assessment is one of the biggest challenges to dietitians. Were the participants asked to recall what they ate yesterday, last week or years ago? Were they fed specific amounts and types of foods in a laboratory setting? Since dietary assessment varies in its reliability, make sure the study uses valid methods of measuring nutrient intake.

Is the story based on a single research study?

It is rare for one study to produce results that would convince scientists to completely change their opinion on a matter of diet and health. Rather than look at any one study in isolation, the results of many studies are compared and analyzed before recommendations are made.

Was the study large or small?

More reliable results are usually obtained from larger rather than smaller studies.

How long did the study take?

Longer-term studies are better able to evaluate the relationship between diet and disease, since it often takes years for a disease to develop. Shorter-term studies may hint at possible outcomes resulting from disease symptoms rather than actual disease.

Dietary changes should not be made based on single media reports without careful evaluation.

WHERE TO GET RELIABLE NUTRITION INFORMATION

In Person

The health professionals best equipped to give advice on diet and health are registered dietitians. A registered dietitian (RD) has completed academic and experience requirements established by the American Dietetic Association, including a minimum of a bachelor's degree, an approved practice program or internship and a qualifying examination. Ongoing professional education is required to maintain registration. Some RDs obtain additional certification in specialized areas, such as weight control, pediatrics and diabetes.

Many states require licensing for dietitians as well. Licensing can make it easier for the public to find competent practitioners by restricting advertisement by unqualified individuals posing as nutrition or diet "experts." Be wary of advice from salespeople and health food store clerks, who may not have formal nutrition training. The American Dietetic Association's Nationwide Nutrition Network may be useful for finding a qualified dietitian in your area. Go to their web site (www.eatright.org) and click on "Find a Nutrition Professional."

Seek a qualified registered dietitian for the most reliable nutrition advice.

Websites

Do an Internet search for "nutrition information" and you will find nearly 100,000,000 entries. Since anyone can put up a web site giving nutrition advice, how is one to discriminate between nutrition facts and fallacy? Here are some web sites offering accurate information on nutrition and health; some of them offer email and print newsletters.

American Diabetes Association: www.diabetes.org
American Dietetic Association: www.eatright.org
American Heart Association: www.americanheart.org
Center for Science in the Public Interest: www.cspinet.org
Eating Well: www.eatingwell.com
Harvard School of Public Health: www.hsph.harvard.edu/
    nutritionsource/
Nutrition Resource Center, Medscape: www.medscape.com/
    resource/nutrition

Tufts University Health and Nutrition Newsletter: www.health-letter.tufts.edu

UC Berkeley Wellness Letter: www.berkeleywellness.com

US Department of Agriculture website: www.nutrition.gov

US Government food safety: www.foodsafety.gov

The Bottom Line

Evaluate media reports carefully before making dietary changes based on them.

Speak with a qualified registered dietitian for nutrition advice.

Seek web and print-based information from reliable sources.

In a Nutshell

As a dietitian, I am frequently asked the question, "What should I eat?" The vast amount of confusing and conflicting nutrition information available to us has made it increasingly difficult to answer this question.

My very short answer is:

Eat less, enjoy it more, exercise, eat plenty of vegetables and fruits and limit processed foods.

I hope that the information in this book makes healthy food choices, shopping and cooking easier for you. My goal is to help you improve your physical and spiritual health through enjoyable and healthy eating.

> "Go eat your bread with joy and drink your wine with a glad heart, for God has already approved your deeds." (*Kohelet* 9:7)
> "May what we ate satisfy us, and what we drank heal us, and what remains should be for a blessing." (Sephardic *Birkat Hamazon*)

Menu Ideas

Planning meals may often seem more daunting than preparing them. Breakfast and lunch may not be that difficult, but by the end of a busy day, most of us are short on ideas for a healthy, tasty dinner.

Make your life easier by creating a week's worth of menus in advance. Solicit ideas from your family and plan on easier, quicker-cooking meals when you know that you will be rushed or under pressure.

When you have time, browse through cookbooks, magazines, newspapers and the web for new recipe ideas. After years of clipping and saving recipes, I always have a handy collection of new recipes to try.

Use the ideas on the following pages to get started and then create your own menus. Be flexible and allow for grocery sales, seasonal produce and spontaneity. Recipes marked with an asterisk (*) can be found in the recipe section of this book.

Sunday	Monday	Tuesday	Wednesday
Breakfast Leftover Challah French Toast* Pure maple syrup Fresh strawberries	**Breakfast** Chana's Granola* Nonfat plain yogurt or nonfat milk or soy milk 1 small banana or ½ large banana Fresh orange juice	**Breakfast** Bran flakes cereal Nonfat milk or soy milk Fresh sliced kiwi Grapefruit juice	**Breakfast** Omelet with leftover vegetables Whole-grain toast All-fruit spread Low-sodium tomato juice
Lunch Pasta Wheels Salad with Tuna* Cherry tomatoes Sliced oranges	**Lunch** Peanut butter, honey and banana sandwich on whole-grain bread Carrot sticks Apple wedges	**Lunch** Turkey sandwich on whole-grain bread with lettuce and tomato Celery sticks Orange wedges	**Lunch** Lentil Salad with Sun-Dried Tomatoes* Carrot sticks Fresh grapes or blueberries Dried Fruit and Nut Bars*
Dinner Spicy Roasted Salmon* Oven-Fried Sweet Potatoes* Tossed green salad Plain yogurt sweetened with fruit spread	**Dinner** Tamale Pie* Tossed green salad with avocado Rice pudding	**Dinner** Sweet and Spicy Tofu* Brown rice Steamed broccoli Baked Pears*	**Dinner** Whole-wheat pasta with marinara sauce Grilled eggplant slices Tossed green salad Unsweetened applesauce with cinnamon

Thursday	Friday	*Shabbat*
Breakfast Homemade oatmeal with raisins Nonfat milk Fresh orange juice Cantaloupe or honeydew melon	**Breakfast** Whole-grain toast All-natural peanut butter Plain, nonfat yogurt Fresh peach, plum or nectarine	***Kiddush*** Unsweetened grape juice or red wine Banana Oatmeal Muffins* Mixed fruit salad
Lunch Egg salad sandwich on whole-grain bread Cherry tomatoes Chocolate Chip Cookie* Banana	**Lunch** Tuna sandwich on whole-grain bread Carrot sticks Oatmeal raisin cookie*	**Lunch** Healthy Whole-Wheat Challah* Italian-Style Sweet and Sour Fish* Potato salad with vinaigrette dressing Israeli salad Easy *Shabbat* Brownies*
Dinner Split Pea and Potato Soup* Corn Muffins* Sliced tomatoes and cucumbers Fresh or juice-packed pineapple slices	***Shabbat* Dinner** Unsweetened grape juice or red wine Healthy Whole-Wheat Challah* Walnut and Lentil Spread* Baked Chicken and Rice* Moroccan-Style Carrot Salad* Braised Swiss chard Fresh fruit crisp*	***Seudah Shlishit*** Healthy Whole-Wheat Challah* Garbanzo Bean and Tuna Salad* Fresh seasonal fruit

PESACH MENU IDEAS

Seder Dinner, Meat	*Seder* Dinner, Dairy
Gefilte Fish Loaf*	Asparagus Soup*
Baked Chicken with Onions*	Baked salmon
Roasted Potatoes*	Spinach Mushroom *Mina**
Zucchini squash	Moroccan-Style Carrot Salad*
Tossed green salad	Israeli salad
Sponge cake	*Pesach* Brownies*
Dried fruit compote	**Fresh fruit**

Weekday Lunch and Dinner Suggestions
Salmon salad
Potato kugel
Steamed broccoli
Ground turkey meatballs with tomato sauce
Spaghetti squash
Tossed green salad
Vegetable soup
Matzah "Lasagna"*
Fresh fruit
Salmon Patties*
Oven-Fried Sweet Potatoes*
Tomato and cucumber slices
Tomato Soup*
Tuna salad
Stuffed Baked Potatoes*
Chicken salad
Sweet Potato Soup*
Sliced tomatoes, cucumber and avocado

Recipes

❧ Grilled Eggplant Rolls (Dairy)

If you want to prepare this in advance, cook the eggplant slices and refrigerate them. Heat them for a few minutes in the microwave oven before rolling, so the cheese filling will be slightly warm. The filling can also be prepared in advance.

INGREDIENTS

2 large eggplants
3 tablespoons extra-virgin olive oil
8 ounces low-fat feta or Bulgarian cheese
¼ cup fresh minced herbs such as parsley, coriander, dill or mint
1 tablespoon fresh lemon juice
Freshly ground black pepper

METHOD

Clean the eggplants well. Cut off the stems and a small slice off of the bottoms. Slice the eggplants lengthwise into thin slices, about ½ an inch thick.

Preheat the broiler or grill to high.

Brush both sides of the eggplant slices with oil, place on a baking sheet and cook until tender, about two minutes on each side. Set aside.

Crumble the feta or Bulgarian cheese in a bowl and mix in the herbs, lemon juice and pepper. Place a spoonful of the cheese mixture on the end of each eggplant slice and roll it up. Arrange the rolls on a plate, seam-side down, and serve warm or at room temperature.

Yields: 15 to 20 rolls

✢⳩ Red Pepper and Walnut Spread (*Parve*)

Serve this Middle-Eastern inspired spread as a condiment or as a spread for challah.

═ INGREDIENTS ═

2 large red peppers, seeded and halved
¼ of a small onion
2 tablespoons extra-virgin olive oil
1 tablespoon lemon juice
2 tablespoons whole-wheat bread crumbs
¼ teaspoon salt
¼ teaspoon ground cumin
¼ teaspoon sugar
1 cup walnut pieces

═ METHOD ═

Broil the peppers, skin-side up, until charred. Put the hot peppers in a paper bag or in a bowl covered with a small plate. (This step produces steam, which helps loosen the skin of the peppers.) When the peppers are completely cool, remove the skins. Cut each pepper half into smaller pieces and set aside.

Place the onion in the food processor and pulse to chop it finely. Add the peppers, olive oil, lemon juice, bread crumbs, salt, cumin and sugar and pulse until chunky. Add the walnuts and pulse again to achieve a spread – it can be smooth or chunky according to your preference.

Yields: approximately 1½ cups

❧ Eggplant Spread (*Parve*)

Cooking the eggplant in the microwave makes this recipe come together quickly. Use this method of cooking for other eggplant recipes that require the whole eggplant to be cooked first.

=== INGREDIENTS ===

1 medium eggplant
¼ cup coarsely chopped onion
1 clove garlic
½ teaspoon salt
⅛ teaspoon freshly ground pepper
2 tablespoons extra-virgin olive oil
2 tablespoons fresh lemon juice
Several sprigs fresh parsley
¼ cup walnut pieces
1 large tomato, diced

=== METHOD ===

Using a sharp paring knife, pierce the eggplant in several places. Place a paper towel on a large dish and put the eggplant on the towel. Microwave the eggplant on high power for 7 to 10 minutes, turning after 5 minutes, until the eggplant is very soft. Remove and cool to room temperature.

Cut the eggplant in half lengthwise, remove the pulp and discard the peel.

Place the onion and garlic in a food processor and pulse until finely chopped. Add the eggplant, salt, pepper, olive oil, lemon juice and parsley and process until fairly smooth and the parsley is chopped. Add the walnuts and process until they are chopped. There should be some texture to the mixture. Stir in the diced tomato and refrigerate to blend flavors.

Serves 4 to 6

✤ Quick and Easy Bean Dip (*Parve*)

Choose mild, medium or hot salsa, depending on your preference. If you keep canned beans and salsa in your pantry, this comes together in minutes. Serve with baked tortilla chips.

═ INGREDIENTS ═

1 can (14 to 16 ounces) black or pinto beans, drained and rinsed
½ cup prepared salsa
2 tablespoons lemon juice
¼ teaspoon ground cumin

═ METHOD ═

Combine all of the ingredients in a food processor and pulse until smooth.

Yields: 1½ cups dip

⚘ Fruit and Nut Snack Mix (*Parve*)

Combine equal amounts of nuts and/or seeds and dried fruits. Choose one or two varieties of nuts and fruits from the following suggestions. Toss in a handful of chocolate chips for a special treat.

═ INGREDIENTS ═════════════════════════════

Nuts and Seeds
Whole, unpeeled almonds
Walnut halves or pieces
Roasted hazelnuts
Unsalted, dry-roasted peanuts
Soy nuts
Sunflower seeds

Fruit
Dried apricot halves or quarters
Unsweetened dried apple slices
Dried cranberries
Raisins
Pitted dates, chopped
Dried cherries or raspberries

❧ Spicy Pistachio Nuts (*Parve*)

Pistachio nuts are a good source of phytosterols, chemicals found in plants that can reduce blood cholesterol levels. These are "special occasion" pistachios, coated with a mixture of Indian-inspired spices.

═ INGREDIENTS ═

3 tablespoons sugar
½ teaspoon salt
1 tablespoon curry powder
2 teaspoons ground coriander
½ teaspoon ground cumin
⅛ teaspoon ground cinnamon
⅛ teaspoon ground ginger
1 tablespoon extra-virgin olive oil
2 cups unsalted shelled pistachio nuts

═ METHOD ═

Line a large baking sheet with parchment or waxed paper and set aside.

Stir together the sugar, salt and spices.

Heat the oil in a large, nonstick skillet. Add the nuts and cook for about 5 minutes, or until they begin to brown. Stir the sugar and spice mixture into the nuts and cook, stirring constantly, until the mixture coats the nuts thoroughly.

Immediately transfer the nuts to the baking sheet to cool.

Yields: 2 cups

MUFFINS, BREAD AND BREAKFAST

✣ Banana Oatmeal Muffins (Dairy)

When we return home from the early Shabbat *morning minyan, we make* Kiddush *and enjoy a cup of tea with these muffins.*

INGREDIENTS

2 ripe bananas, mashed
¾ cup low-fat buttermilk
⅓ cup brown sugar
1 egg
2 tablespoons canola oil
1 cup regular rolled oats
1½ cups whole-wheat pastry flour
1 teaspoon ground cinnamon or nutmeg
1½ teaspoons baking soda

METHOD

Preheat the oven to 375 degrees Fahrenheit. Line 12 muffin cups with paper liners.

In a large mixing bowl, mix together the mashed bananas with the buttermilk, sugar, egg, oil and oats.

In another bowl, whisk together the flour, cinnamon or nutmeg and baking soda. Combine the wet and dry ingredients and stir them together without overmixing.

Fill the muffin cups and bake for 15 to 20 minutes, until golden and a toothpick comes out clean.

Yields: 12 muffins

✿ **Corn Muffins or Bread** (*Parve*)

Corn muffins make a nice accompaniment to soup or chili, for a satisfying lunch or dinner. I also use this recipe for making cornbread stuffing, mixing it with whole-grain bread, vegetables and herbs.

INGREDIENTS

1 cup cornmeal, preferably stone-ground
1 cup whole-wheat pastry flour
3 teaspoons baking powder
½ teaspoon salt
1 egg
¼ cup honey
¼ cup canola oil
1 cup water
1 tablespoon cider vinegar

METHOD

Preheat the oven to 375 degrees Fahrenheit. Line 12 muffin cups with paper liners or spray them with nonstick cooking spray. For cornbread, spray an 8-inch square baking pan with cooking spray.

Stir the cornmeal, flour, baking powder and salt together.

Mix the egg, honey, oil, water and vinegar. Stir into the dry ingredients. Mix briefly just enough to combine the ingredients.

Spoon the batter into the muffin cups or the baking pan and bake until golden, about 15 to 25 minutes.

Serves 12

✿ **Baking Powder Biscuits** (Dairy)

My husband David loves biscuits, and these are the ones I make for him. Most recipes call for white flour and butter or margarine. I substitute whole-wheat pastry flour and canola oil. You can mix and shape these biscuits in the time it takes your oven to preheat. For a simple light dinner, I serve these with a bowl of homemade soup.

═ INGREDIENTS ═

2 cups whole-wheat pastry flour
2 teaspoons baking powder
½ teaspoon baking soda
½ teaspoon salt
1 cup low-fat buttermilk
⅓ cup canola oil

═ METHOD ═

Preheat the oven to 425 degrees Fahrenheit. Lightly grease a baking sheet or line it with parchment paper.

In a mixing bowl, whisk together the flour, baking powder, baking soda and salt.

Mix the buttermilk and oil together. Add them to the dry ingredients and quickly mix them together. Lightly flour a cutting board or kitchen counter, turn out the dough and pat it into a circle about ½ to 1 inch thick. Cut into rounds with a biscuit cutter or the top of a juice glass. Place on the baking sheet and bake for 15 to 20 minutes, until lightly browned.

Yields: 12 biscuits

✌ **Basic Buttermilk Pancakes** (Dairy)

Use your imagination with this recipe: replace ½ cup of the flour with cornmeal or add chopped seasonal fruit or nuts. Serve with a small amount of pure maple syrup, yogurt and fresh fruit.

══ INGREDIENTS ══

1½ cups whole-wheat pastry flour
1 tablespoon sugar
2 teaspoons baking powder
1 teaspoon baking soda
¼ teaspoon salt
2 eggs
2 tablespoons canola oil
1½ cups low-fat buttermilk
1 teaspoon vanilla

══ METHOD ══

Whisk together the flour, sugar, baking powder, baking soda and salt in a bowl.

Mix the eggs, oil, buttermilk and vanilla together. Pour this mixture into the dry ingredients and mix just until combined.

For each pancake, spoon about ¼ cup of batter onto a hot, nonstick griddle or skillet coated with cooking spray. Turn the pancakes when the tops are covered with bubbles. Serve hot.

Yields: 12 to 14 pancakes

❧ **Leftover Challah French Toast** (Dairy)

This recipe depends on good home-baked, or purchased, whole-grain challah. The measurements are approximate, but the idea is to use a large proportion of milk to eggs. The vanilla and cinnamon add a nice sweet flavor, so you will not be tempted to drown these in syrup.

═ INGREDIENTS ═══════════════════════════════

4 to 8 slices of leftover whole-grain challah, sliced
1 to 2 eggs
½ to 1 cup nonfat milk
½ to 1 teaspoon vanilla
¼ to ½ teaspoon ground cinnamon
Canola oil for cooking

═ METHOD ═══════════════════════════════════

Whisk the eggs, milk, vanilla and cinnamon together. Dip each slice of challah in the batter and cook on a lightly oiled griddle or skillet until nicely browned on each side.

Serves 4 to 8

✿ Walnut Raisin Bread (*Parve*)

This Italian-inspired bread is loaded with walnuts and raisins. Use a fruity olive oil and a mild honey for the most delicious flavor. I use a bread machine for this bread, but you can also use a heavy duty mixer with a dough hook or mix and knead the dough by hand. Gluten, which I use to lighten whole-wheat bread dough, is available in whole foods or health food stores.

INGREDIENTS
1¼ cups warm water
¼ cup extra-virgin olive oil
2 tablespoons honey
1½ teaspoons salt
2¾ cups whole-wheat flour
1 tablespoon gluten (also called vital wheat gluten)
1 package (1 tablespoon) active dry yeast
1 cup raisins
1 cup walnut pieces

METHOD
Place the water, oil, honey, salt, flour, gluten and yeast in the pan of the bread machine. Set the machine for the whole-wheat cycle, medium crust. (If your machine does not have a whole-wheat cycle, restart it after the second basic kneading cycle finishes.)

Add the raisins and walnuts when the machine beeps or between the kneading cycles.

When the bread is finished baking, remove from the pan immediately and cool the loaf on a wire rack.

If you are not using a bread machine, allow the dough to rise once, until doubled, in a greased bowl. Shape it into a round loaf and let it rise again on a parchment-lined baking sheet. Bake at 400 degrees Fahrenheit for 35 to 40 minutes.

Yields: 1 loaf

✣ Chana's Granola (*Parve*)

This is what we eat for breakfast most days of the week. We mix in a tablespoon or two of ground flax seed, cut-up, fresh seasonal fruit and unsweetened nonfat yogurt. Feel free to take liberties with this recipe – substitute various rolled grains for part of the oats or try other seeds, nuts and diced dried fruit.

══ INGREDIENTS ══
6 cups regular rolled oats
1 cup shelled sunflower seeds
1 cup shelled pumpkin seeds
½ cup sesame seeds
2 cups walnuts, coarsely chopped
1 tablespoon cinnamon
¼ cup canola oil
¼ cup honey, pure maple syrup or date honey
1 cup raisins

══ METHOD ══
Preheat oven to 325 degrees Fahrenheit.

In a large bowl, mix together the oats, seeds, nuts and cinnamon.

Measure the oil and sweetener in a glass measuring cup; heat in the microwave on high for 30 seconds to liquefy sweetener. Pour over dry ingredients and mix thoroughly, coating the oats, seeds and nuts.

Place the mixture on a large rimmed baking sheet. Bake for 20 to 30 minutes, stirring every 10 to 15 minutes. Remove from the oven when the granola is golden brown, and immediately add the raisins. (The hot mixture will soften the raisins.) Let cool completely. Store the granola in a covered container in the refrigerator.

Yields: 10 cups

SOUPS

❧ Asparagus Soup (*Parve*)

Even now, with most fruits and vegetables available year-round, I think of asparagus as a spring food, especially suited to Pesach. Blanched, with a squeeze of lemon, it makes a lovely side dish with fish or chicken. This soup can be prepared year-round with rice, and with a potato for Pesach.

=== INGREDIENTS ===

1½ pounds fresh asparagus
1 tablespoon extra-virgin olive oil
1 large leek (white and light green parts only), or 1 medium onion, thinly sliced
2 tablespoons raw white rice or 1 medium potato, diced
6 cups water or vegetable broth
½ teaspoon salt
Freshly ground pepper
½ to 1 teaspoon fresh lemon juice

=== METHOD ===

Trim the tough ends from the asparagus and clean the stalks well. Slice the asparagus into ½-inch slices, setting the tips aside to use as garnish, if desired.

Heat the olive oil in a large pot and sauté the leek or onion until soft. Add the rice or potato and sauté for another minute. Add one cup of water or broth, bring to a boil, reduce the heat, cover the pan and simmer for 10 minutes. Add the asparagus, the rest of the water or broth, salt and pepper and cook for about 15 minutes, until the asparagus is tender and the rice or potato is soft.

If you are using the asparagus tips for a garnish, cook them in boiling water for 2 to 4 minutes, or microwave them until tender, but not too soft. Set aside.

Puree with an immersion blender or in a food processor, or pass the soup through a food mill for the smoothest texture. Add the lemon juice and taste for salt and pepper. Garnish with the asparagus tips.

Serves 4 to 6

✿ Tomato Soup (*Parve*)

Cooked tomato products such as sauces and soups are high in the antioxidant lycopene.
Enjoy this delicious soup with a sandwich or salad for lunch or dinner.

═ INGREDIENTS ═

2 28-ounce cans of whole tomatoes
1 tablespoon dark brown sugar
2 tablespoons canola oil
2 medium onions, sliced thinly
1 tablespoon tomato paste
⅛ teaspoon nutmeg
2 tablespoons flour
2 cups water or vegetable broth

═ METHOD ═

Preheat the oven to 475 degrees Fahrenheit. Line a large baking sheet with foil.

Empty the canned tomatoes into a strainer set in a bowl to collect the juice. Open each tomato and break it in half over the strainer, letting the juice and seeds fall into the strainer. Discard the tomato seeds and reserve the juice.

Arrange the tomato halves, cut-side up, on the foil-lined baking sheet. Sprinkle them with brown sugar and roast about 20 minutes or until they start to brown.

Heat the oil in a large saucepan and sauté the onions for about 5 minutes, until soft. Stir the onions while sautéing them. Add the tomato paste and nutmeg and continue to cook and stir for another minute. Add the flour and cook, while stirring, for 1 more minute. Whisk in the water or broth. Add reserved tomato juice and roasted tomatoes. Simmer for about 10 minutes to blend flavors.

Puree the soup in a blender, food processor or immersion blender until smooth.

Serves 4

✤✥ Hungarian Mushroom Soup (Dairy)

Use what you know about good nutrition to create healthy versions of your favorite recipes. The following soup recipe came from an old Portland, Oregon, restaurant. I decreased the total amount of fat (including saturated fat) by using less oil in place of the butter and nonfat milk and low-fat sour cream rather than full-fat versions. Using less salt and low-sodium soy sauce reduces the sodium content.

Healthy Version	Original Version
2 tablespoons canola oil	6 tablespoons butter
1½ cups chopped onion	1½ cups chopped onion
4 teaspoons paprika	4 teaspoons paprika
4 teaspoons dried dill weed	4 teaspoons dried dill weed
1 teaspoon salt	2 teaspoons salt
1 teaspoon black pepper, freshly ground	1 teaspoon black pepper
⅔ cup all-purpose flour	⅔ cup all-purpose flour
1⅔ cups nonfat milk	1⅔ cups whole milk
2⅔ cups water	2⅔ cups water
4 cups sliced mushrooms	4 cups sliced mushrooms
1 tablespoon low-sodium soy sauce	2 tablespoons soy sauce
2 to 3 tablespoons fresh lemon juice	2 tablespoons lemon juice
½ cup low-fat sour cream	½ cup sour cream
3 tablespoons minced parsley	3 tablespoons minced parsley

═ METHOD ═

Heat the oil in a large soup pot. Sauté the onion with the paprika, dill weed, salt and pepper until the onion is soft.

Add the flour and stir for a few minutes to slightly brown the flour.

Slowly whisk in the milk and the water to keep the mixture smooth. Add the mushrooms and bring the mixture to a low boil.

Reduce the heat and simmer the soup for 30 minutes, stirring occasionally. Remove from the heat and stir in the soy sauce, lemon juice, sour cream and parsley. Serve hot.

Serves 6 to 8

‮‬ Sweet Potato Soup (*Parve*)

Two outstanding cooks, Sophie Stern and Doron Degen, gave me similar recipes for sweet potato soup, and I used both of them to create this version. Sophie adds a tablespoon of tomato paste and a carrot to her soup, and Doron adds cream and Thai sweet chili sauce to his. You can also substitute winter squash for the sweet potatoes in this recipe.

═ INGREDIENTS ═

1 tablespoon canola oil
1 medium onion, halved and sliced
1 large or 2 small sweet potatoes (1 pound total), peeled and cut into
  1-inch cubes
1-inch piece of fresh ginger, sliced thinly
4 cups water
½ teaspoon salt
Freshly ground pepper
½ teaspoon soy sauce

═ METHOD ═

Heat the oil in a pot over medium heat. Add the onion and sweet potatoes and cook, stirring frequently, until the onion and sweet potatoes begin to caramelize. This will take about 10 minutes. (They should turn a deep golden brown; be careful not to burn the vegetables.)

Add the ginger and cook, stirring, for another minute. Add the water, salt and pepper and bring the soup to a boil. Reduce the heat and simmer, covered, for about 30 minutes, until the sweet potatoes are completely soft.

Blend the soup with an immersion blender or in a food processor until completely smooth. Add the soy sauce, stir and serve hot.

Serves 4 to 5

✥ **Creamy Cauliflower Soup** (Dairy)

Your family will probably not guess that this mild-tasting soup is made with cauliflower.
It is an excellent, easy and delicious way to include more vegetables in your diet.

= INGREDIENTS =

1 tablespoon canola oil
1 large leek (white part only) or 1 medium onion, thinly sliced
2 to 3 celery stalks, thinly sliced
1 large cauliflower (about 2 pounds), broken into florets and washed
   well
3 cups nonfat milk
3 cups vegetable broth or water
1 medium potato, cubed
1 teaspoon salt
½ teaspoon freshly grated nutmeg
3 to 4 tablespoons fresh lemon juice
Fresh minced parsley

= METHOD =

Heat the oil in a large pot and sauté the leek or onion and the celery until
soft. Add the cauliflower, milk, broth or water, potato, salt and nutmeg. Bring
to a simmer, cover and cook over low heat until the cauliflower is tender,
about 30 minutes.

Remove from the heat and puree until smooth with an immersion blender.
(Alternatively, let the soup cool and puree it in batches using a food processor
or blender.) Add lemon juice to taste and serve hot, garnished with parsley.

Serves 6 to 8

❧ **Sweet and Sour Cabbage Soup** (*Parve*)

This is a quick and easy recipe from my friend Sophie. If you are in a big hurry, don't even sauté the onions. Just put all of the ingredients into a pot, bring them to a boil and simmer until the soup is done.

═ INGREDIENTS ═

2 teaspoons extra-virgin olive oil
1 medium onion, thinly sliced
1 small head cabbage (1 to 1½ pounds), halved, cored and thinly sliced
1 small can (14 to 15 ounces) diced tomatoes, with juice
½ cup tomato puree or ¼ cup tomato paste
4 cups water
3 tablespoons sugar
3 tablespoons freshly squeezed lemon juice

═ METHOD ═

Heat the oil in a large saucepan. Add the onion and sauté until golden, stirring occasionally. Add the remaining ingredients and bring to a boil. Reduce the heat and cover the soup. Cook for 30 to 40 minutes, until the cabbage is completely soft. Taste for seasonings and serve hot.

Serves 6 to 8

⁂ Split Pea and Potato Soup (*Parve*)

This is a very simple split pea soup that takes less than an hour to prepare. Choose either green or yellow split peas.

=== INGREDIENTS ===

2 teaspoons extra-virgin olive oil
1 medium onion, chopped
1 teaspoon dried dill or tarragon
¾ cup split peas, sorted, checked and rinsed
2 medium potatoes (about 1 pound total), cut into 1-inch pieces
4½ cups water or vegetable broth
Salt and fresh ground pepper to taste

=== METHOD ===

Heat the oil in a 3- to 4-quart saucepan and sauté the onions until soft. Add the herbs and stir for another minute. Add the split peas, potatoes and water or broth. Bring to a boil, cover the pan and simmer until the potatoes and split peas are tender, 20 to 30 minutes.

In a food processor or using an immersion blender, process the mixture until smooth. Add more water if necessary and season with salt and pepper to taste. Serve hot.

Serves 4 to 6

✤ **Cold Curried Pea Soup** (*Parve* or Dairy)

═ INGREDIENTS ═════════════════════════════
1 onion, diced
1 tablespoon extra-virgin olive oil
1 tablespoon curry powder
1 bag (16 ounces) frozen peas
3 cups vegetable stock or broth
Salt
Freshly ground pepper
2 teaspoons lemon juice
½ cup nonfat or low-fat plain yogurt (optional)

═ METHOD ═══════════════════════════════
Heat the oil and sauté the onion until soft. Add the curry powder and cook, stirring constantly, for 1 minute. Add the stock and peas and bring to a boil. Cover and simmer for about 4 minutes, until the peas are cooked. Season with salt and pepper to taste.

Blend with an immersion blender until smooth or pass through a food mill for the smoothest texture. Refrigerate for at least several hours until thoroughly chilled. Stir in lemon juice and yogurt, and serve.

Serves 4 to 6

SALADS

✣✤ Moroccan-Style Carrot Salad (*Parve*)

This lively and colorful salad goes well with chicken, fish and vegetarian meals. If you are in a big hurry, use ready-cut fresh carrots, usually found in the produce section of the grocery store.

INGREDIENTS
1 pound carrots, peeled
1 tablespoon balsamic vinegar
¼ cup red wine vinegar
1 tablespoon sweet paprika
1 tablespoon ground cumin
½ teaspoon salt
⅓ cup extra-virgin olive oil
2 cloves garlic, minced
⅓ cup minced parsley

METHOD
Slice the carrots on the diagonal into ⅓-inch thick slices. Place them in a pot and add cold water to cover. Cook until just tender and not too soft. Drain and set aside in a mixing bowl.

Prepare the dressing while the carrots are cooking: Whisk together the balsamic and red wine vinegar, paprika, cumin and salt. Gradually add the oil, whisking until well blended. Stir in the garlic and parsley.

Pour the dressing over the carrots while they are still hot, mixing well. Serve at room temperature.

Serves 4 to 6

✤ Indian-Style Sweet Potato Salad (*Parve*)

Good quality sweet potatoes are terrific served plain and simple – baked and straight from the oven. But here is a more unusual and equally delicious way to use them in a salad. Just be sure not to overbake the sweet potatoes or your salad will be mushy. Serve this as part of an Indian-inspired vegetarian meal or as a side dish with chicken or fish.

═ INGREDIENTS ═

2 pounds sweet potatoes
¼ cup pure maple syrup or honey
3 tablespoons orange juice
3 tablespoons lemon or lime juice
½ teaspoon salt
Freshly ground pepper to taste
½ cup extra-virgin olive oil
⅓ cup cilantro or parsley, finely chopped
2 tablespoons candied ginger, chopped
3 medium tomatoes, peeled, seeded and cut into ½-inch cubes OR
1 cup cherry tomatoes, halved or quartered, depending on their size

═ METHOD ═

Heat the oven to 400 degrees Fahrenheit. Prick potatoes in several places with a paring knife and place on a baking sheet. Bake for 30 to 40 minutes, until baked through, but not too soft. Cool, peel, cut into ½-inch cubes and put into a bowl.

Combine maple syrup or honey, juices, salt, pepper, oil and fresh herbs and mix well. Add the dressing and the ginger to the sweet potatoes and mix well. Refrigerate for at least an hour or overnight. Mix in the tomatoes before serving.

Serves 6

✣ Barley Salad (*Parve*)

Mushroom barley soup comes to mind when most of us think of barley. Here is a salad similar to tabouli that uses barley in a completely different way.

═ INGREDIENTS ═

3 cups water
¼ teaspoon salt
1 cup pearl barley
¼ cup extra-virgin olive oil
¼ cup fresh lemon juice
3 cloves garlic, minced
Salt and fresh ground pepper to taste
3 tomatoes or 12 cherry tomatoes, diced
1 small cucumber, peeled and diced
3 scallions, thinly sliced
¼ to ½ red pepper, diced
1 cup finely chopped Italian parsley

═ METHOD ═

Bring the water and salt to boil in a saucepan. Add the barley, return to a boil, cover and simmer for about 40 to 45 minutes, until tender but not mushy. Drain any excess water and set aside.

Meanwhile, whisk together olive oil, lemon juice, garlic, salt and pepper. Pour over the cooked, warm barley.

Add the diced vegetables and herbs and mix gently. Taste and adjust seasonings if necessary. Serve cold or at room temperature.

Serves 8

❧ Lentil Salad with Sun-Dried Tomatoes
(*Parve* or Dairy)

Plain brown lentils will work with this recipe, but smaller, more delicate black, green or brown varieties produce a more sophisticated salad. Just be sure to check frequently as you are cooking the lentils – you want to be sure that they are done, but not overdone and falling apart.

INGREDIENTS

1½ cups lentils, sorted and rinsed
½ cup sun-dried tomatoes
¼ cup balsamic vinegar
½ cup extra-virgin olive oil
1 tablespoon sun-dried tomato paste (optional)
1 teaspoon dried oregano
½ teaspoon salt
Freshly ground pepper
Feta or Bulgarian cheese, crumbled (optional)

METHOD

Bring a large pot of water to boil and add the lentils. Simmer for 20 to 30 minutes, or until tender, but not falling apart.

Meanwhile, reconstitute the dried tomatoes by pouring boiling water over them. Let them sit for 10 to 20 minutes and then drain off the water. Dice them with a knife or kitchen shears and set aside.

For the dressing, mix the balsamic vinegar, olive oil, sun-dried tomato paste (if using), oregano and salt. Add freshly ground pepper to taste.

When the lentils are cooked, drain the excess water and place them in a mixing bowl. Add the sun-dried tomatoes and the dressing to the warm lentils and mix well. Refrigerate for several hours or overnight. Serve at room temperature, adding the cheese at the last minute, if desired.

Serves 6

❧ Tuna and White Bean Salad (*Parve*)

Cook the beans ahead of time and this salad will come together quickly. For the utmost in convenience, start with rinsed and drained canned white beans. This makes a lovely summer lunch or dinner.

═ INGREDIENTS ═

½ pound dried white beans, soaked for 4 to 8 hours
1 tablespoon olive oil
1 garlic clove, crushed
2 cans tuna, preferably packed in olive oil
1 small red onion, sliced
12 cherry tomatoes, cut in half
¼ cup finely chopped parsley
¼ cup olive oil
¼ cup red wine vinegar
Salt and freshly ground black pepper to taste

═ METHOD ═

Drain soaked beans and then put into a pot with 6 cups of water, olive oil and garlic. Bring to boil, cover and simmer until tender, 45 to 60 minutes. Drain and put into large bowl to cool.

Add drained tuna, breaking it up into chunks with a fork. Gently stir in onion, tomatoes, parsley, olive oil and vinegar. Season with salt and pepper to taste.

Serves 6 to 8

❧ **Pasta Wheels Salad** (*Parve*)

This salad is a big hit with children, who love the shape of the pasta. The sweet and sour dressing is appealing to grown-ups as well. Add a can of tuna fish for a refreshing warm-weather main course.

=== INGREDIENTS ===

2 cups pasta wheels (*rotelle*)
½ cup sweet red onion, finely diced
¼ cup red pepper, diced
1 stalk celery, thinly sliced
1 carrot, diced
1 can tuna, drained (optional)
½ cup low-fat mayonnaise
¼ cup extra-virgin olive oil
1 tablespoon white wine vinegar
1 teaspoon sugar
½ teaspoon salt
Freshly ground pepper to taste
2 tablespoons finely chopped parsley

=== METHOD ===

Cook the pasta in boiling water until firm but not too soft, for 4 to 8 minutes. Drain, rinse, drain again and set aside in a large mixing bowl. Add the onion, vegetables and tuna (if using) to the pasta and mix gently.

Whisk the olive oil, vinegar, sugar, salt and pepper into the mayonnaise until well mixed and smooth. Stir in the parsley. Pour the dressing over the pasta and vegetables and chill for at least half an hour for the flavors to blend.

Serves 4 to 6

✹ Simple Steamed Broccoli (*Parve*)

Vegetables such as broccoli, cauliflower and cabbage are a good source of valuable fiber and antioxidants. Seasoned with lemon juice and olive oil, this tasty broccoli dish is easy to prepare.

═ INGREDIENTS ═
1 bunch broccoli
3 tablespoons extra-virgin olive oil
1 to 3 tablespoons fresh lemon juice
Salt and pepper to taste

═ METHOD ═
Wash, cut and check the broccoli. Peel the stems and finely chop the stems and florets. Steam the broccoli just until tender and bright green. Toss with the olive oil, salt and pepper. Just before serving, add the lemon juice, taste and serve.

Serves 4 to 6

✿ **Sweet and Sour Carrots** (*Parve*)

A nice change from plain cooked carrots, this Italian-inspired recipe is perfect for Shabbat or holidays. Pine nuts give the dish a classy touch but are optional, especially if you are in a hurry. You can serve these carrots warm or at room temperature.

═ INGREDIENTS ═

¼ cup pine nuts (optional)
½ cup raisins
¼ cup unsweetened grape juice
2 tablespoons red wine vinegar
2 tablespoons extra-virgin olive oil
2 pounds carrots, peeled and sliced diagonally, ¼ inch thick
⅛ teaspoon ground cinnamon
½ cup water
½ teaspoon salt

═ METHOD ═

Toast the pine nuts in a dry saucepan (use the same one that you will use to cook the carrots) over medium heat, stirring frequently, until they are golden brown. Remove from the pan and set aside.

Combine the raisins, grape juice and vinegar in a small bowl and set aside.

Heat the olive oil in the saucepan; add the carrots and cinnamon and cook, stirring frequently for about 5 minutes. Add the water, salt and raisins together with their soaking liquid, and bring the mixture to a boil. Cover the carrots and simmer for 15 to 20 minutes, until tender but still somewhat crisp. Add the pine nuts.

Serves 6 to 8

❧ **Peas and Mushrooms** (*Parve*)

Frozen baby peas are good to keep in the freezer – they cook in a few minutes and can be added to any number of pasta, soup, casserole and vegetable dishes for a dash of color and good nutrition. This simple recipe is from Sophie Stern, whose grandchildren often enjoy it for Shabbat *dinner.*

═ INGREDIENTS ═

2 teaspoons extra-virgin olive oil
1 small package (½ pound) fresh "button" mushrooms, washed, trimmed and sliced thinly
1 package frozen baby (*petite*) peas
Salt
Freshly ground pepper to taste

═ METHOD ═

Heat the olive oil in a pan over medium heat. Add the mushrooms and sauté until they are nicely browned and their liquid has evaporated. Add the frozen peas, cover and cook for about 5 minutes, until the peas are tender but still bright green. Season with salt and pepper to taste.

Serves 4 to 6

❧ Sophie's Special Beets (*Parve*)

Here is another of Sophie's vegetable recipes that are especially popular with her grandchildren.

═ INGREDIENTS ═══════════════════════════

4 medium beets, washed and trimmed
6 garlic cloves, washed but left unpeeled
1 tablespoon honey
1 tablespoon lemon juice
1 teaspoon salt
Freshly ground pepper

═ METHOD ════════════════════════════════

Preheat the oven to 400 degrees Fahrenheit. Wrap the beets and the garlic cloves separately in heavy-duty aluminum foil. Seal the foil tightly, place on a baking sheet, and bake for about 30 to 45 minutes, until the beets are tender when pricked with a knife and the garlic is soft. Open the foil and let the beets and the garlic cool.

Meanwhile, prepare the sauce by mixing the honey, lemon juice, salt and pepper together in a small bowl. Squeeze the garlic from their skins with your fingers and mix it into the sauce.

When the beets are cool enough to handle, peel them, cut them in half and slice them thinly. Pour the sauce over the warm beets and serve.

Serves 4 to 6

✺ Cauliflower Kugel (*Parve*)

Cauliflower, broccoli, cabbage, Brussels sprouts and greens such as kale and arugula are cruciferous vegetables containing valuable sulfur compounds. They are also high in vitamins C and K, magnesium, potassium and fiber. Here is a tasty non-potato kugel made with cauliflower.

== INGREDIENTS ==
1 large head cauliflower
2 tablespoons extra-virgin olive oil
1 onion, chopped
2 eggs
1 tablespoon flour
Salt and pepper to taste
Paprika

== METHOD ==
Preheat oven to 375 degrees Fahrenheit.

Cut the cauliflower florets from the stem. Wash, check and steam the cauliflower until very tender. Drain well and set aside.

Sauté the onion in olive oil, stirring occasionally until golden.

Place the cauliflower, eggs, flour, salt and pepper in the bowl of a food processor and pulse to create a slightly chunky mixture. (You can mash the cauliflower with a potato masher or a fork as well.) Mix in the sautéed onions. Pour the cauliflower mixture into an oiled 8 × 8-inch baking dish and sprinkle with paprika. Bake for 30 to 40 minutes.

Serves 4 to 6

VEGETARIAN MAIN COURSES

❧ Rice and Lentil Pilaf *(Parve)*

This stovetop dish is easy to prepare from ingredients that you most likely have on hand. Serve it with a green salad for a quick weekday dinner.

INGREDIENTS

1 small onion, chopped
1 tablespoon extra-virgin olive oil
1 cup raw brown rice, rinsed
1 tablespoon tomato paste
2½ cups water
¼ teaspoon cinnamon
¼ cup raw lentils, sorted and rinsed
1 teaspoon salt
½ cup raisins

METHOD

Heat the oil in a medium-size saucepan; add onion and sauté until soft. Add rice and sauté for another few minutes.

Combine water, tomato paste and cinnamon. Add this mixture to the rice and onions, along with the lentils. Bring to a boil, cover and simmer on low heat for 30 minutes.

Preheat oven to 360 degrees Fahrenheit. Oil an ovenproof casserole or baking dish.

After rice has cooked for 30 minutes, stir in salt and raisins. Add additional water if mixture is too dry, and place in casserole or baking dish. Cover and bake for 20 to 30 minutes.

Serves 4 to 6

✿✿ Curried Brown Rice and Lentil Casserole (*Parve*)

This is a vegetarian dish that is baked in the oven. Serve it with a salad or a green vegetable for an easy mid-week dinner. If you have a heavy enamel pan that can be used in the oven as well as the stovetop, use it here to simplify the recipe even further.

═══ INGREDIENTS ═══

1 cup long-grain brown rice, rinsed and drained
1 tablespoon extra-virgin olive oil
1 tablespoon curry powder
4 cups water
1 cup lentils, sorted and rinsed
1 cinnamon stick
1-inch piece of fresh ginger, peeled and thinly sliced
½ teaspoon salt

═══ METHOD ═══

Preheat the oven to 350 degrees Fahrenheit.

Heat the olive oil in a 1½- to 2-quart saucepan. Add the rice and cook, stirring, until lightly toasted, about a minute or two. Stir the curry powder into the rice and cook for a few seconds more. Add the water, lentils, cinnamon stick and ginger. Bring to a boil.

Transfer the mixture to a casserole or baking dish and cover it tightly. (Or cover the pan you are using if it is ovenproof.) Bake for 45 to 55 minutes, adding more water if necessary if the mixture looks dry. Remove the cinnamon and ginger before serving.

Serves 4 to 6

❧ Tex-Mex Flavored Bulgur (*Parve*)

Serve this flavorful dish as a main course with condiments like shredded low-fat cheese, sunflower seeds, bottled salsa, sliced green onions and low-fat sour cream. It can also be used as a side dish with fish, poultry or a bean dish such as chili.

INGREDIENTS

1 tablespoon extra-virgin olive oil
1 medium onion, chopped
1 cup bulgur wheat
1 stalk celery, sliced thinly
½ red or green pepper, diced
1 teaspoon chili powder
½ teaspoon cumin
2¼ cups water
½ teaspoon salt
Freshly ground pepper to taste

METHOD

Heat the oil in a wide pan over medium heat and sauté the onions until they are nearly soft. Add the bulgur to the pan and continue to sauté, stirring until the onions are soft and the bulgur is lightly toasted. Stir in celery, pepper and spices and cook for several minutes to slightly soften the vegetables. Add water, salt and pepper and bring to a boil. Reduce the heat to low, cover and cook until the water is absorbed, about 20 minutes.

Serves 4 to 6

✸✷ Shortcut Chili (*Parve*)

This recipe can be made with canned kidney beans, which saves time and effort. Be sure to drain and rinse them well to remove as much salt as possible. If you have the time, use home-cooked kidney beans. Fresh-baked cornbread goes nicely with this chili.

=== INGREDIENTS ===

2 tablespoons extra-virgin olive oil
1 tablespoon chili powder
3 medium onions, chopped
1 green or red pepper, chopped
1 tablespoon yellow mustard seeds
1 teaspoon cumin
1 teaspoon unsweetened cocoa powder
¼ teaspoon cinnamon
1 large can (14 to 16 ounces) diced tomatoes
3 cans (16 ounces) kidney beans, drained and rinsed, or 5 cups cooked
   kidney beans
1½ cups water
1 can (6 ounces) tomato paste

=== METHOD ===

In a large pan, heat oil and cook onions and peppers until soft. Add mustard seeds and cook, stirring, for another minute. Add spices, tomatoes, beans, water and tomato paste and mix well. Reduce heat and simmer for 30 to 40 minutes, until the chili has thickened.

Serves 6 to 8

✴ **Tamale Pie** (Dairy)

Tamale pie is a classic combination of beans and grains – complementary vegetarian protein. To save time, use canned beans and ready-made salsa or Mexican-style cooking sauce instead of the sauce in this recipe. Serve with a tossed salad for a nutritious mid-week meal.

INGREDIENTS

2 cups cooked kidney, pinto or black beans
1 tablespoon extra-virgin olive oil
1 medium onion, diced
1 clove garlic, minced
2 teaspoons chili powder
½ teaspoon salt
2 tablespoons tomato paste
½ cup ripe olives, sliced
½ cup frozen corn, thawed
3 cups water
1 cup cornmeal, preferably stone-ground
½ teaspoon salt
¼ cup grated Cheddar cheese

METHOD

Oil an 8 × 8-inch baking pan or spray with nonstick cooking spray.

Preheat the oven to 350 degrees Fahrenheit.

Mash the beans coarsely and set aside.

Heat the olive oil in a saucepan and sauté the onion until soft. Add the garlic and chili powder and sauté for another minute, stirring constantly. Mix the mashed beans, tomato paste, olives and corn into the onion mixture and cook until hot.

In another pan, bring 2 cups of the water to a boil. Mix the remaining cup of water, cornmeal and salt and add it to the boiling water, stirring constantly. (A whisk works well for this.) Cook and stir until the mixture boils and thickens.

Spread half of the cornmeal mixture on the bottom of the baking pan. Spoon the bean mixture over this and spread the remaining cornmeal over the beans. Sprinkle the cheese on top and bake for about 30 minutes.

Serves 4 to 6

✸✿ Stuffed Baked Potatoes (Dairy)

Children are especially fond of potatoes, and this stuffed version is sure to be a favorite. Potatoes and broccoli provide vitamins, minerals, fiber and antioxidants in this tasty combination that is also low in fat. For faster preparation, cook the potatoes in the microwave. You can even prepare this dish in advance, keep it refrigerated and heat just before serving. Double or triple the recipe if you are serving a crowd.

=== INGREDIENTS ===

2 large baking potatoes, scrubbed
1 large stalk broccoli, checked and washed
¼ teaspoon salt
1 tablespoon extra-virgin olive oil
1 tablespoon nonfat or low-fat milk
2 tablespoons grated Parmesan or Cheddar cheese

=== METHOD ===

Preheat the oven to 400 degrees Fahrenheit. Make a shallow cut in the middle of each potato. (This will make it easier to cut them in half later.) Place the potatoes on a baking dish and bake until soft, about 1 hour.

Cut the fibrous ends from the broccoli and peel the stalks. Lightly steam the broccoli, for just a few minutes, until the color changes to bright green. It should be tender but still crunchy. Drain and chop it into very small pieces.

When the potatoes are baked and cool enough to handle, scoop the insides into a bowl, leaving a small amount of potato on the skin to hold the filling. Mash the potatoes and add the salt, olive oil, cheese and broccoli.

Place the filling inside the potato shells and heat until warm.

Serves 4

❧ **Pasta with Zucchini Sauce** (Dairy)

=== INGREDIENTS ===

2 tablespoons extra-virgin olive oil
1 small onion, minced
5 to 6 medium zucchini, thinly sliced
2 cups nonfat milk
1 pound pasta tubes or spirals
¼ cup grated Parmesan cheese
Freshly ground pepper

=== METHOD ===

Heat the oil in a large pan and sauté the onion until soft. Add the zucchini and cook, stirring until slightly soft.

Add the milk and bring to a simmer. Cook uncovered over very low heat, until most of the milk has evaporated, stirring the mixture occasionally so that the bottom of the pan does not burn. Allow up to an hour of cooking for the milk to cook down with the zucchini into a sauce.

When the sauce is about half cooked, bring a large pot of water to boil and cook the pasta. Drain the pasta, rinse, drain again and set aside.

Add the cheese and ground pepper to the cooked sauce and mix with the pasta.

Serves 6 to 8

✿ Swiss Chard with Soba Noodles (*Parve*)

Chard or spinach cooked with raisins and pine nuts is common in many Sephardic cuisines. Soba, or buckwheat noodles, come to us from Japan. This dish combines them both! One hundred percent buckwheat noodles are more assertive in flavor than those made with a blend of buckwheat and regular flour. You can find soba noodles at whole or health food stores.

═ INGREDIENTS ═

1 to 1½ pounds Swiss chard
2 tablespoons pine nuts
2 tablespoons extra-virgin olive oil
4 garlic cloves, minced
½ teaspoon salt
12 ounces soba noodles
¼ teaspoon red pepper flakes (optional)
¼ cup raisins
Salt to taste

═ METHOD ═

Wash the chard carefully. Cut the chard stems into ½-inch dice. Chop the leaves coarsely. Set the stems and leaves aside, keeping them separate.

In a large nonstick skillet, toast the pine nuts, stirring frequently, until lightly toasted. Remove the nuts from the pan and set them aside.

In the same skillet, heat the olive oil. Add the chard stems and cook until they begin to soften. Add the garlic and red pepper flakes (optional) to the chard stems and cook for another minute. Add the chard leaves and salt, cover and cook until wilted, stirring occasionally.

Bring a large pot of water to boil and cook the soba noodles until *al dente*. Reserve ½ cup of the cooking liquid and then drain the noodles. Rinse them and drain again.

Mix the raisins and the noodles into the chard and heat them for a few minutes. Add the pine nuts and serve hot.

Serves 4 to 6

✴ Tofu Stir-Fry with Peanut Sauce and Napa Cabbage (*Parve*)

This method of cutting and cooking the tofu produces a great taste and texture that many people who normally don't like tofu will enjoy. Use this basic tofu preparation method with the following peanut sauce and Napa cabbage, or use your favorite homemade or store-bought sauce and vegetables of your choice for an easy stir-fry meal.

Tofu

═ INGREDIENTS ═
1 package firm tofu (14 to 16 ounces)
2 teaspoons canola or peanut oil

Peanut Sauce

═ INGREDIENTS ═
6 tablespoons water
4 tablespoons natural peanut butter
1 tablespoon vinegar
2 teaspoons soy sauce
2 teaspoons honey
2 teaspoons minced ginger
2 cloves garlic, minced

Vegetables

═ INGREDIENTS ═
4 cups Napa cabbage, sliced
1 cup mushrooms, sliced

═ METHOD ═
Drain and pat the tofu until dry. Slice it crosswise into 6 to 8 slices, ½ inch thick. Crumble the slices into small, uneven pieces. Whisk the sauce ingredients in a small bowl and set aside.

Heat the oil in a large skillet over high heat. Add the tofu and cook until it turns golden brown. Stir gently and continue to cook until all of the sides are golden brown. Add the sauce and the vegetables and cook, stirring, just until the vegetables are tender-crisp.

Serves 4

❧ Sweet and Spicy Tofu (*Parve*)

This is another easy tofu recipe. Use your imagination with different spices to produce a variety of flavors. Curry powder, for instance, would work well, as would baharat, *a Mediterranean spice blend. Substitute 1½ tablespoons of either of these for the spice mixture supplied in the recipe.*

═ INGREDIENTS ═

1 package firm tofu (14 to 16 ounces)
1 tablespoon hot or sweet paprika
1 teaspoon ground coriander
1 teaspoon ground cumin
½ teaspoon salt
2 tablespoons lemon juice
1 tablespoon honey
3 tablespoons hot water
1 tablespoon canola oil

═ METHOD ═

Drain the tofu and pat dry with a paper or regular towel. Cut the tofu crosswise into eighths.

Mix the spices and salt together and place them in a shallow dish. Dip each piece of tofu into the spice mixture to coat all sides.

Mix the lemon juice, honey and hot water in a small bowl and set aside.

Heat the oil in a nonstick skillet and cook the tofu pieces until they are well browned on all sides. Carefully add the sauce mixture and stir to coat the tofu.

Serves 4

FISH

✣ Soy-Glazed Salmon (*Parve*)

You will probably have most of the ingredients for this dish on hand. Try this glaze with other fish fillets as well.

=== INGREDIENTS ===

1 tablespoon canola oil
1 tablespoon low-sodium soy sauce
1 tablespoon honey
1 tablespoon Dijon mustard
1 to 1½ pounds salmon fillets

=== METHOD ===

Preheat oven to 400 degrees Fahrenheit.

Mix together oil, soy sauce, honey and mustard in a small bowl.

Place salmon fillets in a lightly oiled baking dish. Pour most of the sauce mixture on the salmon, leaving some on the side.

Bake until salmon is done. It should flake easily with a fork and look opaque. Spoon the remaining sauce over the fish and serve.

Serves 4 to 6

✤✤ Oven-Steamed Fish with Vegetables (*Parve*)

This one-dish meal can be prepared using salmon, tuna, cod, halibut or other fish fillets. You can use a variety of other vegetables as well, and add fresh or dried herbs of your choice.

═ INGREDIENTS ═══════════════════════

4 fish fillets (see suggestions above), 6 ounces each
2 tablespoons lemon juice
1 pound Yukon Gold or other boiling potatoes, peeled and sliced ½ inch thick
4 medium carrots, peeled and sliced ½ inch thick
1 medium onion, cut into ½-inch dice
1 tablespoon extra-virgin olive oil
Salt and freshly ground black pepper
2 medium sized zucchini squash, sliced ¼ inch thick

═ METHOD ═══════════════════════

Preheat oven to 400 degrees Fahrenheit. Sprinkle the fish with 1 tablespoon of the lemon juice and set aside in the refrigerator.

Combine potatoes, carrots and onions in a 9 × 13-inch baking dish. Mix in the olive oil, salt and pepper to coat the vegetables. Bake, stirring occasionally, until the potatoes are almost tender, 20 to 30 minutes. Stir in the zucchini and bake for another 10 minutes. Stir the remaining tablespoon of lemon juice into the vegetables.

Arrange the fish fillets on top of the vegetables and cook for another 10 minutes, or until fish is completely cooked.

Serves 4

✌ **Spicy Roasted Salmon** (*Parve*)

══ INGREDIENTS ═══════════════════════════
¼ cup orange juice
2 tablespoons lemon juice
4 salmon fillets, 6 ounces each
2 tablespoons brown sugar
4 teaspoons chili powder
½ teaspoon ground cumin
2 teaspoons grated lemon rind
¼ teaspoon cinnamon

══ METHOD ════════════════════════════════
Place fish in a shallow glass container. Combine orange and lemon juice and pour it over the fish. Marinate in the refrigerator for about an hour.

Preheat oven to 400 degrees Fahrenheit.

Combine brown sugar, chili powder, cumin, lemon rind and cinnamon in a small bowl. Drain excess marinade from the fish and rub the spice mixture into the fillets.

Coat a baking dish with cooking spray and arrange fish fillets in a single layer. Bake for 10 to 15 minutes or until the fish flakes easily.

Serves 4

❧ Italian-Style Sweet and Sour Fish *(Parve)*

Firm white fish fillets work well with this recipe – my favorite choice is tilapia. You can bake this dish ahead of time, refrigerate it and serve it at room temperature, or enjoy it hot. We often enjoy eating this for lunch on Shabbat.

═══ INGREDIENTS ═══
6 fish fillets (about 6 ounces each)
⅓ cup golden raisins
2 tablespoons pine nuts (optional)
¼ cup water
1 tablespoon honey
2 tablespoons lemon juice
2 tablespoons extra-virgin olive oil

═══ METHOD ═══
Preheat the oven to 400 degrees Fahrenheit. Lightly oil a baking pan and arrange the fish in the pan in a single layer. Sprinkle the raisins and pine nuts evenly over the fish.

Mix together water, honey, lemon juice and olive oil. Pour this mixture over the fish.

Bake uncovered for 10 to 20 minutes, until fish is thoroughly cooked.

Serves 6

✌ **Crispy Baked Fish** (*Parve*)

Try this healthy version of crisp-coated fish fillets and you may never go back to buying frozen fish sticks. Use a firm-textured fish such as cod, scrod, orange roughy or halibut. Serve these with homemade tartar sauce made with low-fat mayonnaise, diced dill pickle and a dash of lemon juice.

═══ INGREDIENTS ═══════════════════════════

⅓ cup dry bread crumbs
⅓ cup cornmeal
½ teaspoon salt
¼ teaspoon freshly ground pepper
1 large egg
1 pound fish fillets, cut into four equal pieces

═══ METHOD ═══════════════════════════════

Preheat the oven to 450 degrees Fahrenheit.

Line a baking sheet with aluminum foil and oil well or spray with nonstick cooking spray.

In a shallow bowl or on a piece of waxed paper, mix together the bread crumbs, cornmeal, salt and pepper.

In another shallow bowl, beat the egg lightly.

Dip each piece of fish in the beaten egg and then in the crumb mixture. Place the fish on the prepared baking pan.

Bake for 8 to 10 minutes, until the fish is crispy and cooked through. (This will depend a lot on the thickness of the fish fillets.) Serve hot.

Serves 4

✿ Salmon Patties (*Parve*)

With a can of salmon and a few other ingredients that you probably have on hand, this simple main course comes together quickly for a mid-week dinner. Use bread crumbs during the year and matzah meal for Pesach. My mother always served these patties with creamed peas, but I prefer plain frozen cooked peas or a tossed green salad and oven-fried potato wedges on the side.

=== INGREDIENTS ===

1 small onion, quartered
1 small handful parsley
1 can (15 to 16 ounces) salmon, including liquid
1 egg
1 tablespoon fresh lemon juice
½ cup whole-grain bread crumbs or *matzah* meal
Freshly ground pepper
Olive oil for cooking

=== METHOD ===

Put the onion and parsley in the food processor and pulse until chopped. Add the salmon, egg, lemon juice, bread crumbs (or *matzah* meal) and pepper. Pulse again to mix all of the ingredients.

Alternatively, mince the onion and parsley with a knife, mash the salmon with a fork and mix the ingredients together in a bowl.

Add more bread crumbs (or *matzah* meal) if necessary to hold the mixture together.

Heat the oil in a nonstick skillet. Form the salmon mixture into patties, using between ¼ and ½ cup for each one. Sauté the patties in the oil until brown. Turn them over and sauté on the other side. Serve hot.

Serves 4 to 6

POULTRY

⁂ Baked Chicken and Rice (Meat)

This is a quick and easy recipe using chicken, brown rice and Sephardic-style seasonings. One of them, baharat, *is a Mediterranean blend that often includes cinnamon, cloves and chili peppers. If the spices in this recipe do not appeal to you, substitute others, such as oregano, dill or tarragon.*

= INGREDIENTS =
1 tablespoon extra-virgin olive oil
1 large onion, minced
1½ cups brown rice, rinsed
2 teaspoons ground cumin
2 teaspoons ground coriander
1 teaspoon ground turmeric
1 teaspoon ground paprika
½ teaspoon freshly ground pepper
½ teaspoon ground *baharat* (optional)
½ teaspoon salt
3 cups water
2½ to 3 pounds chicken, cut into pieces and skin removed

= METHOD =
Preheat the oven to 350 degrees Fahrenheit.

Heat the oil in a skillet and sauté the onion, stirring, until golden. Put the onion into a large shallow baking dish or casserole. Add the rice to the onions and mix together.

Mix the spices and salt in a small bowl. Set aside a few teaspoons of the mixture and add the remaining spices to the water. Pour this over the rice in the baking dish. Place the chicken pieces on top and sprinkle with the remaining spice mixture.

Cover tightly and bake for 1 hour. Uncover and bake for another 15 minutes, until the chicken is thoroughly cooked and browned.

Serves 4 to 6

✣ Tali's Israeli Couscous and Chicken Salad (Meat)

My daughter-in-law, Tali, shared this elegantly presented warm salad recipe with me. Similar to pasta, Israeli couscous is much larger than regular couscous. It can be eaten warm as a side dish, made into a salad with added vegetables or used in any number of creative ways, as in this recipe.

═ INGREDIENTS ═

Couscous:
1 tablespoon extra-virgin olive oil
2 cups Israeli couscous
2½ cups water
½ cup orange juice
¼ teaspoon salt

Dressing:
2 tablespoons olive oil
¼ cup orange juice
¼ teaspoon salt
Freshly ground pepper
½ teaspoon cinnamon
½ teaspoon cumin
½ teaspoon turmeric
2 tablespoons olive oil
4 pieces skinless, boneless chicken breasts, flattened
2 seedless oranges, peeled and thinly sliced
4 cups mixed baby greens or tender lettuce, torn into small pieces

═ METHOD ═

Heat 1 tablespoon olive oil in a saucepan over medium heat. Add the couscous, and toast, stirring often, until golden, 3 to 5 minutes. Add the water, orange juice and salt and bring to a boil. Reduce the heat to low, cover and cook until the couscous has absorbed the liquid, 10 to 15 minutes. Set aside to cool.

Make the dressing by mixing together olive oil, orange juice, salt and pepper. Set aside.

Mix spices into a paste with 2 tablespoons of olive oil. Rub the mixture onto both sides of the chicken breasts.

Heat a nonstick skillet and sauté the chicken breasts until brown on each side and cooked through. Remove to a cutting board and cut into strips.

Arrange the baby greens or lettuce on 4 to 6 dinner plates. Drizzle a little dressing over the greens. Fluff the couscous with a fork and divide it equally over the greens. Arrange the orange slices and chicken over the couscous and divide the remaining dressing over each salad. Serve while still warm.

Serves 4 to 6

✣ **Fragrant Baked Chicken and Onions** (Meat)

Here is an easy and delicious chicken dish that works well during the week as well as on Shabbat and holidays. Remove the skin from the chicken before baking for the leanest dish. Otherwise, remove all of the visible fat before baking and take the skin off before eating the chicken. The leanest cuts of chicken are the white meat (breasts), while dark meat cuts (legs, thighs) contain more fat.

=== INGREDIENTS ===

2 large onions, sliced thickly
2 teaspoons cumin
1 teaspoon coriander
1 teaspoon sweet or hot paprika
1 teaspoon turmeric
½ teaspoon fresh ground pepper
3 pounds chicken pieces (or a whole, cut-up chicken)

=== METHOD ===

Preheat the oven to 375 degrees Fahrenheit.

Spray a roasting pan with nonstick spray and arrange the onions in the pan.

Mix the spices together in a small bowl. Using your hands, rub the spice mixture into each piece of chicken. Place the chicken pieces on top of the onions in the pan. Cover the pan and bake for 45 minutes.

Remove the cover and bake for an additional 10 to 20 minutes, until chicken is cooked through and browned.

Serves 6

❧ Chicken with Bulgur and Prunes (Meat)

One-half to one cup of dried cherries or cranberries can be substituted for the prunes, if you prefer. Here is an easy and delicious way to "stretch" chicken breasts by combining them with bulgur wheat.

INGREDIENTS

1½ pounds skinless, boneless chicken breasts
2 tablespoons extra-virgin olive oil
6 green onions, sliced
2 tablespoons minced fresh ginger
1 tablespoon minced fresh garlic
10 large pitted prunes cut in quarters
1½ cups bulgur
1 cup orange juice
2 cups water
Freshly ground pepper

METHOD

Cut chicken breasts into large cubes.

Heat the oil in a nonstick pan and sauté the chicken until golden. Remove the chicken from the pan with a slotted spoon so that the oil remains. Set the chicken aside.

In the same pan sauté the green onions, ginger and garlic for 1 minute. Add the prunes, bulgur, orange juice, water and pepper to the pan. Bring to a boil, reduce the heat, cover and cook for 10 to 15 minutes, until the liquid is absorbed. Add the chicken to the pan and cook for another several minutes.

Serves 6 to 8

✿✿ Honey Mustard Chicken (Meat)

Store-bought sauces are often very high in sodium. Here is an example of a delicious and healthier sauce that you can prepare in just a few minutes. And most likely you will have most of the ingredients in your pantry.

═ INGREDIENTS ═══════════════════════════════

⅓ cup balsamic vinegar
⅓ cup honey
¼ cup Dijon mustard
3 cloves fresh garlic, minced
1 tablespoon extra-virgin olive oil
8 skinless, boneless chicken breast halves (2 pounds total), ½ inch thick

═ METHOD ═══════════════════════════════════

For the sauce, combine the vinegar, honey, mustard and garlic in a bowl and set aside.

Heat the oil in a large nonstick pan and cook the chicken until well browned. Turn the chicken over and cook until brown on the other side. Reduce the heat and add the sauce to the pan. Cover and cook until the chicken is completely cooked.

Serves 8

DESSERTS

✺ Chocolate Chip Cookies (*Parve* or Dairy)

Canola oil replaces margarine in this popular recipe. Whole-wheat pastry flour gives the cookies a nice texture without tasting heavy. They can be prepared quickly, making them an easy, last-minute dessert. These are parve *cookies, unless you use dairy chocolate chips.*

═ INGREDIENTS ═

½ cup canola oil
⅓ cup white sugar
⅓ cup brown sugar
1 egg
1 teaspoon vanilla extract
1¾ cup whole-wheat pastry flour
½ teaspoon salt
½ teaspoon baking soda
½ cup chocolate chips
½ cup chopped walnuts
(Or use 1 cup chocolate chips and omit walnuts)

═ METHOD ═

Preheat oven to 350 degrees Fahrenheit. Coat two baking sheets with cooking spray or line with parchment paper.

Whisk together flour, salt and baking soda in a small bowl. Combine oil, sugars, egg and vanilla in a mixing bowl and mix well. Add in the dry ingredients and mix thoroughly. Mix in the chocolate chips and the walnuts.

Form the dough into balls the size of a tablespoon and place on the baking sheet, about an inch apart. Bake for 10 to 12 minutes, until golden brown and firm around the edges. Cool for a few minutes on the pan and then transfer to a wire rack to cool completely.

Yields: about 2½ dozen cookies

✣ Suretta's Oatmeal Raisin Cookies (*Parve*)

My friend Suretta loves to bake. Between the two of us, there was always something in the oven when our boys were growing up. I played with her recipe, substituting whole-wheat flour and reducing the amount of oil and sugar. If you enjoy the taste of olive oil, use a fruity extra-virgin variety. Otherwise, use light olive oil or canola oil.

=== INGREDIENTS ===

1¾ cups whole-wheat pastry flour
1 teaspoon baking soda
½ teaspoon salt
1 cup sugar
½ cup plus 2 tablespoons olive or canola oil
2 eggs
2 tablespoons water
2 teaspoons vanilla
2½ cups rolled oats (uncooked oatmeal)
½ cup raisins
½ cup walnut pieces, chopped (optional)

=== METHOD ===

Preheat oven to 375 degrees Fahrenheit. Line two baking sheets with parchment paper or spray with nonstick cooking spray.

Whisk together the flour, baking soda and salt in a large mixing bowl.

Mix together the sugar, oil, eggs, water and vanilla. Add these to the dry ingredients and mix well. Add the oats, raisins and walnuts, if using, and mix well.

Form the mixture into balls, about a heaped tablespoon each. Place on baking sheet, about 2 inches apart. Use a fork to press down on each cookie to flatten it.

Bake for 12 to 14 minutes, until firm and golden brown.

Yields: about 3 dozen cookies

✿ Dried Fruit and Nut Bars (*Parve*)

These could be described as "health food bars," but they are much tastier than anything you might find in the store. Filled with dried fruit, nuts and sesame seeds, they make a nice snack and would even be good for breakfast served with yogurt or a glass of skim milk.

══ INGREDIENTS ══

½ cup chopped almonds or walnuts
⅓ cup sesame seeds
½ cup whole-wheat flour
1 teaspoon cinnamon
¾ teaspoon baking powder
⅛ teaspoon salt
2½ cups dried unsweetened chopped fruit (see suggestions below)
⅓ cup canola or mild olive oil
⅓ cup brown sugar
2 large eggs
1 teaspoon vanilla
9-inch square baking pan

══ METHOD ══

Preheat oven to 325 degrees Fahrenheit.

Spread the nuts in the baking pan and toast in the oven for about 5 minutes, until they begin to smell fragrant; add the sesame seeds to the pan with the nuts and continue baking until the nuts and seeds are lightly toasted, another minute or two.

Remove nuts and seeds to a small bowl and set aside.

When cool enough to handle, line the baking pan with aluminum foil and oil lightly or spray with nonstick cooking spray.

Adjust the oven temperature to 375 degrees Fahrenheit.

Whisk together the flour, cinnamon, baking powder and salt in a large mixing bowl. Add dried fruit, nuts and sesame seeds.

Mix together oil, brown sugar, eggs and vanilla, and then stir into dry ingredients, mixing until well combined. The batter will be thick.

Spread batter evenly into baking pan. Bake until golden, 25 to 30 minutes. Cool completely before removing from the pan and cutting into bars.

Dried fruit suggestions: pitted and chopped dates (especially good with walnuts), diced apricots (dice them easily with kitchen shears), chopped figs, peaches, nectarines or raisins

Yields: about 25 small bars

✣ **Lemon Olive Oil Cake** (*Parve*)

═ INGREDIENTS ════════════════════════════════
1⅓ cups all-purpose flour
1 cup sugar, divided
½ teaspoon salt
4 eggs, separated
Grated zest of 1 lemon
2 tablespoons fresh lemon juice
2 tablespoons lemon or orange liqueur or orange juice
⅓ cup fruity extra-virgin olive oil
1 teaspoon almond extract

═ METHOD ═════════════════════════════════════
Preheat oven to 325 degrees Fahrenheit. Set aside a 9-inch ungreased springform pan.

Combine the flour, ⅔ cup sugar and salt in a small bowl and whisk together.

Whisk the egg whites until soft peaks begin to form. Gradually add the remaining ⅓ cup of sugar to the whites and continue to whisk until stiff peaks form. Remove to a clean bowl and set aside.

Without cleaning the bowl you used for the egg whites, combine the egg yolks, lemon zest, lemon juice, liqueur or juice, olive oil and almond extract. Beat until pale yellow. Mix in the flour mixture lightly, only until blended.

Beat ⅓ of the beaten whites into the yolk mixture; fold in the remaining whites by hand.

Pour the batter into the pan and bake for 45 to 50 minutes, or until the center feels dry. Remove to a cake rack to cool. When completely cool, run a knife around the edge to loosen sides before removing the cake from the pan.

Serves 10 to 12

✣ Lemon Cake with Variations (*Parve*)

The following recipe was developed by substituting unsweetened applesauce for half of the oil called for in the original recipe. The amount of sugar was reduced as well.

══ INGREDIENTS ═══════════════════════

3 cups all-purpose flour
2 teaspoons baking powder
½ teaspoon baking soda
½ teaspoon salt
½ teaspoon citric acid
½ cup canola oil
1½ cups sugar
Zest of 1 lemon
4 eggs
2 teaspoons vanilla extract
½ cup unsweetened smooth applesauce
½ cup lemon juice
¾ cup water
10-inch tube pan or two 8 × 4-inch or 9 × 5-inch loaf pans

══ METHOD ═══════════════════════════

Oil the pans and line bottoms with parchment paper.

Preheat oven to 350 degrees Fahrenheit.

In a medium-size bowl whisk together flour, baking powder, baking soda, salt and citric acid. Set aside.

In a large mixing bowl, blend oil, sugar and lemon zest until light and fluffy. Blend in eggs, one at a time. Add vanilla, applesauce, lemon juice and water and mix well. Add the flour mixture to the egg mixture and mix well.

Pour the batter into the pan(s). Bake in a large tube pan for 55 to 65 minutes or in loaf pans for 40 to 50 minutes, or until cake tester comes out clean. Leave in pan for 15 to 20 minutes before turning out onto a cake rack.

Variations:
Fold into batter ½ cup poppy seeds or 1 cup chocolate chips or 1 cup chopped dried apricots or 1 cup raisins or currants. (Plump dried fruit in hot water and drain well before adding to the batter.)

Serves 12

❧ **Carrot Cake or Cupcakes** (*Parve*)

This carrot cake recipe uses prune puree to replace much of the oil called for in traditional recipes. Crushed pineapple and carrots add moisture as well. The amount of sugar has been reduced, and whole-wheat pastry flour replaces the white flour called for in the original recipe.

═ INGREDIENTS ═

1 small can (8 oz) crushed pineapple packed in juice
2 cups grated fresh carrots (about 4 carrots)
1 cup pitted prunes
⅓ cup hot water
2¼ cups whole-wheat pastry flour
2 teaspoons baking powder
1½ teaspoons baking soda
½ teaspoon salt
2 teaspoons ground cinnamon
3 large eggs
1 cup sugar
⅓ cup canola oil
9 × 5-inch loaf pan + small muffin pan (6 cupcakes) OR
2 large muffin pans (12 each) or two 9-inch, round cake pans

═ METHOD ═

Preheat oven to 350 degrees Fahrenheit. Coat pans with cooking spray or line muffin tins with paper liner.

Drain the pineapple and set aside.

Use a food processor (with shredding disc) to grate the carrots. Set them aside.

Combine prunes and hot water in the processor (with the metal blade) and process until smooth.

Mix together flour, baking powder, baking soda, salt and cinnamon in a bowl and set aside.

In a large bowl, whisk together eggs, sugar and canola oil until smooth. Add prune puree and mix well.

Add the dry ingredients to the egg mixture and mix to blend. Stir in the pineapple and carrots.

Divide the batter between the prepared pans and bake until cake tester comes out clean, about 20 minutes for cupcakes, 25 to 30 minutes for round pans and 40 minutes for loaf pan.

Remove the cakes from the baking pans and cool on a baking rack.

Serves 12

✣ Doron's Banana Walnut Cupcakes
(Parve)

Doron Degen trained as a pastry chef in Canada and now lives in Beer Sheva. I gave him a basic banana cake recipe to play with and he came up with this delicious version. If you are short on time, you can prepare the recipe without sautéing the bananas, but it won't taste quite as sophisticated.

═ INGREDIENTS ═

½ cup walnuts
⅔ cup whole-wheat pastry flour
⅓ cup all-purpose white flour
1 tablespoon cornstarch
¾ teaspoon baking powder
¾ teaspoon baking soda
¼ teaspoon salt
¼ teaspoon freshly grated nutmeg
3 large, very ripe bananas
¼ teaspoon cinnamon
½ tsp unsweetened cocoa
⅓ cup brown sugar
1 large egg
¼ cup canola oil
12-cup muffin pan

═ METHOD ═

Preheat oven to 375 degrees Fahrenheit.

Line muffin pan with paper liners.

Whisk together the whole-wheat flour, white flour, cornstarch, baking powder, baking soda, salt and nutmeg and set aside.

Cut peeled bananas into large pieces and place in the large mixing bowl of an electric mixer. Beat until coarsely mashed and transfer to a measuring cup. You should have 1½ cups of mashed bananas. In a lightly oiled pan, gently sauté the bananas with the cinnamon, unsweetened cocoa, and 1 teaspoon of the brown sugar until slightly softened.

Beat the rest of the brown sugar, egg, and oil using the electric mixer and the same mixing bowl (no need to wash it out). Add the bananas to mix and then add the dry ingredients. Mix only until blended. Stir in the walnuts.

Place batter in muffin pans and bake for 20 to 25 minutes, until the tops spring back when gently pressed. Remove from pan and cool on a rack.

Serves 12

✣ **Surprise Cupcakes** (*Parve*)

These cupcakes are one way to "sneak" vegetables past fussy children. Choose from carrots, zucchini or beets – they all add moisture, but their taste is not detected. This is another of Sophie's grandchildren's favorite recipes.

═══ INGREDIENTS ═══════════════════════════

2 large eggs
1 cup sugar
1 square (1 ounce) unsweetened chocolate, melted
2 tablespoons canola oil
1 teaspoon vanilla extract
¾ cup all-purpose or whole-wheat pastry flour
¼ cup unsweetened cocoa powder
1 teaspoon baking soda
1½ cups raw grated carrots, zucchini or beets

═══ METHOD ═══════════════════════════════

Preheat oven to 350 degrees Fahrenheit. Line 12 muffin cups with paper liners.

Beat eggs and sugar in an electric mixer for 1 minute, until smooth. Add melted chocolate, oil and vanilla and mix well.

Sift flour, cocoa powder and baking soda together and add to the egg mixture. Stir the grated vegetables into the batter. Spoon into the muffin cups and bake for 20 to 30 minutes, until a toothpick inserted into the center of a cupcake comes out clean. Cool the cupcakes on a wire rack.

Yields: 12 cupcakes

✢✿ Chocolate Jam Cake (*Parve*)

This cake is not exactly healthy, but it has a lot less sugar and fat than most purchased chocolate cakes. With a microwave, it comes together quickly, and you are likely to have most of the ingredients on hand. Choose high-quality cherry, raspberry or apricot jam or orange marmalade. A tablespoon or two of liqueur of the same flavor as the jam can be added for an extra fancy touch.

═ INGREDIENTS ═

1 cup cake flour
1 teaspoon baking powder
¼ teaspoon salt
⅓ cup canola oil
4 ounces bittersweet chocolate, cut into small pieces
⅓ cup sugar
1 cup jam or marmalade (see suggestions above)
2 eggs, beaten

═ METHOD ═

Preheat the oven to 350 degrees Fahrenheit.

Line the bottom of an 8-inch springform pan with baking paper and spray the pan with nonstick cooking spray.

Whisk together the flour, baking powder and salt in a mixing bowl and set aside.

Put the oil and the chocolate into a 4-cup Pyrex measuring cup. Microwave for 3 minutes on low power, or until the chocolate is melted. Whisk the chocolate and oil together. Add the sugar, jam and eggs to the chocolate, mixing well with a spoon or rubber spatula. Add this to the dry ingredients a little at a time until everything is mixed together. Pour the batter into the pan.

Bake for 40 to 50 minutes, until a wooden skewer comes out clean. Cool on a rack for 10 minutes before removing the sides and bottom of the pan.

Serves 8 to 12

✣ Oven Baked Pears (*Parve*)

This simple method of preparation may change your attitude towards pears. It makes an especially nice dessert during the winter. Use one small or half of a large pear per serving.

INGREDIENTS

Fresh pears
Fresh lemon juice
Cinnamon-sugar (½ teaspoon cinnamon to ¼ cup sugar)

METHOD

Preheat the oven to 375 degrees Fahrenheit. Lightly spray a shallow baking pan or casserole dish with nonstick cooking spray or brush lightly with oil.

Peel and core the pears. Cut them in half or in thick slices. Brush all of the surfaces with lemon juice and place in the baking dish.

Sprinkle the pears with the cinnamon-sugar mixture.

Cover tightly and bake for 20 to 30 minutes, depending on the variety and ripeness of the pears.

❧ Blueberry and Peach Casserole (*Parve*)

Here is a colorful fruit dessert that uses a minimum amount of sugar and fat. You can substitute other berries or pitted cherries for the blueberries, and nectarines for the peaches.

═══ INGREDIENTS ═══════════════════════

1 to 1½ pounds blueberries, washed and drained
2 pounds peaches, blanched, peeled and sliced thickly
½ cup + 2 tablespoons sugar, divided
1 cup all-purpose or whole-wheat pastry flour
1 teaspoon baking powder
¼ teaspoon salt
1 egg
¼ cup canola oil
1 teaspoon cinnamon

═══ METHOD ═══════════════════════════

Preheat the oven to 375 degrees Fahrenheit. Lightly oil or spray a 9 × 13-inch baking pan or casserole dish with cooking spray.

Put the sliced peaches into the baking pan and top with the blueberries. Sprinkle with 1 tablespoon of the sugar.

In a bowl, mix together the ½ cup sugar, flour, baking powder and salt with a whisk. Add the unbeaten egg to the flour mixture and mix with a fork just until crumbly. Use your hands to sprinkle this mixture evenly over the fruit. Drizzle the oil evenly over the topping. Mix the cinnamon with the remaining 1 tablespoon of sugar and sprinkle it over the top.

Bake uncovered for 15 minutes. Increase the oven temperature to 400 degrees Fahrenheit and bake for an additional 10 to 15 minutes, until fruit is soft and topping is golden.

Serves 6 to 8

❧ No-Roll Pie Crust (*Parve* or Dairy)

The beauty of this recipe is that it uses liquid oil and can be mixed quickly right in the pie pan. It can be used for pies or savory tarts. Use milk for a dairy crust and soy or rice milk for parve. You can prebake it for a pudding or fresh fruit tart, or bake the crust and filling together for cooked fruit or custard pies.

═ INGREDIENTS ═

1½ cups whole-wheat pastry flour
¾ teaspoon sugar (for sweet pies)
¾ teaspoon salt
⅓ cup + 3 tablespoons canola oil
2 tablespoons milk (soy or rice milk for a *parve* crust)
9-inch pie plate

═ METHOD ═

Combine the flour, salt and optional sugar in the pie pan. Mix together the oil and milk and add it to the flour mixture. Use a fork or your fingers to mix the dough until it holds together. Add more milk, if necessary.

Press the dough evenly over the bottom and sides of the pan and crimp the edges.

To prebake the crust: Preheat the oven to 425 degrees Fahrenheit. Line the dough with aluminum foil and fill it with dry beans or pie weights. Bake the crust for 10 minutes. Lower the oven temperature to 350 degrees Fahrenheit, remove the beans and foil and bake for an additional 10 to 15 minutes, until golden brown.

Yields: one 9-inch pie crust

✣ Quick and Easy Microwave Chocolate Pudding (Dairy)

This recipe will convince you that homemade pudding can be easy, delicious and healthier than store-bought varieties. Serve it in small individual dishes or line a pie crust (see preceding recipe) with sliced bananas and pour this pudding over them for a chocolate-banana cream pie.

═ INGREDIENTS ═

3 tablespoons cornstarch
¼ to ⅓ cup sugar
⅓ cup unsweetened cocoa powder (preferably Dutch process)
1 teaspoon cinnamon (optional)
2 cups nonfat or low-fat milk
1 teaspoon vanilla extract

═ METHOD ═

Put the cornstarch, sugar, cocoa and cinnamon in a 4-cup glass measuring cup. Mix the ingredients together with a whisk.

Slowly mix in the milk, using the whisk to keep the mixture smooth and free from any lumps of cocoa. Stir in the vanilla.

Cook in the microwave on high for 3 minutes. Remove and whisk the mixture until smooth. Return to the microwave and cook on high for 2 to 5 minutes, until it comes to a boil and thickens.

Pour the pudding into individual serving dishes or one serving bowl and refrigerate until cold.

Serves 4 to 5

SHABBAT

✣✣ Healthy Whole-Wheat Challah (*Parve*)

I use the "dough" setting on my bread machine to prepare this challah dough on Thursday. When it finishes rising in the machine, I transfer the dough to an oiled plastic bag, close it tightly and place it in the refrigerator overnight. On Friday morning, I bring the dough to room temperature, braid it, let it rise once more until double in size and then bake the loaves. The ratio of 3 cups of whole-wheat flour to 1 cup of white flour is one that most people enjoy, as opposed to using all whole-wheat flour. The gluten helps lighten the loaves, and the potato flakes add moisture. Both can be purchased at a health food store. You can also use these ingredients to mix the dough by hand or in an electric mixer.

═ INGREDIENTS ═

¾ cup water
3 eggs
¼ cup canola oil
¼ cup honey
3 cups whole-wheat flour
1 cup all-purpose or bread flour
3 tablespoons gluten
1 tablespoon instant potato flakes
2 teaspoons salt
2½ teaspoons instant dry yeast

═ METHOD ═

If you are using a bread machine, place all of the ingredients in the machine and set it on the "dough" setting. While the dough is mixing, check that it remains moist and not dry. If necessary, add a little more water.

Follow the directions above if you are preparing the dough a day before baking it. Otherwise, remove the dough from the bread machine, divide it into however many loaves you want to make and braid them. Let the dough rise on baking sheets until double in size.

You can brush the loaves with an egg wash and sprinkle them with sesame seeds before baking, or spray them with water for a crisper crust.

Depending on the size of the loaves, bake them for 15 to 25 minutes at 350 degrees Fahrenheit.

Yields: two 1-pound loaves or a number of smaller loaves and rolls

✿ **Walnut and Lentil Spread** (*Parve*)

Serve this tasty and healthy parve *spread on* Shabbat *in place of chopped liver.*

== INGREDIENTS ==

1 cup walnut pieces
1 cup brown lentils, sorted, rinsed and drained
2 cups vegetable broth or water
1 tablespoon extra-virgin olive oil
1 large onion, thinly sliced
Salt and freshly ground pepper

== METHOD ==

Spread the walnuts on a small baking sheet and bake at 325 degrees Fahrenheit for 5 to 7 minutes, until fragrant. Set them aside.

Cook the lentils and broth or water in a saucepan for about 30 minutes, until tender. Add water if necessary to prevent sticking.

Sauté the onions in oil until they start to brown.

Process lentils, onions and walnuts in a food processor until they are just slightly chunky, or smoother, as desired. Season with salt and pepper as desired. Refrigerate several hours or overnight.

Serves 6 to 8

❧ **Sephardic-Style Red Lentil Soup** (*Parve*)

Although regular brown lentils can be used in this recipe, small red lentils cook more quickly and give this soup a golden hue. Sort and inspect the lentils in advance if you know you will be running short on time for Shabbat *preparations.*

═ INGREDIENTS ═══════════════════════════════════
1 tablespoon extra-virgin olive oil
1 medium onion, chopped
1 clove garlic, chopped
½ teaspoon ground cumin
½ teaspoon ground coriander
½ teaspoon ground cinnamon
Dash cayenne pepper, optional
6 cups water or vegetable broth
1½ cups red lentils, sorted, checked and rinsed well in a strainer
1 small can diced tomatoes (14 to 16 ounces), with their juice
Salt and freshly ground pepper to taste
1 to 2 tablespoons fresh lemon juice

═ METHOD ═══════════════════════════════════════
Heat the olive oil in a large soup pot and sauté the onion until soft. Add the garlic and spices and cook, stirring for a minute or two.

Add the water or broth, lentils and tomatoes, and bring to a boil. Lower the heat and simmer the soup, partially covered, until the lentils are cooked and the soup is thick. You may want to add more water if the soup is too thick. Season the soup with salt, pepper and lemon juice to taste.

Serves 6 to 8

❧ **Italian Tuna Loaf** (*Parve*)

The Italians have a special way with canned tuna. This recipe appears in different forms in several Italian-Jewish cookbooks. Some versions contain parmesan cheese and others include fresh herbs, which you may choose to use as well. I have simplified the recipe and included a "shortcut" sauce. We often enjoy this loaf for Shabbat lunch during the summer. It also works well as a first course or appetizer.

Tuna Loaf

═ INGREDIENTS ═

2 cans of tuna (6 ounces each), packed in oil (olive oil is preferable)
2 eggs
½ cup soft bread crumbs (leftover challah crumbs work well)
1 tablespoon dried dill or 2 tablespoons fresh dill
½ teaspoon freshly ground pepper
Cheesecloth and 2 pieces of string
Fresh dill sprigs and/or thin lemon slices for garnish, optional

Sauce

═ INGREDIENTS ═

½ cup low-fat mayonnaise
2 tablespoons fresh lemon juice
½ teaspoon dried dill
1 to 2 tablespoons finely chopped pickled lemon (optional but
  delicious)

═ METHOD ═

Fill a wide saucepan with water and bring it to a boil while preparing the tuna.

In a mixing bowl, mix together the tuna, eggs, bread crumbs, dill and pepper. Break up the chunks of tuna to form a smooth but textured mixture.

Cut a double piece of cheesecloth into an approximate 12-inch square and lay it on a large dinner plate. Turn the tuna mixture onto the cheesecloth and form it into a round loaf about 8 inches long. Wrap the roll in the cloth and tie both ends with string. (I just twist each end of the cheesecloth, without using string, a technique you may want to try as well.)

Carefully put the tuna loaf into the boiling water, cover and simmer over low heat for 30 minutes.

Remove the tuna loaf to a plate using a large slotted spoon. Drain off any excess water and let it cool for a short time. Place the loaf on a plate, cover with another plate and place a heavy weight on the top plate (a large can of tomatoes works well) and refrigerate for several hours or overnight.

Prepare the sauce by mixing all of the ingredients together. Chill to blend the flavors.

Remove the cheesecloth from the tuna loaf, slice it and garnish it with dill sprigs and/or lemon slices. Serve with the sauce.

Serves 6 to 8

❧ Garbanzo Bean and Tuna Salad (*Parve*)

This is a favorite Shabbat *lunch dish when preparations are rushed. With canned garbanzo beans and tuna in the pantry, this salad comes together quickly. If you are fortunate to have kosher, Italian-style tuna packed in olive oil, use it in this salad. Drain the oil and use it as part of the oil called for in the recipe.*

═ INGREDIENTS ═

1 can (15 ounces) garbanzo beans (chickpeas), drained and rinsed
10 green or black olives, sliced
¾ cup minced fresh parsley
4 green onions (scallions), thinly sliced
¼ cup extra-virgin olive oil
¼ cup fresh lemon juice
1 can tuna, drained and rinsed (see note above if using tuna packed in olive oil)
Freshly ground pepper

Optional ingredients:
1 small cucumber, peeled and diced
1 tomato or a handful of cherry tomatoes, diced or sliced
¼ to ½ cup feta cheese, crumbled

═ METHOD ═

Combine garbanzo beans, olives, parsley and green onions in a bowl. Add the olive oil and lemon juice and mix together. Break up the tuna into the bean mixture and stir to combine. Add ground pepper to taste, and more lemon juice if necessary. Cover and chill for several hours before serving.

If you are using the optional ingredients, mix them into the salad just before serving.

Serves 4

✿ Zucchini and Mozzarella Quiche (Dairy)

Here is another recipe makeover. This quiche originally called for a ready-made pie crust, which is high in saturated and trans fat. I have reduced the amount of cheese and substituted nonfat or low-fat milk for the light cream. Increase the amount of zucchini and sauté it for added flavor with little extra fat.

We especially enjoy vegetable-filled quiches like this one for Shabbat *lunch during the summer.*

Healthy Version	Original Version
1 No-Roll Pie Crust (see recipe under desserts)	1 ready-made pie crust
1 cup part-skim shredded mozzarella cheese	1½ cups shredded mozzarella cheese
½ cup dry-pack sun-dried tomatoes, sliced	½ cup oil-packed sun-dried tomatoes, sliced
Boiling water	1 small zucchini, thinly sliced
2 teaspoons extra-virgin olive oil	2 large eggs
2 small zucchini, thinly sliced	1 cup light cream (half and half)
2 large eggs, beaten	¼ teaspoon salt
1 cup nonfat or low-fat milk	¼ teaspoon fresh ground pepper
¼ teaspoon salt	6 tablespoons plus ¼ cup grated Parmesan cheese
¼ teaspoon fresh ground pepper	
¼ cup grated Parmesan cheese	

═ METHOD ═

Preheat oven to 350 degrees Fahrenheit.

In a small bowl, pour boiling water over the sun-dried tomatoes to cover them. Set aside to plump.

Heat the olive oil in a nonstick skillet and sauté the zucchini, stirring frequently, until they are golden and any liquid has evaporated. Set aside.

Prepare the pie crust in a 9-inch pie pan. Sprinkle the mozzarella cheese over the bottom of the crust.

Beat the eggs and mix them with the milk, salt and pepper. Pour this mixture over the cheese in the crust.

Drain the sun-dried tomatoes and arrange them, along with the sautéed zucchini, on top of the quiche. Sprinkle with grated Parmesan.

Place the pie pan on a baking sheet and bake for 30 to 40 minutes until the filling is firm. Remove from the oven and serve warm or at room temperature.

Serves 6 to 8

✌ *Shabbat* Chicken Breasts (Meat)

This is an easy and versatile "recipe" that we enjoy regularly on Erev Shabbat. *It involves little in the way of time and effort, especially if skinless, boneless chicken breasts are available. Some ideas are below, but let your creativity and seasonal ingredients guide you. The quantity of ingredients will depend on how many people you are serving.*

═ INGREDIENTS ═══════════════════════
Sauce (see suggestions below)
Chicken breasts
Extra-virgin olive oil
All-purpose flour
Spices (see suggestions below)

═ METHOD ═══════════════════════════
Mix the sauce ingredients together in a glass measuring cup and set aside.

Trim the chicken breasts of any fat or tendons, and cut each breast in half.

Heat the olive oil in a large, nonstick skillet.

Mix the flour and spices together on a flat dish or waxed paper, and dredge both sides of the chicken breasts in the mixture. Sauté the chicken, a few pieces at a time, in the olive oil until lightly browned on both sides. Remove the cooked chicken to a platter or serving dish while you cook the rest. When all of the chicken is cooked, return it to the pan and add the sauce ingredients. Cover the pan and cook just until the chicken is done.

Spices
Tarragon, thyme, dill, or Bonnes Herbes
Curry powder
Oregano, basil, Italian sauces
Cumin, coriander, *baharat*
Chinese five-spice, ginger

Sauce
White wine or broth, Dijon mustard, lemon juice
Broth, orange juice, tomato sauce
Tomato sauce, red wine, onion, garlic, red wine vinegar
Tomato sauce, broth, sliced olives, tomatoes
Garlic, soy sauce, rice wine vinegar, sesame oil

✣ Sweet and Sour Cherry Sauce (*Parve*)

This tangy sweet and sour sauce originates in the Syrian Jewish community. It makes a delicious sauce for sautéed chicken breasts (see preceding recipe) as well as with ground chicken, turkey, low-fat beef or vegetarian "meatballs." Be sure to use Morello or sour cherries and not canned sweet cherries. Pomegranate molasses makes an exotic touch when available.

═ INGREDIENTS ════════════════════════

1 tablespoon extra-virgin olive oil
½ cup finely chopped onions
¼ teaspoon ground cinnamon
¼ teaspoon ground allspice
Freshly ground pepper to taste
1 jar (24 ounces) sour (Morello) cherries, drained, liquid reserved
1 can (4–6 ounces) tomato paste or puree
⅓ cup water
2 tablespoons lemon juice
2 tablespoons light or dark brown sugar
1 tablespoon pomegranate molasses, optional

═ METHOD ═════════════════════════════

Heat the olive oil in a wide saucepan. Add the onions and sauté, stirring occasionally, until soft. Add the cinnamon, allspice and a few grinds of pepper. Sauté for another minute.

Add the cherry juice, tomato paste, water, lemon juice, brown sugar and pomegranate molasses to the onions. Mix well and simmer for 5 to 10 minutes to blend flavors. Taste, and add lemon juice and/or brown sugar if necessary to achieve a sweet and sour flavor. Add the cherries and cook for another few minutes.

Yields: enough for 8 chicken breasts

❧ **Chocolate Mousse** (*Parve*)

Try this chocolate mousse for dessert on Shabbat. *No one will guess that it is made with tofu.*

══ INGREDIENTS ════════════════════════════════

2 packages soft silken tofu (12-ounce aseptic package)
1 bar (3 to 4 ounces) good quality *parve* bittersweet chocolate, finely
   chopped
½ cup unsweetened Dutch-process cocoa powder
½ cup boiling water
1 teaspoon vanilla
2 teaspoons freshly grated orange zest or other flavoring (see below)
¾ cup powdered sugar

══ METHOD ════════════════════════════════════

Puree tofu in a food processor, scraping down the sides as needed, until completely smooth. This may take several minutes.

Combine chocolate and cocoa in a medium bowl. Slowly add boiling water and stir until completely smooth.

Stir in vanilla and orange zest. Add the chocolate mixture and the sugar to the tofu in the food processor and puree until smooth.

Pour into individual serving containers or one serving bowl. Cover and chill for at least one hour.

Additional flavor ideas (in place of the orange zest):

3 tablespoons instant coffee or espresso powder dissolved in the boiling water

1 or 2 tablespoons of your favorite liqueur

Serves 8

✣ **Easy** *Shabbat* **Brownies** (*Parve*)

=== INGREDIENTS ===

1 cup all-purpose or whole-wheat pastry flour
½ cup cocoa powder, preferably Dutch process
¼ teaspoon salt
¼ teaspoon baking powder
1 teaspoon instant coffee powder
1 teaspoon hot water
¼ cup canola oil
1 cup sugar
2 eggs
1 teaspoon vanilla extract

=== METHOD ===

Preheat oven to 350 degrees Fahrenheit. Lightly oil an 8-inch square baking pan or line with parchment paper.

Whisk together flour, cocoa, salt and baking powder and set aside. Dissolve coffee powder in hot water. Mix together oil, sugar, eggs, vanilla and dissolved coffee. Add the dry ingredients and mix until well blended.

Pour batter into pan and bake for 20 to 25 minutes, until slightly sticky in center. Cool on a rack.

Cut into 16 squares when cool.

✿ **Cocoa Spice Cake** (*Parve*)

This cake comes together very quickly, so it is perfect when you are in a hurry just before Shabbat.

For an equally easy "frosting," sprinkle the hot cake with chocolate chips, wait a few minutes until they melt and spread them evenly over the cake with a knife.

═ INGREDIENTS ═══════════════════════════

1½ cups all-purpose flour
⅓ cup unsweetened cocoa powder
1½ teaspoons cinnamon
1 teaspoon baking soda
3 tablespoons canola oil
¾ cup sugar
1 egg
1⅓ cups unsweetened applesauce

═ METHOD ════════════════════════════════

Preheat oven to 350 degrees Fahrenheit. Oil a 9-inch square baking pan or line it with parchment paper.

Whisk together the flour, cocoa, cinnamon, ginger and baking soda in a bowl.

Mix together well the oil, sugar and egg in a mixing bowl.

Add the dry ingredients and applesauce alternately to the sugar and oil mixture, beating well after each addition.

Bake for 25 to 35 minutes, until a toothpick or cake tester comes out clean.

Serves 6 to 8

✿ As-You-Like-It Fresh Fruit Crisp (*Parve*)

Choose your favorite seasonal fruits for this recipe. The amount of sugar and flour used will vary according to the sweetness and juiciness of the fruit. I like to prepare a double batch of the crisp topping and store it in the freezer for an easy, last-minute dessert.

═ INGREDIENTS ══════════════════

Winter Fruit
2 to 3 pounds peeled, cored and thinly sliced apples or pears (or use a
   mixture)
1 teaspoon cinnamon or a mixture of cinnamon, ginger and nutmeg
1 to 2 tablespoons sugar
1 tablespoon lemon juice

Summer Fruit
2 to 3 pounds peaches, nectarines, plums or apricots (cherries or
   berries can be substituted for some of the fruit)
2 to 4 tablespoons sugar
1 to 3 tablespoons flour

Topping
¾ cup brown sugar
⅔ cup whole-wheat pastry flour
½ cup rolled oats
½ cup chopped walnuts or sliced almonds
1 teaspoon cinnamon
⅓ cup canola oil

═ METHOD ════════════════════════

Mix together the brown sugar, flour, oats, nuts and cinnamon in a medium-sized bowl. Add the oil and mix with a fork until the mixture is crumbly.

In a large bowl, mix the fruit with the spices, sugar, lemon juice and flour, depending on the type of fruit you are using. Place the fruit mixture in an oiled shallow baking or gratin dish and sprinkle with crisp topping. Set on a baking sheet to catch any drips. Bake at 375 degrees Fahrenheit for 30 to 60 minutes (summer fruits cook faster than winter fruits), until the top is nicely browned and the fruit is tender and bubbly.

Serves 6 to 8

⸙ **Braised Swiss Chard** (*Parve*)

Chard is a deep green (or red) leafy vegetable that is versatile, nutritious and easily available. It grew prolifically in my grandfather's garden, so we ate it regularly. Use it in place of spinach, in soups or as a wrapper for stuffed vegetables or grains. Chard (or beet greens) is one of the vegetables used for the brachot said before the Rosh Hashanah meal in many Sephardic families.

INGREDIENTS

1 or 2 bunches Swiss chard (2 pounds), washed well
1 medium onion, minced
1 clove garlic, minced
¼ cup fresh cilantro (coriander), minced OR
½ teaspoon each ground cumin and coriander
½ cup extra-virgin olive oil
¼ cup water
1 teaspoon paprika
½ teaspoon salt
Freshly ground pepper to taste

METHOD

Cut the chard stems from the leaves and dice the stems. Holding several leaves at a time, slice them into thin ribbons. Put the chard stems and leaves in a pan and add the rest of the ingredients. Cover tightly and cook over low heat for 30 to 45 minutes, or until the chard is very soft. Check occasionally and add more water if necessary to prevent sticking. Taste for salt and pepper. Serve hot or at room temperature.

Serves 4 to 6

✣ Braised Leeks (*Parve*)

Leeks are traditionally served as part of the Rosh Hashanah *meal in Sephardic homes. Here is an easy and delicious way of preparing this often neglected member of the onion family. Just be sure to clean the leeks carefully, as explained in the recipe instructions.*

=== INGREDIENTS ===

2 pounds leeks
2 tablespoons extra-virgin olive oil
½ teaspoon dried tarragon, thyme or Bonnes Herbes
¼ cup vegetable broth or white wine
Salt and freshly ground pepper

=== METHOD ===

Trim the coarse dark green leaves from the leeks and discard (or set them aside for use in soup stock). You will be using only the white and light green parts of the leek. Cut off the root ends and halve the leeks lengthwise. Soak them in salted water (or a mixture of water and vinegar) for a few minutes to remove any dirt. Rinse well between the layers and slice the leeks thinly.

Heat the olive oil in a saucepan over medium heat and add the leeks and herbs. Cover and cook over a low heat, stirring occasionally for about 5 minutes. Be careful not to let the leeks brown. Add the stock or wine, cover and cook for another 10 to 15 minutes, until tender. Add salt and pepper to taste.

Serves 4 to 6

✿ Baked Kasha and Bow-Tie Pasta *(Parve)*

Kasha and bow-tie noodles are a traditional Ashkenazic dish. This version goes into the oven, making it especially convenient to prepare in advance of the holiday meal.

═ INGREDIENTS ═

3 tablespoons extra-virgin olive oil
2 medium onions, halved and sliced
1 teaspoon sweet paprika
8 ounces mushrooms, washed and sliced, optional
8 ounces bow-tie pasta
1 egg
1 cup kasha
½ teaspoon salt
Freshly ground pepper
2 cups vegetable broth or water
2 eggs

═ METHOD ═

Preheat the oven to 350 degrees Fahrenheit. Spray a 2-quart baking dish with nonstick cooking spray.

Heat 2 tablespoons of oil in a large pan with a cover and sauté the onions, stirring frequently, until nicely browned. Place the onions in a large mixing bowl. Add the mushrooms to the same pan and sauté just until they begin to brown. Add the paprika and cook for another minute. Add the mushrooms to the onions. Set the pan aside without washing it.

Cook the pasta in a large pot of boiling water for 3 to 4 minutes, until tender but not thoroughly cooked. Drain, rinse and add to the onions.

Beat 1 egg in a bowl and add the kasha to it. Mix thoroughly.

Heat 1 tablespoon of oil in the pan. Add the kasha and stir constantly until the grains are toasted. Add salt, pepper and broth or water and bring to a boil. Reduce temperature to low, cover and cook for about 15 minutes, until liquid is absorbed. Add the cooked kasha to the noodle and onion mixture and gently mix together. Taste for salt and pepper.

Beat the remaining two eggs and add them to the kasha and noodles. Place in the sprayed baking dish and sprinkle with paprika.

Bake, uncovered, for 30 to 45 minutes, until thoroughly cooked.

Serves 6 to 8

❧ Mom's Honey Cake (*Parve*)

I have been making this honey cake ever since my mother gave me the recipe many years ago. The preparation is somewhat unusual – baking soda is added to hot honey which bubbles up in a chemical reaction of acid and base. This cake has a moist texture similar to a sponge cake, and since honey is a natural preservative, you can bake it several days before Rosh Hashanah.

═ INGREDIENTS ═

2 cups honey
2 teaspoons baking soda
1 cup strong hot coffee (brewed or instant)
3 cups all-purpose flour
1 teaspoon ground cinnamon
1 teaspoon ground ginger
1 teaspoon ground allspice
3 eggs, at room temperature
1 cup sugar

═ METHOD ═

Generously spray a large *bundt* pan or two 9 × 5-inch loaf pans with baking spray.

Preheat oven to 300 degrees Fahrenheit.

Heat the honey in a very large pan until it begins to bubble slightly. Remove the pan from the heat and stir in the baking soda. The mixture will bubble and foam up to the top of the pan. Stir in the coffee and set the mixture aside to cool.

Whisk together the flour and spices and set aside.

With an electric mixer, beat the eggs until creamy. Add the sugar, a little at a time, until the mixture is thick and pale.

Add the cooled honey and the flour mixture alternately to the eggs, a little at a time, mixing on low speed to combine. Pour the mixture into the baking pan(s) and bake for 45 to 60 minutes, depending on the size of the pan. The cake should start to come away from the sides of the pan and a toothpick inserted into the center should come out dry when ready.

Cool the cake(s) on a wire rack.

Serves 12 to 16

SUKKOT

✿ Eggplant Rolls (Dairy)

Eggplant is usually abundant and flavorful in the fall, just in time for Sukkot. You can prepare this recipe ahead of time without the final heating, and refrigerate it overnight. Then just heat it the next day until thoroughly hot.

By baking rather than frying the eggplant, you save a great deal of fat without losing flavor. Use this technique for recipes calling for cubed eggplant as well, tossing the cubes with olive oil and baking until browned.

═ INGREDIENTS ═
2 to 3 large eggplants (2½ to 3 pounds total)
2 tablespoons extra-virgin olive oil
1 cup grated, part-skim, mozzarella cheese
1½ cup part-skim ricotta cheese
2 cloves garlic, minced
1½ teaspoons dried oregano
¼ teaspoon fresh ground pepper
1 egg
2 cups marinara or spaghetti sauce (homemade or store-bought)
½ cup freshly grated Parmesan cheese

═ METHOD ═
Preheat the oven to 425 degrees Fahrenheit.

Cut the eggplant into lengthwise slices, ½ to ¾ inch thick. Brush both sides of the eggplant with olive oil and arrange in a single layer on a baking pan. (You may need more than one baking pan, or repeat the process until all of the eggplant is baked.) Bake for 15 to 20 minutes, until the bottoms are lightly browned. Turn the slices and bake until the second side is browned. Remove from the oven.

While the eggplant is baking, mix together the mozzarella cheese, ricotta cheese, garlic, oregano, pepper and egg in a bowl.

When the eggplant is finished baking, lower the oven temperature to 350 degrees Fahrenheit.

Spray a 9 × 13-inch baking dish with nonstick cooking spray or oil lightly.

Pour ¾ cup of the marinara sauce into the pan and spread it evenly on the bottom.

When the eggplant slices are cool enough to handle, place about 2 tablespoons of the cheese mixture on the short end of each slice and roll to enclose the cheese. Place each eggplant roll, seam-side down, on the sauce in the baking pan. Pour the remaining sauce over the eggplant rolls. Sprinkle with Parmesan cheese.

Bake for 25 to 30 minutes, until hot.

Serves 6 to 8

🎋 Eggplant *Mousaka* (Dairy)

Casseroles, soups and stuffed vegetables are convenient main courses to serve during Sukkot. Lasagna is one of our favorites, as is this vegetarian version of the Greek dish mousaka. Goat cheese is often high in fat, but a little goes a long way. If it is not available, substitute cream cheese. This recipe calls for preparing two separate sauces – tomato and white. You may prefer to save time by using 3 cups of bottled marinara or spaghetti sauce instead of making your own.

═ INGREDIENTS ═

3 large eggplants (3 pounds total)
¼ cup extra-virgin olive oil, divided
1 large onion, diced
3 cloves garlic, minced
2 cans (28 ounces each) diced tomatoes
½ cup dry red wine
1 tablespoon tomato paste
1 teaspoon dried oregano
2 tablespoons extra-virgin olive oil
4 tablespoons all-purpose flour
2 cups nonfat milk
¼ teaspoon freshly grated nutmeg
¼ teaspoon salt
Freshly ground pepper
1 egg yolk
2 ounces goat cheese, crumbled
3 tablespoons dry bread crumbs

═ METHOD ═

Preheat the oven to 425 degrees Fahrenheit.

Cut the eggplant into ½ inch-thick rounds, brush with 3 tablespoons of the olive oil and bake in a single layer on a baking sheet until brown, 15 to 20 minutes. Turn each slice over and continue baking until the other side is brown.

Prepare the tomato sauce by heating the remaining tablespoon of olive oil in a large pan. Sauté the onion, stirring until soft. Add the garlic and sauté for another minute. Stir in the tomatoes, wine, tomato paste and oregano. Simmer the sauce for about 20 minutes or until thickened.

In another pan, heat the 2 tablespoons of olive oil over low heat. Whisk in the flour and heat, stirring constantly for a minute or two. Slowly add the milk, whisking to keep the sauce smooth. Bring to a slow boil and simmer until thick, stirring constantly. Stir in the salt and nutmeg. Lightly beat the egg yolk and whisk it into the white sauce. Stir in the crumbled goat cheese.

Lower the oven temperature to 350 degrees Fahrenheit.

Spray a 9 × 13-inch baking dish with nonstick cooking spray or lightly coat with olive oil. Sprinkle the bread crumbs over the bottom of the dish.

Arrange a third of the eggplant slices on the bread crumbs. Spoon half of the tomato sauce over the eggplant. Arrange another third of the eggplant slices over the sauce and cover them with the remaining tomato sauce. Place the remaining eggplant slices on top of the tomato sauce and pour the white sauce over the eggplant.

Bake uncovered for 45 to 60 minutes.

Serves 6 to 8

✤✤ Stuffed Peppers (*Parve*)

The idea for this "non-recipe" came from one of our local newspapers. The instructions were very complex, involving much time and many ingredients. However, the basic idea of using fresh grapes was intriguing, so I adapted the technique and simplified the whole recipe.

Feel free to use other vegetables, such as zucchini, eggplant, tomatoes or cabbage leaves. Substitute bulgur for the rice if you prefer. Season the cooked grain liberally with diced, sautéed onions, garlic, fresh herbs, salt and pepper. A handful of dried cranberries, raisins and almonds are also a nice addition to the grain. Use your imagination!

═ INGREDIENTS ═

Large red peppers – ½ a pepper for each serving
Cooked and seasoned brown rice – about ⅓ cup per serving
Fresh grapes, washed thoroughly, on the stem
Extra-virgin olive oil

═ METHOD ═

Preheat the oven to 400 degrees Fahrenheit.

Cut each pepper in half lengthwise (through the stem). Remove the seeds.

Lightly oil the bottom of a heavy, ovenproof pan or casserole dish. Fill each pepper half with rice. Arrange the peppers in the baking dish. It is all right if they overlap or are layered on top of each other. Place the bunch of grapes (stem and all) over the stuffed peppers. Drizzle a spoonful of olive oil over the vegetables and grapes.

Cover the pan and bake for about half an hour. Uncover and continue baking until the peppers and grapes are completely soft and have started to brown. Serve hot or at room temperature.

❧ Cabbage Flan (Dairy)

A savory flan is similar to a quiche without a crust. You could also call it a sophisticated kugel. This recipe transforms cabbage into a gourmet main course. Serve it with baked sweet potatoes and a fresh green salad for a perfect Sukkot meal.

═ INGREDIENTS ═

½ head green cabbage (8 cups total), shredded
1 tablespoon extra-virgin olive oil
1 medium onion, thinly sliced
3 tablespoons chopped fresh dill or 1 tablespoon dried dill
3 eggs
⅓ cup all-purpose flour
½ teaspoon salt
Freshly ground pepper
1¼ cups nonfat milk
½ cup grated Cheddar cheese

═ METHOD ═

Preheat the oven to 375 degrees Fahrenheit.

Spray a shallow 8-cup baking dish with nonstick cooking spray.

Cook the shredded cabbage in a large pot of boiling water, just until tender, about 5 minutes. Drain and rinse the cabbage. Press out as much water as possible and place it in a large bowl.

Heat the oil in a skillet and sauté the onion until soft. Add the onions and dill to the cabbage.

Whisk together the eggs, flour, salt and pepper until smooth and then whisk in the milk. Add this mixture to the cabbage. Add the grated cheese and combine everything. Pour into the baking dish.

Bake for 40 to 50 minutes, until firm and golden.

Serves 4 to 6

CHANUKAH

✿ Oven-Fried Potatoes *(Parve)*

Most of us think of latkes, or potato pancakes, during Chanukah. *Here is a healthy alternative to fried latkes. This recipe also works well with sweet potatoes. Chile powder, curry or other spices can be used instead of the paprika for a spicier taste.*

═ INGREDIENTS ═══════════════════════════

2 pounds potatoes
1 tablespoon extra-virgin olive oil
¼ teaspoon paprika
Salt and pepper to taste

═ METHOD ═══════════════════════════════

Preheat oven to 425 degrees Fahrenheit. Spray a baking sheet with cooking spray.

Cut each potato into wedges or sticks of equal size. Toss the potatoes in a bowl with the olive oil, paprika, salt and pepper.

Arrange the potatoes in a single layer on the baking sheet and bake for 15 to 20 minutes. Use a spatula to turn the potatoes and bake for another 10 to 15 minutes, until nicely browned.

Serves 6

✣ Ricotta Pancakes (Dairy)

Another change from latkes, these pancakes are also nice for a special breakfast or brunch. You can keep these warm by placing them in a single layer on a baking sheet in a 200-degree Fahrenheit oven, for about 15 minutes.

=== INGREDIENTS ===

1½ cups whole-wheat pastry flour
2 tablespoons sugar
1 teaspoon baking soda
½ teaspoon salt
1½ cups low-fat buttermilk
2 eggs, separated
1 tablespoon grated lemon rind
⅓ cup part-skim ricotta cheese

=== METHOD ===

Whisk together the flour, sugar, baking soda and salt.

Mix together the buttermilk, egg yolks, lemon rind and ricotta. Stir this mixture gently into the dry ingredients.

With a mixer on high speed, beat the egg whites until soft peaks form. Fold the whites into the pancake batter.

Use about ¼ cup of batter for each pancake and cook on a nonstick griddle or skillet that has been sprayed with cooking spray. Turn the pancakes when they begin to brown on the bottom and the edges begin to look dry.

Yields: 12 to 16 pancakes

❧ **Spanish Potato Tortilla** (*Parve*)

This is not a flour or corn tortilla, but a Spanish version of an omelet or frittata. Another alternative to latkes, this dish makes a nice mid-week entrée. Serve it with a tossed salad or the orange, fennel and avocado salad that follows. Leftover cooked potatoes may also be used.

═ INGREDIENTS ═

2 tablespoons extra-virgin olive oil
1 medium onion, thinly sliced
¾ teaspoon salt
½ teaspoon freshly ground pepper
2 pounds boiling potatoes (Yukon gold are nice), thinly sliced
⅓ cup water
5 eggs

═ METHOD ═

Heat the oil in a 10- to 12-inch nonstick ovenproof skillet over medium heat. When the oil is hot, add the onion and cook, stirring until soft. Add the salt, pepper and potato slices and mix together in the pan.

Add the water, bring to a boil and reduce the heat to low. Cover and cook until the potatoes are tender, about 10 minutes. Evaporate any liquid that remains by removing the cover and boiling for a few minutes.

Beat the eggs in a large bowl and add the potato mixture, mixing well. Place the unwashed skillet back on the stovetop over medium heat. When the pan is hot, pour the egg and potato mixture into it and cook for 5 to 10 minutes, until the eggs are set and the bottom is lightly browned.

Slide the tortilla onto a large plate and invert back into the pan to cook the other side.

Loosen the tortilla and invert it onto a large serving platter. Cut into wedges and serve warm or at room temperature.

Serves 8 to 10

✣ Orange, Fennel and Avocado Salad (*Parve*)

Here is a salad made with winter fruits and vegetables. It goes nicely with a mid-week Chanukah meal and is easy to put together.

INGREDIENTS

2 navel oranges
1 large fennel bulb
1 large avocado
¼ teaspoon salt
¼ teaspoon fresh ground pepper
1½ tablespoons white wine vinegar
¼ cup extra-virgin olive oil

METHOD

Peel the oranges, cut them in half and slice thinly. Trim off the fennel stalks, cut it in half and remove the core if it is large and/or tough. Slice the fennel into very thin slices. Peel and pit the avocado and cut it into ½ inch-thick slices.

In a small bowl, whisk together the salt, pepper and vinegar. Add the oil slowly, whisking until combined.

Gently mix the orange, fennel and avocado slices with the dressing and serve.

Serves 4 to 6

❧ Lentil and Swiss Chard Soup (*Parve*)

Lentils and chard make a delicious, nutritious, whole-meal or first-course soup, especially during the winter months. Cumin, coriander and lemon are popular flavorings throughout the Middle East and add a lively zest to otherwise fairly bland lentils.

INGREDIENTS

1½ cups brown lentils, sorted, checked and rinsed
2 tablespoons extra-virgin olive oil
1 medium onion, finely chopped
3 cloves garlic, minced
1 teaspoon ground cumin
½ teaspoon ground coriander
6 cups water or vegetable broth
1 large bunch Swiss chard (about 1 pound), cleaned thoroughly and
  chopped
Salt and freshly ground pepper
2 tablespoons fresh lemon juice
¼ cup fresh chopped cilantro (coriander), optional

METHOD

Heat the oil in a large soup pan and sauté the onions until soft and golden. Add the garlic, ground cumin and coriander and cook, stirring, for another minute.

Add the lentils and water or broth to the pan and bring to a boil. Cover and simmer over a low heat for 30 to 40 minutes, until the lentils are soft. Add the Swiss chard, salt and pepper to the soup and simmer for another 10 minutes. If the soup is too thick, add more water or broth. Add the lemon juice and fresh cilantro, and serve hot.

Serves 6 to 8

PURIM

✣ Vegetable Stew with Garbanzo Beans (*Parve*)

Queen Esther would have enjoyed this vegetarian entrée. We serve it to our vegetarian guests on Shabbat as well. Feel free to add or substitute other vegetables, such as green beans, red pepper or peas.

=== INGREDIENTS ===

1 cup water
2 medium carrots, peeled and cut into ½ inch-thick, diagonal slices
3 to 4 zucchini cut in half lengthwise and sliced ½ inch thick
1 tablespoon extra-virgin olive oil
4 cloves garlic, chopped
1 can (14 to 15 ounces) diced tomatoes
1 can (8 ounces) tomato sauce
1½ teaspoons ground cumin
1 can (15 ounces) garbanzo beans
⅓ cup raisins
½ teaspoon hot sauce, or to taste (optional)
Salt and pepper to taste

=== METHOD ===

Cook the carrots and water in a covered saucepan for 5 minutes. Add the zucchini and cook for about 3 minutes, until just tender. Remove the vegetables from the broth and set aside. (Use the broth for a soup or sauce.) When the saucepan is cool, dry it with a paper towel.

In the same saucepan, heat the olive oil and sauté the garlic for a few seconds. Add the tomatoes, tomato sauce, cumin, salt and pepper. Bring to a boil and simmer, uncovered, for a few minutes. Stir in the garbanzo beans and raisins and simmer another few minutes. Add hot sauce, zucchini and carrots and simmer a few more minutes. Taste for salt and pepper.

Serves 4 to 6

❧ **Peanut Butter Cookies** (*Parve*)

These cookies are especially popular with children. They make a nice addition to Purim mishloach manot.

═ INGREDIENTS ═
2½ cups whole-wheat pastry flour
1 teaspoon baking powder
1 teaspoon baking soda
½ teaspoon salt
2 cups brown sugar
½ cup natural peanut butter
¼ cup canola oil
2 eggs
2 teaspoons vanilla extract
5 teaspoons water

═ METHOD ═
Preheat oven to 350 degrees Fahrenheit.

Lightly oil two baking sheets or cover them with parchment paper.

Whisk together the flour, baking powder, baking soda and salt and set aside.

In the bowl of an electric mixer, combine sugar, peanut butter, oil, eggs and vanilla. Add the water and mix until smooth. Add the dry ingredients and mix just until combined.

Using your hands, form 1-inch balls of dough and place them 2 inches apart on the baking sheet. Flatten the cookies with a fork dipped into flour.

Bake for 8 to 10 minutes, or until golden. Cool on a wire rack.

Yields: approximately 48 cookies

✦ **Gingerbread Cupcakes** (*Parve*)

Another favorite with children, these spice cupcakes are quick and easy to prepare.

=== INGREDIENTS ===

1 cup whole-wheat pastry flour
1 teaspoon baking soda
¼ teaspoon salt
1 teaspoon ground ginger
½ teaspoon ground cloves
½ teaspoon cinnamon
1 whole egg
1 egg yolk
½ cup sugar
½ cup molasses
½ cup canola oil
1 tablespoon instant coffee powder, dissolved in
½ cup boiling water

=== METHOD ===

Preheat oven to 400 degrees Fahrenheit.

Line 16 muffin cups with paper liners.

Sift or whisk together flour, baking soda, salt and spices and set aside.

Beat eggs together, add the sugar, molasses and oil and mix. Mix in dry ingredients and coffee. The mixture will be thin.

Pour the batter into the muffin cups. (You can do this easily with a glass measuring cup.)

Bake for 18 to 20 minutes, or until cakes spring back when gently touched. Remove cupcakes to a rack to cool.

Yields: 16 cupcakes

❧ Ginger and Walnut Biscotti (*Parve*)

Include these sophisticated biscotti in mishloach manot for adults. The combination of sharp candied, powdered ginger and walnuts is a winner!

INGREDIENTS

1 cup sugar
½ cup canola oil
2 tablespoons ground ginger
¾ cup candied ginger, chopped
1 cup walnut pieces, chopped
½ cup chocolate chips, optional
2 eggs
2¼ cups whole-wheat pastry flour
1 tablespoon baking powder

METHOD

Combine sugar, oil and ginger and mix well. Add candied ginger, walnuts and chocolate chips (optional) and mix to combine. Stir in the eggs.

Whisk together flour and baking powder and add to the egg mixture. Cover and chill for 2 to 3 hours.

Preheat oven to 375 degrees Fahrenheit. Line a baking sheet with parchment paper.

Divide the dough in half, and, using lightly floured hands, shape it into 12-inch logs. They should each be about 2 inches wide and ½ inch thick. Place the logs at least 2 inches apart on the baking sheet and bake for 15 to 20 minutes, until golden brown.

Remove and let cool for 10 minutes. Place the logs onto a cutting board and slice diagonally into ½-inch slices. Place the slices on their sides on the baking sheet (you may need another baking sheet for this) and return to the oven for 5 minutes. Turn the slices over with a spatula and bake for an additional 5 minutes. Cool on a wire rack.

Yields: 3 to 4 dozen biscotti

✿ Gefilte Fish Loaf *(Parve)*

Most of us appreciate cooking shortcuts, especially during Pesach. *This loaf is much easier to prepare than traditional gefilte fish balls. I like to use some salmon in the mixture, but you can choose whitefish, pike, cod or other fish that appeal to you. If you have the option, have the fish ground at the market. Then you can grate or mince the onion and carrot at home, and add the rest of the ingredients to the ground fish to make your life even easier.*

INGREDIENTS

1 pound fish fillets, cut into cubes
1 medium onion, quartered
1 medium carrot, thickly sliced
1 egg
1 tablespoon canola oil
2 tablespoons water
¼ cup *matzah* meal
½ cup parsley sprigs
¾ teaspoon salt
¼ teaspoon white pepper
½ teaspoon sugar, optional

METHOD

Oil or spray an 8 x 4-inch loaf pan with nonstick cooking spray. Line the pan with waxed paper and oil or spray the paper. Set aside.

Preheat the oven to 350 degrees Fahrenheit.

Grind or process the fish (use a food grinder or processor) in batches with the onion and carrot. Add the egg, oil, *matzah* meal, parsley, salt, pepper and sugar, if using. Pulse the mixture until smooth. Spoon the mixture into the baking pan, smoothing the top so that it is flat.

Bake for 40 to 50 minutes or until firm and fully cooked. Cool for about 15 minutes and invert the loaf on a serving plate. Chill and slice.

❧ Spinach Mushroom *Mina* (Dairy)

In Portland, I cooked for Pesach with my good friend Suretta. Our joint Sedarim included our families as well as new immigrants and local students. The menu usually included fresh local salmon and this Sephardic layered dish known as a mina. Multiply the recipe if you are feeding a large crowd, and use fresh spinach if frozen is not available for Pesach.

═ INGREDIENTS ═

1 tablespoon extra-virgin olive oil plus extra for greasing the pan
1 medium onion, chopped
1 large clove garlic, minced
½ pound mushrooms, finely chopped
2 10-ounce packages frozen spinach, thawed and drained
¾ cup feta cheese, crumbled
Salt and freshly ground pepper to taste
6 *matzah* squares
3 eggs, beaten

═ METHOD ═

Grease a 7 × 11-inch baking dish with olive oil and set aside. Preheat oven to 375 degrees Fahrenheit.

Heat the oil in a large skillet. Add the onion and cook until soft, stirring occasionally. Add the garlic and sauté for another minute. Add the mushrooms and cook until most of the liquid released from the mushrooms has evaporated, 3 to 5 minutes.

Remove from the heat and stir in the spinach, feta cheese, salt and pepper.

Working with two *matzot* at a time, dip them in water for about 30 seconds, and then into the beaten eggs. Place the *matzot* in the bottom of the oiled pan and distribute half of the filling over them. Add a second layer of softened *matzah* dipped in the eggs, and cover with the remaining filling. Top with the last two soaked and egg-dipped *matzot*. Reserve the remaining beaten egg in the refrigerator.

Cover the pan tightly with aluminum foil. Bake for 20 minutes. Remove the foil and brush the top with the remaining beaten eggs. Continue to bake for 5 to 10 minutes, until the top is golden brown.

Serves 6 to 8

⁂ *Matzah* Lasagna (Dairy)

Matzah stands in for lasagna noodles in this mina, or matzah *pie. To make it even easier, use ready-made tomato or marinara sauce.*

═ INGREDIENTS ═══════════════════════════

3 to 4 whole-wheat or regular *matzot*
1 tablespoon extra-virgin olive oil
1 medium onion, diced
2 cloves garlic, minced
2 8-ounce cans of tomato sauce
1 10-ounce package frozen, chopped spinach, thawed and drained well
1 cup nonfat or low-fat cottage cheese
2 eggs
¾ cup grated mozzarella cheese

═ METHOD ═══════════════════════════════

Oil an 8- or 9-inch square baking dish or spray it with nonstick cooking spray.

Preheat the oven to 375 degrees Fahrenheit.

Dip the *matzah* in warm water for 1 minute and then set aside to drain on a towel.

Heat the olive oil and sauté the onions until soft. Add the garlic and sauté for another minute. Add the tomato sauce and cook for 5 minutes, until the flavors are blended. (If you are using prepared tomato or marinara sauce, skip this step.)

Mix together the spinach and cottage cheese.

Beat the eggs in a shallow plate. Dip a piece of *matzah* in the egg and arrange in the baking pan. Use another piece of *matzah* dipped in egg if necessary to cover the bottom of the pan. Spread half of the spinach and cottage cheese mixture on the *matzah*. Cover with half of the tomato sauce. Repeat with another layer of *matzah*, the remaining spinach and cheese, and top with the remaining sauce. Cover with the grated mozzarella cheese.

Bake for 30 to 40 minutes, until the filling is firm. Cool for a short while and cut into squares to serve.

Serves 4 to 6

❧ Farfel Apple Kugel (*Parve*)

The addition of grated apples to this kugel keeps it light and not too sweet. I have been making this recipe for years, and usually serve it with chicken.

INGREDIENTS

2 cups *matzah* farfel or broken up *matzah*
2 eggs
¼ cup walnut or olive oil
⅓ cup orange juice
½ teaspoon salt
¼ cup sugar
⅓ cup raisins
3 large tart apples, peeled and coarsely grated

METHOD

Preheat the oven to 350 degrees Fahrenheit. Oil a large casserole or baking dish or spray it with nonstick cooking spray.

Place the farfel or broken *matzah* in a strainer and pour cold water over it to soften it slightly. (Do not let the *matzah* become mushy.) Put the *matzah* in a large mixing bowl.

Beat the eggs and add them to the *matzah* along with the oil, orange juice, salt, sugar, raisins and grated apples. Mix well and pour into baking dish.

Bake for one hour, or until golden brown and thoroughly baked.

Serves 6 to 8

❧ Asparagus *Matzah Brei* (*Parve*)

Adding vegetables increases the nutritional value of traditional matzah brei. *Consider using other vegetables as well.*

═ INGREDIENTS ═══════════════════════

½ pound asparagus
2 tablespoons extra-virgin olive oil
1 onion, sliced
5 pieces of *matzah*
6 eggs, beaten
Salt and pepper

═ METHOD ═══════════════════════════

Trim and wash asparagus. Steam or cook in boiling water just until tender, but still bright green. Drain and set aside.

Heat 1 tablespoon of the olive oil in a large skillet and sauté onions until golden. Add onions to asparagus.

Crumble the *matzot* and soak them for about a minute in water. Drain and squeeze out excess water. Mix *matzah* with beaten eggs, add asparagus and onions, and season with salt and pepper.

Heat remaining oil in the same skillet and cook the egg mixture for several minutes, until set. Slide onto a large plate and flip it back into the pan to finish cooking on the other side.

Serves 4 to 6

✿ **Rubin Family Favorite** *Charoset* (*Parve*)

Chock full of fresh fruits, dried fruits and nuts, this healthy Turkish-style charoset gets raves from our Seder guests. I prepare a double recipe and use it to spread on matzah during the whole week of Pesach – a good breakfast and snack idea as well.

═ INGREDIENTS ═══════════════════════════════

1 seedless orange, peeled and cut into eighths
1 apple, peeled, cored and cut into eighths
1 cup dates, pitted and halved
1 cup raisins
½ cup walnut pieces or halves
½ cup almonds
2 tablespoons orange juice

═ METHOD ═══════════════════════════════════

Put all of the ingredients into the bowl of a food processor. Process until the mixture becomes a soft but rather coarse paste. Add more juice if necessary. Refrigerate to blend the flavors.

Yields: 3 cups

❧ *Pesach* **Apple Cake** (*Parve*)

You will not even notice that this cake, bursting with apples and cinnamon, is a Pesach *recipe.*

═ INGREDIENTS ═══════════════════

2 to 3 pounds tart apples, peeled, cored and thinly sliced
½ cup brown sugar (you can use white sugar as well)
2 teaspoons cinnamon
1 teaspoon lemon juice
6 eggs (or substitute whites for some of the whole eggs)
1 cup walnut or light olive oil
2 cups sugar
2 tablespoons potato starch
2 cups cake meal
1 teaspoon salt
½ to 1 cup raisins (optional)
½ to 1 cup chopped walnuts (optional)

═ METHOD ═══════════════════════

Preheat oven to 350 degrees Fahrenheit. Oil a 9 × 13-inch baking pan.

Mix apples with brown sugar, cinnamon and lemon juice and set aside while preparing the cake batter.

Beat eggs. Add oil, sugar, potato starch, cake meal and salt and mix well. Fold apples into batter, and add raisins and/or nuts if using.

Pour batter into oiled baking pan and bake for about an hour, until a cake tester comes out dry.

This recipe can be cut in half and baked in an 8-inch square pan.

Serves 8 to 10

✌ *Pesach* **Brownies** (*Parve*)

My friend Mitzi was just voted "English teacher of the year" in Israel. She has a special knack for cooking as well, and enjoys creating healthier versions of traditional recipes. I tasted these brownies at her house during Pesach *and found them hard to resist.*

═ INGREDIENTS ═

¾ cup walnut or canola oil
½ cup unsweetened cocoa powder
4 eggs
1¾ cups sugar
1 cup *matzah* cake meal
½ teaspoon salt
½ cup prepared hot coffee
½ cup walnuts, chopped (optional)

═ METHOD ═

Preheat oven to 350 degrees Fahrenheit. Lightly oil a 9 × 13-inch baking pan.

Whisk together the oil and cocoa until smooth. Set aside.

Beat the eggs and sugar together until frothy. Mix in the oil and cocoa mixture, cake meal, salt, coffee and walnuts, if using.

Pour into prepared pan and bake for 20 to 25 minutes, until a toothpick comes out clean.

Yields: approximately 24 brownies

༖ **Almond Cookie Slices** (*Parve*)

=== INGREDIENTS ===
1½ cups blanched almonds
⅓ cup sugar
2 egg whites
Cake meal
⅓ cup fruit preserves or all-fruit jam

=== METHOD ===
Line a small cookie sheet with parchment paper.

Place the almonds and sugar in the bowl of a food processor and process until very fine. Add one egg white through the feed tube and process briefly. Beat the second egg white briefly, and add a little at a time to the almond mixture, just until the mixture forms a firm paste.

Sprinkle a small amount of cake meal onto a smooth surface and place the nut mixture on it. Mold it into an 11-inch long log. Transfer to the cookie sheet and brush off excess cake meal. With a wet finger, form a trench down the middle of the dough, leaving a "border" at each end.

Let stand uncovered, overnight.

Preheat oven to 350 degrees Fahrenheit.

Stir the preserves to soften and then place in the trench. Bake for about 25 minutes, until the cookie is lightly browned.

Cool cookie completely before slicing diagonally into 1-inch thick cookies.

Yields: 12 cookies

✿✿ Cheese Blintz Loaf (Dairy)

*This is a shortcut way of getting the taste of blintzes without all the fuss. We enjoy it on
Shavuot and to break the Yom Kippur fast. It comes together in minutes with a food
processor, and you can double the recipe to feed a crowd. As it is fairly high in fat, serve
small portions and include several vegetable dishes along with it.*

Filling

INGREDIENTS

1 pound low-fat or fat-free cottage or farmer's cheese
1 tablespoon low-fat or fat-free sour cream
1 egg
1 tablespoon sugar
¼ teaspoon salt
¼ teaspoon cinnamon
1 teaspoon lemon juice

Batter

INGREDIENTS

¼ cup (½ stick) butter, at room temperature
¼ cup canola oil
2 tablespoons sugar
2 eggs
¾ cup nonfat milk
1 teaspoon baking powder
1¼ cups all-purpose flour

METHOD

Preheat oven to 350 degrees Fahrenheit.

Combine the filling ingredients in a food processor and process until
completely smooth. Remove to a bowl and set aside.

Without cleaning the bowl of the food processor, combine the batter
ingredients and process until smooth.

Spray an 8-inch square baking dish with cooking spray.

Pour half of the batter into the baking dish and smooth it with a spatula until it covers the bottom. Gently spoon the filling over the batter, smoothing it into an even layer. Pour or spoon the rest of the batter over the filling and smooth it to cover the filling evenly.

Bake for 45 to 60 minutes, until firm and golden brown. Cut into squares and serve warm.

Serves 6 to 8

❧ **Spinach Ricotta Dumplings** (Dairy)

Serve these unusual dumplings with homemade or bottled tomato or marinara sauce. They go nicely with polenta, brown rice and spaghetti as well. You can prepare these ahead of time, mix them with the sauce and reheat before eating.

═ INGREDIENTS ═

1 package (10 ounces) frozen chopped spinach, thawed
1 cup part-skim ricotta cheese
1 egg
½ cup fine dry bread crumbs (preferably whole wheat)
½ cup grated Parmesan cheese
⅛ teaspoon fresh ground nutmeg
⅛ teaspoon fresh ground pepper
All-purpose flour
1 to 2 cups tomato sauce

═ METHOD ═

Squeeze thawed spinach to remove extra moisture. Mix in a large bowl with remaining ingredients, except for the flour.

Bring a large pot of water to a gentle boil.

Sprinkle a few tablespoons of flour onto a plate or a piece of waxed paper. Use your hands to shape the cheese mixture into 1½-inch balls or ovals, and roll in the flour to coat lightly.

Drop the balls into the water. When the water returns to a boil, reduce the heat and simmer gently for 10 minutes. Use a slotted spoon to remove the balls from the pot and place in a colander to drain. Serve with tomato sauce.

Serves 4 to 6

✸✸ Cauliflower Quiche (Dairy)

With slivered almonds and a touch of mayonnaise, this is not your typical quiche. It's a nice way to enjoy cauliflower and a tasty dairy main course.

═ INGREDIENTS ══════════════════════

One recipe whole-wheat No-Roll Pie Crust (see recipe under desserts)
½ cup slivered almonds
1 small head cauliflower (about 1 pound), cut into ½-inch pieces
1 cup shredded low-fat Cheddar cheese
½ cup low-fat mayonnaise
½ cup nonfat milk
2 eggs
⅛ teaspoon fresh ground nutmeg
⅛ teaspoon fresh ground pepper

═ METHOD ══════════════════════════

Preheat oven to 400 degrees Fahrenheit.

Prepare pie crust in a 9-inch pie pan. Bake for 10 minutes and then cool on a wire rack.

Reduce the oven temperature to 350 degrees Fahrenheit. Spread the almonds on a small baking sheet and toast for 3 to 5 minutes, until lightly browned.

Wash, check and steam the cauliflower just until tender, but still crisp. Arrange the cauliflower in the bottom of the cooled pie crust. Sprinkle with the shredded cheese and the toasted almonds.

Use a whisk or food processor to combine the mayonnaise, milk, eggs, nutmeg and pepper. Pour this mixture over the cauliflower.

Bake for 25 to 35 minutes, until the center is set.

Serves 6

✣ **Ricotta Cheesecake** (Dairy)

This is an Italian-style cheesecake – rich tasting and not too sweet. We especially enjoy serving this on Shavuot, *when dairy foods are traditional.*

Crust

═ INGREDIENTS ════════════════════
½ cup walnuts
¼ cup low-sugar cereal, such as bran flakes, Grape Nuts or Cheerios
½ teaspoon ground cinnamon
2 tablespoons canola oil

Filling

═ INGREDIENTS ════════════════════
½ cup golden raisins
¼ cup orange juice
1¾ cups (16 ounces) part-skim ricotta cheese
6 tablespoons (3 ounces) low-fat cream cheese, at room temperature
¼ cup nonfat plain yogurt
¼ cup all-purpose flour
½ cup sugar
2 eggs
1 tablespoon fresh lemon juice
2 teaspoons grated lemon zest

═ METHOD ════════════════════════
Preheat oven to 325 degrees Fahrenheit. Coat an 8-inch springform pan lightly with oil or cooking spray.

Combine walnuts, cereal and cinnamon in a food processor and process until finely ground. While the processor is running, slowly add the oil through the feed-tube until the crumb mixture holds together. Pat the mixture evenly into the bottom of the baking pan and set aside.

In a small, heatproof bowl, combine the raisins and orange juice. Warm in the microwave for 30 to 60 seconds, mix together and set aside to plump the raisins. (You can do this in a small saucepan as well.)

Rinse the bowl and blade of the food processor. Process the ricotta cheese, cream cheese and yogurt together until very smooth. Add the remaining ingredients and process until the mixture is completely smooth.

Drain the raisins and stir them into the cheese mixture. Pour the batter over the crust in the baking pan. Bake for 45 to 55 minutes, until the edges are puffy but the middle is slightly soft. Turn off the heat and leave the cake in the oven, with the door closed, for 30 minutes. Remove the cake from the oven and cool it completely on a wire rack.

Cover and refrigerate until cold.

Serves 8 to 10

REFERENCES

BOOKS AND ARTICLES

Albert CA, Hennekens CH, O'Donnell CJ, et al. 1998. Fish consumption and risk of sudden cardiac death. *The Journal of the American Medical Association* 279 (1): 23–28.

Aldoor WH, Giovannucci EL, Rockett HR, et al. 1998. A prospective study of dietary fiber types and symptomatic diverticular disease in men. *The Journal of Nutrition* 128 (4): 714–719.

Anderson JW, Johnstone BM and ME Cook-Newell. 1995. Meta-analysis of effects of soy protein intake on serum lipids in humans. *The New England Journal of Medicine* 333 (5): 276–282.

Appel LJ, Moore TJ, Obarzanek E, et al. 1997. A clinical trial of the effects of dietary patterns on blood pressure. *The New England Journal of Medicine* 336 (16): 1117–1124.

Armstrong J, Reill JJ and the Child Health Information Team. 2002. Breastfeeding and lowering the risk of childhood obesity. *The Lancet* 359 (9322): 2003–2004.

Barton BA, Eldridge AL, Thompson D, et al. 2005. The relationship of breakfast and cereal consumption to nutrient intake and body mass index: the National Heart, Lung, and Blood Institute growth and health study. *The Journal of the American Dietetic Association* 105 (9): 1383–1389.

Booth SL, Broe KE, Gagnon DR, et al. 2003. Vitamin κ intake and bone mineral density in women and men. *American Journal of Clinical Nutrition* 77 (2): 512–516.

Camargo CA, Jr, Stampfer MJ, Glynn RF, et al. 1997. Prospective study of moderate alcohol consumption and risk of peripheral arterial disease in US male physicians. *Circulation* 95 (3): 577–580.

Campbell VA, Crews JE and L Sinclair (reported by). 2002. State-specific prevalence of obesity among adults with disabilities – Eight States and the District of Columbia, 1998–1999. *Morbidity and Mortality Weekly Report* 51 (36): 805–808. www.cdc.gov/mmwr.

Cohen V. 2000. Milei D'Chasida. In *The Soul of the Torah: Insights of the Chasidic Masters on the Weekly Torah Portion*, 383 & 348. Northvale, New Jersey: Jason Aronson Inc.

Connor WE, De Francesco CA and SL Connor. 1993. N-3 fatty acids from fish oil: effects on plasma lipoproteins and hypertriglyceridemic patients. *Annals of the New York Academy of Sciences* 638 (1): 16–34.

Chen WY, Colditz GA, Rosner B, et al. 2002. Use of postmenopausal hormones, alcohol, and risk for invasive breast cancer. *Annals of Internal Medicine* 137 (10): 798–804.

Conigrave KM, Hu BF, Camargo CA, Jr., et al. 2001. A prospective study of drinking patterns in relation to risk of type 2 diabetes among men. *Diabetes* 50 (10): 2390–2395.

DeVrese MA, Stegelmann B and Richter B, et al. 2001. Probiotics compensation for lactase insufficiency. *American Journal of Clinical Nutrition* 73 (2): 421s.

Dietary Guidelines for Americans. 2005. Department of Health and Human Services and the Department of Agriculture.

Duffy C, Cyr M. 2003. Phytoestrogens: potential benefits and implications for breast cancer survivors. *Journal of Women's Health* 12 (7): 617–631.

Engler MB, Engler MM, Chen CY, et al. 2004. Flavonoid-rich dark chocolate improves endothelial function and increases plasma epicatechin concentrations in healthy adults. *Journal of the American College of Nutrition* 23 (3): 197–204.

Erdman JW, Jr. 2000. AHA Science Advisory. Soy protein and cardiovascular disease: a statement for healthcare professionals from the Nutrition Committee of the AHA. *Circulation* 102 (20): 2555–2559.

Fung TT, Hu FB, Pereira MA, et al. 2002. Whole-grain intake and the risk of type 2 diabetes: a prospective study in men. *American Journal of Clinical Nutrition* 76 (3): 535–540.

Feskanich D, Willett WC, Stampfer MJ, et al. 1996. Protein consumption and bone fractures in women. *American Journal of Epidemiology* 143 (5): 472–479.

Goldberg IJ, Mosca L, Piano MR and EA Fisher. 2001. Science Advisory: Wine and your heart: a science advisory for healthcare professionals from the Nutrition Committee, Council on Epidemiology and Prevention, and Council on Cardiovascular Nursing of the American Heart Association. *Circulation* 103 (3): 472–475.

Guthrie JF and JF Morton. 2000. Food sources of added sweeteners in the diets of Americans. *The Journal of the American Dietetic Association* 100 (1): 43–51.

Hakim I, Weisberber U, Harris R, et al. 2000. Preparation, composition and consumption patterns of tea-based beverages in Arizona. *Nutrition Research* 20 (12): 1715–1724.

Hetherington MM and L Burnett. 1994. Ageing and the pursuit of slimness: dietary restraint and weight satisfaction in elderly women. *British Journal of Clinical Psychology* 33 (3): 391–400.

Hibbeln JR, Davis JM, Steer C, et al. 2007. Maternal seafood consumption in pregnancy and neurodevelopmental outcomes in childhood: an observational cohort study. *The Lancet* 369 (9568): 578–585.

Higdon JV and B Frei. 2006. Coffee and health: a review of recent human research. *Critical Reviews in Food Science and Nutrition* 46 (2): 101–123.

Hollenberg NK, Martinez G, McCullough M, et al. 1997. Aging, acculturation, salt intake and hypertension in the Kuna of Panama. *Hypertension* 29 (1): 171–176.

Hollenberg NK, Schmitz H, Macdonald I and N Poulter. 2004. Cocoa, flavanols and cardiovascular risk. *British Journal of Cardiology* 11 (5): 379–386.

Hollman PC, Van Het Hof KH, Tijburh LB and MB Katan. 2001. Addition of milk does not affect the absorption of flavanols from tea in man. *Free Radical Research* 34 (3): 297–300.

Hu FB, Stampfer MJ, Rimm EB, et al. 1999. A prospective study of egg consumption and risk of cardiovascular disease in men and women. *The Journal of the American Medical Association* 281 (15): 1387–1394.

Hung HC, Joshipura KJ, Jiang R, et al. 2004. Fruit and vegetable intake and risk of major chronic disease. *Journal of the National Cancer Institute* 96 (21): 1577–1584.

Janszky I, Ericson M, Blom M, et al. 2005. Wine drinking is associated with increased heart rate variability in women with coronary heart disease. *Heart* 91 (3): 314–318.

Jensen MK, Koh-Banerjee PK, Hu FB, et al. 2004. Intakes of whole grains, bran, and germ and the risk of coronary heart disease in men. *American Journal of Clinical Nutrition* 80 (6): 1492–1499.

Johnson IT. 2004. New approaches to the role of diet in the prevention of cancers of the alimentary tract. *Mutation Research* 13 (1): 551, 1–2, 9–28.

Kaplan, Rabbi Aryeh. 1983. *Made in Heaven*, 84. Jerusalem: Moznaim.

Key TJ, Schatzkin A, Willett WC, et al. 2004. Diet, nutrition and the prevention of cancer. *Public Health Nutrition* 7 (1a): 187–200.

Kisch B. 1953. Salt-poor diet and Jewish dietary laws. *The Journal of the American Medical Association* 153 (16): 1472.

Koh-Banerjee P, Franz M, Sampson L, Liu S, Jacobs DR, Spiegelman D, Willett W and E Rimm. 2004. Changes in whole-grain, bran, and cereal fiber consumption in relation to 8-y weight gain among men. *American Journal of Clinical Nutrition* 80 (5): 1237–1245.

Kolata G. 2006. Low-fat diet does not cut health risks, study finds. *New York Times*, February 8.

Leitzmann MF, Stampfer MJ, Willett WC, et al. 2002. Coffee intake is associated with lower risk of symptomatic gallstone disease in women. *Gastroenterology* 123 (6): 1823–1830.

Leitzmann MF, Giovannucci EL, Stampfer MJ, et al. 1999. Prospective study of alcohol consumption patterns in relation to symptomatic gallstone disease in men. *Alcoholism: Clinical and Experimental Research* 23 (5): 835–841.

Liu S, Willett WC, Manson JE, et al. 2003. Relation between changes in intakes of dietary fiber and grain products and changes in weight and development of obesity among middle-aged women. *American Journal of Clinical Nutrition* 78 (5): 920–927.

Mattes RD and D Donnelly. 1991. Relative contributions of dietary sodium sources. *Journal of the American College of Nutrition* 10 (4): 383–393.

McDowell MA, Briefel RR, Alaimo K, et al. 1994. Energy and macronutrient intake of persons age 2 months and over in the US: Third National

Health and Nutrition Examination Survey – Phase 1988–1991. In *Vital and Health Statistics publication 255*. Hyattsville, MD: National Center for Health Statistics.

McGartland CP, Robson PJ, Murray LJ, et al. 2004. Fruit and vegetable consumption and bone mineral density: the Northern Ireland Young Hearts Project. *American Journal of Clinical Nutrition* 80 (4): 1019–1023.

Messina M, Gardner C and S Barnes. 2002. Gaining insight into the health effects of soy but a long way still to go: commentary on the fourth International Symposium on the Role of Soy in Preventing and Treating Chronic Disease. *The Journal of Nutrition* 132 (3): 547S–551S.

Mokdad AH, Ford ES, Bowman BA, et al. 2003. Prevalence of obesity, diabetes, and obesity-related health risk factors, 2001. *The Journal of the American Medical Association* 289 (1): 76–79.

Moore TJ, Vollmer WM, Appel LJ, et al. 1999. Effect of dietary patterns on ambulatory blood pressure: results from the Dietary Approaches to Stop Hypertension (DASH) trial. *Hypertension* 34 (3): 472–477.

Mozaffarian D and EB Rimm. 2006. Fish intake, contaminants, and human health. *The Journal of the American Medical Association* 296 (15): 1885–1899.

Mrdjenovic G and Levitsky DA. 2005. Children eat what they are served: the imprecise regulation of energy intake. *Appetite* 44 (3): 273–282.

National Institute on Alcohol Abuse and Alcoholism. 2000. *10th Annual Report to the US Congress on Alcohol and Health*. Washington, DC.

NHANES Survey 1999–2000. Center for Disease Control and Prevention, National Center for Health Statistics, Hyattsville, MD.

Nielsen SJ and BM Popkin. 2003. Patterns and trends in food portion sizes, 1977–1998. *The Journal of the American Medical Association* 289 (4): 450–453.

NIH Consensus Conference Statement: Optimal Calcium Intake. June 6–8, 1994. 12 (4): 3.

Oomen CM, Ocké MC, Feskens EJ, et al. 2001. Association between trans fatty acid intake and 10-year risk of coronary heart disease in the Zutphen Elderly Study: a prospective population-based study. *The Lancet* 357 (9258): 746–751.

Park DK, Bitton G and R Melker. 2006. Microbial inactivation by microwave radiation in the home environment. *Journal of Environmental Health* 69 (5): 15–17.

Ra'avad, Rabbi Abraham ben David. 1993. *Ba'alei Ha'nefesh*, 125–126. Jerusalem: Mossad ha'Rav Kook. 5th edition.

Rimm EB, Ascherio A, Giovannucci E, Spiegelman D, Stampfer MJ and WC Willett. 1996. Vegetable, fruit, and cereal fiber intake and risk of coronary heart disease among men. *The Journal of the American Medical Association* 275 (6): 447–451.

Rosenberg IH. 2002. Fish – food to calm the heart. *The New England Journal of Medicine* 346 (15): 1102–1113.

Schneerson, Rabbi Menachem. 2005. As quoted in *Hayom Yom: Adar 2/26*. Brooklyn, New York: Kehot Publication Society.

Schulze MB, Manson JE, Ludwig DS, et al. 2004. Sugar-sweetened beverages, weight gain, and incidence of type 2 diabetes in young and middle-aged women. *The Journal of the American Medical Association* 292 (8): 927–934.

Semba RD and G Dagnelie. 2002. Are lutein and zeaxanthin conditionally essential nutrients for eye health? *Medical Hypotheses* 61 (4): 465–472.

Simopoulos AP. 1997. Omega-3 fatty acids in the prevention-management of cardiovascular disease. *Canadian Journal of Physiology and Pharmacology* 75 (3): 234–239.

Stampfer MD, Kang JH, Chen J, et al. 2005. Effects of moderate alcohol consumption on cognitive function in women. *The New England Journal of Medicine* 352 (3): 245–253.

Steinberg FM, Bearden MM and CL Keen. 2003. Cocoa and chocolate flavanoids: implications for cardiovascular health. *The Journal of the American Dietetic Association* 103 (2): 215–223.

Taveras EM, Rifas-Shiman SL, Berkey CS, et al. 2005. Family dinner and adolescent overweight: obesity research 2005. *The North American Association for the Study of Obesity* 13 (5): 900–906.

Taha W, Chin D, Silverberg AI, et al. 2001. Reduced spinal bone mineral density in adolescents of an ultra-orthodox Jewish community in Brooklyn. *Pediatrics* 107 (5): E79.

Weber P. 2001. Vitamin K and bone health. *Nutrition* 17 (10): 880–887.

Weinreb O, Mandel S, Amit T and MB Youdim. 2004. Neurological mechanisms of green tea polyphenols in Alzheimer's and Parkinson's diseases. *The Journal of Nutritional Biochemistry* 15 (9): 506–516.

Weitzman G. 1999. Orot Hakodesh, Volume III. In *Sparks of Light: Essays on the Weekly Torah Portions Based on the Philosophy of Rav Kook*, 163 & 292. Northvale, New Jersey: Jason Aronson Inc.

Willett WC and A Ascherio. 1994. Trans-fatty acids: Are the effects only marginal? *American Journal of Public Health* 84 (5): 722–724.

Wylie-Rosett J. 2002. Fat substitutes and health – an advisory from the Nutrition Committee of the AHA. *Circulation* 105 (23): 2800–2804.

Young VR and PL Pellett. 1994. Plant proteins in relation to human protein and amino acid nutrition. *American Journal of Clinical Nutrition* 59 (5 Suppl): 1203S–1212S.

Yusuf S, Hawken S, Ounpuu S, et al. 2005. Obesity and the risk of myocardial infarction in 27,000 participants from 52 countries: a case-control study. *The Lancet* 366 (9497): 1640–1649.

Zhang S, Hunter DJ, Hankinson SE, et al. 1999. A prospective study of folate intake and the risk of breast cancer. *The Journal of the American Medical Association* 281 (17): 1632–1637.

Zhang X, Shu X-O, Li H, et al. 2005. Prospective cohort study of soy food consumption and risk of bone fracture among postmenopausal women. *Archives of Internal Medicine* 165 (16): 1890–1895.

INTERNET SITES

Cardozo, Rabbi Nathan Lopes. "Thoughts to Ponder: Halacha and 'Trivialities,'" www.cardozoschool.org (accessed August 8, 2005).

Food Standards Agency. "Survey of Caffeine Levels in Hot Beverages. Food Survey Information Sheet 53/04, Food Standards Agency," www.food.gov.uk (accessed November 2, 2005).

Harvard Health Beat www.health.harvard.edu/healthbeat (accessed August 2005).

NIH Office of Dietary Supplements. "Facts about Dietary Supplements: Vitamin A," www.ods.od.nih.gov (accessed June 16, 2005).

Partnership for Food Safety Education, www.fightbac.org (accessed August 4, 2005).

United States Department of Health and Human Services. "Surgeon General's Report, 2005," www.surgeongeneral.gov (accessed August 4, 2005).

USDA National Nutrient Database for Standard Reference, Release 17 (2004), http://www.nal.usda.gov/fnic/foodcomp/search/index.html (accessed August 10, 2005).

USDA Human Nutrition. "Kids Eating More – Food Surveys Research Group, Beltsville, MD," ARS Quarterly Report. www.ars.usda.gov (accessed July 6, 2005).

USDA-ARS. "Added-Sugar Intake on the Rise," http://www.ars.usda.gov/is/AR/archive/jun00/sugar0600.htm (accessed June 20, 2005).

USFDA Center for Food Safety and Applied Nutrition. "How to Understand and Use the Nutrition Facts Label," http://www.cfsan.fda.gov/~dms/foodlab.html (accessed August 18, 2005).

USFDA Center for Food Safety and Applied Nutrition (a) http://www.cfsan.fda.gov/~dms/hclaims (accessed September 18, 2005).

USFDA Center for Food Safety and Applied Nutrition (b). "What You Need to Know about Mercury in Fish and Shellfish: 2004 EPA & FDA Advice for Women Who Might Become Pregnant, Women Who Are Pregnant, Nursing Mothers, Young Children," http://www.cfsan.fda.gov/~dms/admehg3.html (accessed September 18, 2005).

USFDA Center for Food Safety and Applied Nutrition (c), "FDA/CFSAN Resources Page," http://www.cfsan.fda.gov/index.html (accessed August 23, 2005).

1. Weitzman 1999.
2. Cohen 2000.
3. Schneerson 2005.
4. Taveras, Rifas-Shiman, Berkey, et al. 2005.
5. Kaplan 1983.
6. Hetherington and Burnett 1994.
7. NHANES Survey 1999–2000.
8. Mokdad, Ford, Bowman, et al. 2003.
9. Campbell, Crews, Sinclair 2002.
10. Yusuf, Hawken, Ounpuu, et al. 2005.
11. Center for Food Safety and Applied Nutrition (a).
12. Ibid.
13. McDowell, Briefel, Alaimo et al. 1994.
14. Connor, De Francesco and Connor 1993.
15. Oomen, Ocké, Feskens, et al. 2001.
16. Willett and Ascherio 1994.
17. Rosenberg 2002; Marchioli, Barzi, Bomba, et al. 2002; Hu, Bronner, Willett, et al. 2002.
18. Wylie-Rosett 2002.
19. Kolata 2006.
20. USDA-ARS.
21. Guthrie and Morton 2000.
22. Nurses' Health Study and Health Professionals Follow-Up Study 2004; Jensen, Koh-Banerjee, Hu, et al. 2004.
23. Koh-Banerjee, Franz, Sampson, et al. 2004.
24. Rimm, Ascherio, Giovannucci, et al. 1996; Brown, Rosner, Willett, et al. 1999.
25. Fung, Hu, Pereira, et al. 2002; Liu, Willett, Stampfer, et al. 2000.
26. Liu, Willett, Manson, et al. 2003; Spieth, Harnish, Lenders, et al. 2000.
27. Aldor, Giovannucci, Rockett, et al. 1998.
28. Nielsen and Popkin 2003.
29. Connor, De Francesco and Connor 1993.

30. Simopoulos 1997.
31. Albert, Hennekens, O'Donnell, et al. 1998.
32. Hibbeln, Davis, Steer, et al. 2007.
33. USFDA Center for Food Safety and Applied Nutrition (b).
34. USFDA Center for Food Safety and Applied Nutrition (c).
35. Mozaffarian and Rimm 2006; Seafood choices 2006.
36. Hu, Stampfer, Rimm, et al. 1999.
37. Partnership for Food Safety Education.
38. Park, Bitton, Melker 2006.
39. Young and Pellet 1994.
40. Messina, Gardner and Barnes 2002.
41. Zhang, Shu, Li, et al. 2005.
42. Anderson, Johnstone and Cook-Newell 2005; Zhan and Ho 2005.
43. Erdman 2000.
44. Duffy 2003.
45. Schulze, Manson, Ludwig, et al. 2004.
46. Hakim, Weisberber, Harris, et al. 2000.
47. Hollman, Van Het Hof , Tijburh, Katan 2001.
48. Higdon and Frei 2006.
49. Food Standards Agency.
50. Conigrave, Hu, Camargo, et al. 2001.
51. Leitzmann, Giovannucci, Stampfer, et al. 1999.
52. National Institute on Alcohol Abuse and Alcoholism 2000.
53. Chen, Colditz, Rosner, et al. 2002.
54. Zhang, Hunter, Hankinson, et al. 1999.
55. Stampfer, Kang, Chen, et al. 2005.
56. Goldberg, Mosca, Piano, Fisher 2001.
57. Camargo, Stampfer, Glynn, et al. 1997.
58. Janszky 2005.
59. Dietary Guidelines for Americans.
60. Bone Health and Osteoporosis: A Report from the US Surgeon General, October 14, 2004.
61. Ibid.
62. NIH Consensus Conference Statement: Optimal Calcium Intake 1994.
63. McGartland, Robson, Murray, et al. 2004.
64. Taha, Chin, Silverberg, et al. 2001.
65. Weber 2001.
66. Booth, Broe, Gagnon, et al. 2003.
67. Feskanich, Willett, Stampfer, et al. 1996.
68. DeVrese, Stegelmann, Richter, et al. 2001.

69. Hung, Joshipura, Jiang, et al. 2004.
70. Appel, Moore, Obarzanek, et al. 1997.
71. Johnson 2004.
72. Semba and Dagnelie 2002.
73. Key, Schatzkin, Willett, et al. 2004.
74. Moore, Vollmer, Appel, et al. 1999.
75. Mattes and Donnelly 1991.
76. Dietary Guidelines for Americans 2005.
77. Mattes and Donnelly 1991.
78. Kisch, 1953.
79. United States Department of Health and Human Services.
80. Armstrong, Reill and the Child Health Information Team 2002.
81. Israel Heart Fund, Long-Term Effects of a Combined Dietary Behavioral and Physical Activity Intervention for Childhood Obesity 2004.
82. USDA Human Nutrition.
83. Barton, Eldridge, Thompson, et al. 2005.
84. Mrdjenovic 2005.
85. Engler, Engler, Chen, et al. 2004.
86. Hollenberg, Martinez, McCullough, et al. 1997.
87. Steinberg, Bearden and Keen 2003.
88. Hollenberg, Schmitz, Macdonald and Poulter 2004.
89. Cohen 2000.

Food has interested me for years.

As a young girl, I filled blintzes and baked cookies at my mother's side. When she began working outside of the home, I helped with the shopping and cooking. By high school I was cooking dinner several nights a week. Those were "hippie" years and I baked bread, grew herbs and cooked lentils and brown rice, much to the chagrin of my meat-and-potato-loving father.

At the local Jewish community center I worked as a camp counselor and group leader. My after-school cooking class was a favorite with the children.

When I came to Israel in the early seventies, I lived on a kibbutz in the Upper Galilee. Unlike the other volunteers, I was a failure at picking fruit. My real strength was in the kitchen, and soon I was cooking breakfast and vegetarian meals.

Back in the United States, I earned a degree in dietetics from Oregon State University, raised three sons, volunteered with various Jewish organizations, taught preschool, tutored *bar* and *bat mitzvah* students and started The Kosher Connection, a kosher gourmet gift business. I have worked as a dietitian in a Jewish nursing home, hospitals, schools and as a consultant to physicians.

I started teaching cooking and nutrition to adults in Portland, Oregon, and later taught in the Chicago area as well.

In 2003 I returned to Israel. My husband and I live in Beer Sheva, where I work in our family business, write and continue to teach nutrition and healthy cooking. I am the mother of three grown sons and the *savta* (grandmother) of one beautiful granddaughter.

Shevat 5768
January 2008